CAR

== A Hoi

CARPE DIEM
A HORACE READER

GILBERT LAWALL
University of Massachusetts, Amherst, Mass., Emeritus

BRUCE ARNOLD
Mount Holyoke College, South Hadley, Mass.

ANDREW ARONSON
Sidwell Friends School, Washington, D.C.

BRIAN W. BREED
University of Massachusetts, Amherst, Mass.

JOHN HIGGINS
The Gilbert School, Winsted, Conn.

HELENE LERNER
Wayland High School, Wayland, Mass., Emerita

and

SALLY MURPHY
The Winsor School, Boston, Mass.

A Prentice Hall Latin Reader

PEARSON
Prentice
Hall

Glenview, Illinois
Boston, Massachusetts
Upper Saddle River, New Jersey

CREDITS

The authors are grateful to the following for their help with this book:

John Oksanish, Yale University Graduate student, for help collecting bibliography on Horace and the poems included in this book

Elizabeth Baer, Berkshire Country Day School, Lenox, Mass., and Jamie Keller, Lenox Memorial High School, Lenox, Mass., for proofreading the manuscript at various stages

Cover photo: Relief of a Banqueter, Roman, late Republican period, about 50 B.C., marble. Museum of Fine Arts, Boston, Lillie Pierce Fund.

Other acknowledgements and photo credits appear on page 335-336.

ISBN 0-13-166105-1

4 17

CONTENTS

Contents

INTRODUCTION

HORACE AND HIS POETRY

No Latin phrase is so prominently displayed on coffee mugs, t-shirts, bumper stickers, and in pop culture exhortations as the one coined by Horace and chosen as the title of this book, **Carpe diem**. Time and again Horace in his poetry counsels his audience to "seize the day" and live as if there would be no tomorrow. Horace's imperative to enjoy life while you can becomes a theme that weaves its way through his body of work like an underlying musical motif and has been associated with him through the centuries. Many of his poems touch on themes of how to live well with a proper understanding of the big issues of life such as the fleeting passage of time, awareness of what one can and what one cannot control, and mortality. For Horace, one's life should be enjoyable and as free as possible from worry about the future, if only because one's life will not last.

Quintus Horatius Flaccus was born on December 8, 65 B.C. He was, like Vergil and Octavian (the later Augustus), part of the generation that grew up and matured during a decade of bloody civil wars that were triggered by Julius Caesar's crossing of the Rubicon (49 B.C.) and continued in the aftermath of his assassination by Brutus and Cassius and other conspirators (44 B.C.), leading ultimately to the collapse of the Roman Republic and the ascendancy of Octavian as sole ruler. Although Horace was the son of a freedman, his father, despite his limited means, met the large expenses of bringing him to Rome and giving him the best education. As a young man, he went to Athens to study philosophy and there became fatefully embroiled in the Republican cause supported by the assassins of Caesar and championed by Brutus, who was gathering a large army to defend himself against Octavian and Antony, who were intent upon avenging the murder of Caesar. Horace served as a military tribune in command of a legion at Philippi where the forces of Brutus and Cassius fought against those of Octavian and Antony and suffered a crushing defeat (42 B.C.). In *Odes* 2.7 Horace offers a poetic reflection on that life-changing crisis using the poetic formula made famous by the early Greek poets Archilochus, Alcaeus, and Anacreon of abandoning his shield on the battlefield and running away to save his life. Horace embellishes the scene by attributing his miraculous escape to the providential assistance of Mercury, a patron god of poets.

After the defeat of the Republican cause at Philippi, Horace returned to Rome humbled and impoverished by the punitive confiscation of his father's estate near Venusia. Horace, however, was fortunate enough to be pardoned by the victorious Octavian. He took up employment in

Rome as a clerk to a quaestor (**scrība quaestōrius**) in order to make a living, and he also began to write poetry and attracted the notice of the poets Vergil and Varius. In 38 B.C., they presented him to Maecenas, the friend of Octavian and patron of literature, who in time admitted him to his literary circle and a few years later (33 B.C.) gave him a farm in the Sabine territory near the modern town of Licenza. This farm afforded him the financial security that was critical to sustaining his vocation as a poet.

By 29 B.C., Horace had published two books of *Satires* and his *Epodes*. In the present collection, *Satires* 1.9 is offered as an example of the former. In it Horace tells a funny story about his attempts to shake off a social climber who is seeking admittance to Maecenas's literary circle and who insists that he knows our poet and is determined to follow him around the Forum like a pest.

Following the battle of Actium in 31 B.C., where Octavian defeated Antony, and through the early years of Octavian's consolidation of power that culminated in the Senate granting him the title "Augustus" (27 B.C.), Horace began his most ambitious project, writing lyric poetry in the Greek tradition. The result was a collection of eighty-eight poems, arranged in three books, which he published in 23 B.C. The hallmark of the collection is its great variety of subject matter, styles, meters, occasions, and addressees.

In his programmatic first ode, Horace expresses his aspiration to strike the stars with uplifted head if included by Maecenas among the lyric poets of Greece. He singles out *the lyre of Lesbos* (**Lesbōum . . . barbiton**, 34) as a particular emblem of his inspiration, indicating the special sense of poetic craftsmanship and the subject matter that he shared with Alcaeus and Sappho, archaic Greek poets from the island of Lesbos. The affiliation with Alcaeus is explained more extensively in *Odes* 1.32, where Alcaeus is held up as a model for Horace of the lyric poet who is equally adept at singing of passionate love affairs and of armed strife and political turmoil—both large themes treated in Horace's collection of *Odes*. In *Odes* 1.22, he acknowledges his debt as a love poet both to Catullus and to Sappho by alluding to famous verses of Sappho that Catullus had translated in his poem 51. In addition, the influence of the lyre of Lesbos is documented by several poems in the collection that begin with specific allusions to known poems by Alcaeus, such as the Soracte and Cleopatra odes (1.9 and 1.37) in this collection.

Despite giving special acknowledgment to Alcaeus's influence, Horace is eclectic in absorbing literary and philosophical influences. A consistent literary feature of the *Odes* is the wide range of Greek lyric influences and meters that the author draws on, including, in addition to Alcaeus and Sappho, Anacreon, Bacchylides, and Pindar. He also owes a debt to the refined Hellenistic poetic practice of Callimachus. An important influence on Horace was Catullus, his Roman predecessor in the writing of highly allusive and sophisticated lyric poetry (see especially *Odes* 1.5, 1.13, 1.22, 1.24, and 3.9 in this collection for Horace's debt to Catullus). Horace also shares many themes with his Epicurean predecessor Lucretius, and in his love poems he often consciously distances himself from the contemporary elegiac love poets Tibullus and Propertius, while playing freely with their favorite themes. His contemporary and friend Vergil, whom he calls *half of my soul* (**animae dīmidium meae**, *Odes* 1.3.8), must also be rated as a major influence on Horace's art and thinking. To read the *Odes* in the fullest way possible requires that one be acquainted with the Greek and Roman poetry that was known to the well-educated Roman of the late Republic. Through the inclusion of many passages for comparison from Greek and Latin poetry, this book offers valuable opportunities to view and to understand Horace's poems within their larger literary context.

Horace's *Odes* touch upon many vital currents of political and personal experience in the latter half of the first century B.C. Everywhere in the collection Horace portrays himself as being a mature and sensible observer and mentor. In Horace's practice, lyric poetry is less a direct engagement with the world than it is a reflection of life that requires a detached observer. Age (Horace was in his mid-thirties to early forties when he wrote the *Odes*) and circumstances appear to have favorably conspired to offer Horace that perfect observation post from which to work in the classical lyric form. The value of such detachment is signaled for the reader in many ways throughout the *Odes*, most significantly perhaps through the symbolic distance of Horace's Sabine farm, located far enough from Rome to offer a place of contemplative retreat and self-sufficiency poised against the bustling business and pressing anxieties of the capital. Horace reclines within his own version of what the ancients called a **locus amoenus** or *pleasant place* made up usually of elements such as the shade of trees, a soft bed of grass, and a spring or stream of running water. From his charmed sanctuary he often evokes the protective bulwark of Augustus, *a powerful god* (**praesēns dīvus**, *Odes* 3.5.2) and dispenser of peace to a weary Roman world. Having experienced the ups and downs of love in his former days, Horace can represent himself as a wise source of advice to others less experienced than himself, as in *Odes* 1.5. At other times, however, as in *Odes* 1.13 and 1.25, both addressed to a courtesan named Lydia, Horace presents himself as boiling with passion and with frustrated desire as intense as any expressed by Catullus.

Undergirding much of the present collection and providing it with a consistent thematic thread is Horace's incorporation of popular philosophy and ethics. His most consistent attitude toward life is expressed in the **carpe diem** theme, which takes different forms, sometimes foregrounded, at other times more muted. The expression **carpe diem** itself appears in *Odes* 1.11. The phrase exhorts the reader to consider the brevity of life, the imminence of death, and the need to take advantage of life's pleasures and joys while there is still time. A related principle is the need to cultivate **aurea mediocritās**, *the golden mean*, a term deriving from *Odes* 2.10, which suggests the crucial ethical imperative to avoid excess in all its forms and to cultivate equanimity amid life's vicissitudes. Hence, it is no accident that many of the scenes Horace evokes in his poems involve the **locus amoenus** or the Greek symposium or drinking party, both suitable places for moderate drinking, poetic performances, love affairs, the culti-vation of friendship, and imparting sound advice with the poet as men-tor. All such settings reflect a general Epicurean orientation in Horace's values and are in accord with the Epicurean emphasis on pleasure, prop-erly understood as taken in moderation and cultivated apart from the pressures and anxieties of the public world. Such thinking and lifestyles, derived from the Hellenistic Greek world, had made great inroads in Roman society. Horace refers to himself jokingly as *a pig from Epicurus's herd* (**Epicūrī dē grege porcum**, *Epistles* 1.4.16), but while Epicureanism forms the strongest strain of his ethical orientation, he is not a doctrinaire Epicurean. He appears to accept much conventional Roman religion and to endorse a greater degree of civic participation than would a thorough-going Epicurean, such as Lucretius, whose poetry exerted considerable influence on Horace. Our poet, however, reflects a wider range of ethical values. For example, he often refers to the ennobling value of **virtūs**, *virtue*, and to the inner self-sufficiency of the wise man much as a Stoic might, and he takes up diatribes against **luxuria**, *conspicuous consumption* (*Odes* 3.1), as might a Cynic. The lasting value of the ethical views that Horace expounds in the *Odes* centers around the cultivation of equanim-ity, self-restraint, and pleasure as properly understood. In other words, Horace advocates values such as characterized the life of well-educated Romans influenced by popular moral philosophy.

After the publication of the first three books of *Odes* in 23 B.C., Horace never again took on any comparably ambitious poetic program. His sub-sequent production, two books of poetic *Epistles*, one additional book of *Odes*, and the *Ars poetica* has often struck readers as lacking the same level of inspiration and represents something of a departure from his earlier poetic ambitions. His personal reputation, however, soared, and he func-tioned under the Augustan regime as something of a poet laureate and was commissioned to write the great ode to accompany Augustus's re-vival of the **Lūdī Saeculārēs** (*Centennial Games*) in 17 B.C., the *Carmen saeculare*.

Horace died in November of 8 B.C. at the age of fifty-seven, just fifty-nine days after the death of his great friend and patron, Maecenas, to whom he owed much for the success of his career as a poet.

For further background reading: "Introduction to Horace, Especially the Odes," in William S. Anderson, *Why Horace? A Collection of Interpretations*, Wauconda: Bolchazy-Carducci Publishers, 1999, pages v–xv.

TIME LINE

Information about Horace is in boldface.

70	Birth of Vergil.
65	**Birth of Horace, December 8.**
63	Cicero consul; conspiracy of Catiline.
	Birth of Octavian (Augustus).
60	Pompey, Caesar, and Crassus form the First Triumvirate.
59	Caesar consul.
58	Cicero exiled.
58–51	Caesar's conquest of Gaul.
57	Cicero recalled.
55	Possible year of Lucretius's death and of Tibullus's birth.
55–54	Caesar invades Britain.
54	Possible year of Catullus's death.
53	Death of Crassus at Carrhae.
52	Pompey sole consul.
50	Birth of Propertius.
49–46	War of Caesar with the senatorial faction.
48	Battle of Pharsalus; Caesar versus Pompey; death of Pompey.
ca. 46	**Horace goes to Athens to study philosophy.**
44	March 15: assassination of Julius Caesar by Brutus, Cassius, and other conspirators.
	September: Brutus in Athens, recruiting soldiers to fight Octavian and Antony, the avengers of Julius Caesar; **Horace joins Brutus's army and is appointed tribune of the soldiers.**
43	Birth of Ovid.
	Octavian consul; Antony, Lepidus, and Octavian form the Second Triumvirate.
42	Battles of Philippi; Octavian and Antony against Brutus and Cassius; victory of Octavian and Antony; suicides of Brutus and Cassius; **Horace escapes.**
41	**Horace returns to Rome and becomes a quaestor's clerk.**
38	**Vergil and Varius introduce Horace to Maecenas.**
37	Second term of the Triumvirate begins.
	Vergil's *Eclogues* published.
36	Defeat of Sextus Pompey; Lepidus removed from the Triumvirate.

33	**Horace receives Sabine farm from Maecenas.**
34	**Book 1 of Horace's *Satires* published.**
31	Battle of Actium; Antony and Cleopatra defeated by Octavian.
30	Death of Antony and Cleopatra.
29	**Book 2 of Horace's *Satires* published; Horace's *Epodes* published.**
	Book 1 of Propertius's *Elegies* published.
	Vergil's *Georgics* published; Vergil begins writing the *Aeneid.*
27	Octavian **prīnceps** and named Augustus; the principate of Augustus begins and extends to his death in A.D. 14.
	Book 1 of Tibullus's *Elegies* published.
26	Book 2 of Propertius's *Elegies* published.
23	**Books 1–3 of Horace's *Odes* published.**
23–20	Book 3 of Propertius's *Elegies* published.
20	Diplomatic treaty with Parthia.
19	**Book 1 of Horace's *Epistles* published.**
	Death of Vergil, September 20.
18	Julian law on marriage.
	Poem 2 of Book 2 of Horace's *Epistles* published.
17	**Horace's *Carmen saeculare* performed.**
16	Book 4 of Propertius's *Elegies* published.
	16 or later: second edition of Ovid's *Amores* published; *Heroides* published somewhat earlier.
15	**Poem 1 of Book 2 of Horace's *Epistles* published.**
13	**Or later: Book 4 of Horace's *Odes* published; Horace's *Ars poetica* published later yet.**
12	Augustus pontifex maximus.
8	Death of Maecenas, September 29.
	Death of Horace, November 27.

USING THIS BOOK

The running vocabularies facing the Latin passages contain most of the words that are not in *ECCE ROMANI*, Books I and II, published by Prentice Hall. A word that is in *ECCE ROMANI*, Books I and II, is, however, included in the running vocabulary if it is being used in a sense different from the sense in which it is used in that series. Words not given on the facing pages will be found in the vocabulary at the end of the book, thus allowing this book to be used after completion of any standard Latin program. When words that appear in the running vocabularies reappear in later poems, they are glossed again on the facing page. This facilitates reading of the poems in any order; the vocabulary aids will always be there regardless of the order in which the poems are read. Note that a word that is glossed on the facing page and then reappears later in the same poem is not normally glossed at this later reappearance and may not appear in the end vocabulary. Look for the word in the earlier glosses for the poem. The format of vocabulary entries is similar to that in the *ECCE ROMANI* series. Information about the Latin words themselves—in particular, information about the individual parts of compound verbs and sometimes of adjectives and nouns—is given in square brackets. Words borrowed from Greek are often followed by square brackets containing the Greek word and, where appropriate, its component parts. A Greek alphabet for reference is given on page 334.

Several definitions are usually given for Latin words, with the most basic meaning of the word coming first and an appropriate meaning for the context coming last. Definitions and translations are given in italics. Words or phrases that help round out a definition but are not part of the definition itself are enclosed in parentheses. Words or phrases that fill out a suggested translation to make it more complete or to make it better English are placed in square brackets.

Exploration questions accompany each segment of each poem and are designed to focus attention on what is being said and on how it is being said. Questions are asked about the sequence of thought from segment to segment of the poem and about poetic and rhetorical devices and figures of speech. The questions are intended to help you build up your own interpretation of each poem. Sometimes these questions invite comparison with other poems printed below or on the facing page.

Coming right after the vocabulary notes, poem segments, and exploration questions is a full-text version of the poem. You may photocopy this version and use it as you work through the segments into which the poem is divided. This will help you see the poem as a whole and will give you a text that you may mark up with your own observations on meaning, poetic devices, structure, and so forth.

These full-text versions of the poems are accompanied by discussion questions that address the overall structure and the larger meanings of the poems. Often these questions direct your attention to passages for comparison from Horace and other authors. The passages for comparison that accompany the exploration and discussion questions will help you understand what Horace is saying by showing how he responds in his poetry to the poetry of his predecessors and contemporaries. Careful attention to the passages for comparison will help you situate Horace in the larger literary world of antiquity and will give you a better sense of what Horace is saying, how he is saying it, and why he is saying it.

The Latin texts of the poems of Horace are printed in this book largely as they appear in the Oxford Classical Text edition of the poems of Horace, edited by Edward C. Wickham (Oxford University Press, 1901) and revised by H. W. Garrod (1912). Some editors and commentators have preferred readings other than those in the Oxford Classical Text edition, and we have noted some of these in special sections labeled **Text**.

In preparing the vocabularies and notes on the left-hand pages and the questions accompanying the poems, numerous books and scholarly articles were consulted. The following reference books were heavily used. The authors wish to acknowledge their debt to them and to encourage you to consult them for further information about the language and interpretation of the poems of Horace in this book:

Grammar:
> Greenough, J. B., and G. L. Kittredge, A. A. Howard, and Benjamin L. D'Ooge. *Allen and Greenough's New Latin Grammar for Schools and Colleges.* Boston: Ginn and Company, 1931.

Dictionaries:
> Glare, P. G. W. *Oxford Latin Dictionary.* Oxford: Clarendon Press, 1982.
>
> Hornblower, Simon, and Antony Spawforth. *Oxford Classical Dictionary.* 3rd ed. Oxford: Oxford University Press, 1996.
>
> Smith, Sir William, and Sir John Lockwood. *Chambers Murray Latin-English Dictionary.* Cambridge: Cambridge University Press, 1933.

Commentaries:
> Nisbet, R. G. M., and Margaret Hubbard. *A Commentary on Horace: Odes Book I.* Oxford: Clarendon Press, 1970.
>
> Nisbet, R. G. M., and Margaret Hubbard. *A Commentary on Horace: Odes Book II.* Oxford: Clarendon Press, 1978.
>
> Nisbet, R. G. M., and Niall Rudd. *A Commentary on Horace: Odes Book III.* Oxford: Oxford University Press, 2004.

Essays:
> Anderson, William S. *Why Horace? A Collection of Interpretations.* Wauconda: Bolchazy-Carducci Publishers, 1999.

POETIC AND RHETORICAL DEVICES AND FIGURES OF SPEECH

The following poetic and rhetorical devices and figures of speech occur in the selections from Horace's poetry included in this book. Those included in the *Teacher's Guide to Advanced Placement Courses in Latin* are marked with asterisks. Definitions are followed by representative examples (some of the definitions in this section and the section on metrical terms are formulated to be consistent with those in *Love and Transformation: An Ovid Reader*, edited by Richard A. Lafleur and published by Prentice Hall, 2nd ed., 1999).

Adversative asyndeton: see Asyndeton; the absence of a conjunction when one might expect one to indicate a contrast in thought with what comes before, e.g., *Odes* 1.1.29.

*__Allegory__: Gr., *speaking differently*, a prolonged metaphor, i.e., a type of imagery involving the extended use of a person or object to represent some concept outside the literal narrative of a text, e.g., the voyage of life in *Odes* 2.10.1–4 and 22b–24.

*__Alliteration__: from Lat. **ad-**, *to, toward* + **littera**, *letter*, deliberate repetition of sounds, usually of initial consonants but also of initial stressed vowels, in successive words, for emphasis and for musical and occasionally onomatopoetic effect, e.g., *Odes* 1.1.2, **dulce decus**; cf. Assonance and Consonance.

*__Anaphora__: Gr., *carrying back*, repetition of words or phrases at the beginning of successive clauses, often with asyndeton, for emphasis and emotional effect, e.g., *Odes* 1.22.23–24, **dulce rīdentem Lalagēn amābō, / dulce loquentem.**

Antithesis: Gr., *set against, in opposition*, sharp contrast of juxtaposed ideas or words, e.g., **virentī** and **canitiēs** in **dōnec virentī cānitiēs abest / mōrōsa** (*Odes* 1.9.17–18a).

*__Apostrophe__: Gr., *turning away*, a break in a narrative to address some person or personified thing present or absent, sometimes for emotional effect, sometimes to evoke a witness to a statement being made, e.g., *Satires* 1.9.11b–12a, **"Ō tē, Bōlāne, cerebrī / fēlīcem!"**

*__Ascending Tricolon__: Gr., *having three members*, a climactic series of three examples, illustrations, phrases, or clauses, each (or at least the last) more fully developed or more intense than the preceding, e.g., *Odes* 1.22.5–8.

*__Assonance__: Lat., *responding to*, repetition of internal or final vowel or syllable sounds in successive words, for musical and sometimes onomatopoetic effect, e.g., *Odes* 1.22.23, **Lalagēn amābō.**

*__Asyndeton__: Gr., *without connectives*, omission of conjunctions where one or more would ordinarily be expected in a series of words, phrases, or clauses, underscoring the words in the series, e.g., *Odes* 1.13.2–3a, **cervīcem roseam, cērea Tēlephī / laudās bracchia.**

*__Chiasmus__: Gr., *crossing*, arrangement of words, phrases, or clauses in an oppositional, ABBA order, often to emphasize some opposition or to draw the elements of the chiasmus closer together, e.g., *Odes* 1.13.2–3a, **cervīcem : roseam :: cērea : bracchia** (noun A : adjective A :: adjective B : noun B).

Conduplicatio: Lat., *doubling*, for emphasis and emotional effect, e.g., *Odes* 2.14.1, **Postume, Postume.**

Consonance: Lat., *sounding together*, repetition of consonants at the beginning, middle, or end of words (thus overlapping with the term *al-*

literation), e.g., *Odes* 1.22.23–24, du<u>l</u>ce . . . <u>L</u>a<u>l</u>agēn . . . / du<u>l</u>ce <u>l</u>o-quentem; cf. Alliteration.

*Ellipsis: Gr., *falling short*, omission of one or more words necessary to the sense of a clause but easily understood from the context; often a form of the verb **sum**, e.g., *Odes* 2.10.17b, **sī male nunc** (supply **est**).

Embedded Word Order: framing of one word or pair of related words by another pair of words related to one another, e.g., *Odes* 1.1.22b, <u>aquae</u> <u>lēne</u> <u>caput</u> <u>sacrae</u>.

*Enjambment: Fr., *straddling*, delay of the final word or phrase of a sentence (or clause) to the beginning of the following verse, to create suspense or emphasize an idea or image, e.g., *Odes* 1.1.16–17a and 17b–18a.

Golden Line: an arrangement of words with an adjective and its noun at beginning and end of the line, another adjective and noun next within, and the verb in the center, e.g., *Odes* 3.1.16, **omne capāx movet urna nōmen** (adjective A : adjective B :: verb :: noun B : noun A).

*Hendiadys: Gr., *one through two*, use of two nouns connected by a conjunction to express a single complex idea, instead of having one noun modified by an adjective or a genitive; the usual effect is to give equal prominence to an image that would ordinarily be subordinated, especially some quality of a person or thing, e.g., *Odes* 1.23.4, **aurārum et siluae**, not *of breezes and the forest*, but *of breezes of the forest, of forest breezes*.

Homoioteleuton: Gr., *like ending*, the use of similar endings to words, phrases, or clauses, e.g., *Odes* 3.30.1–2, **perenn<u>ius</u> / . . . alt<u>ius</u>**; cf. Assonance and Polyptoton.

Hyperbaton: Gr., *stepping over, transposition*, a departure from usual word order for special effect, e.g., the distant separation of adjective from its noun in *Odes* 2.3.1–2: **Aequam . . . / . . . mentem**.

*Hyperbole: Gr., *throwing beyond, excess*, self-conscious exaggeration for rhetorical effect, e.g., *Odes* 2.14.26, <u>centum</u> clāvibus.

* Hysteron Proteron: Gr., *the latter put as the former*, a reversal of the natural, logical, or chronological order of terms or ideas, e.g., *Odes* 1.37.10b–12a, **quidlibet impotēns / spērāre fortūnāque dulcī / ēbria**; the drunkenness would come first and then the crazed hope for anything and everything, but the speaker wishes to highlight the wild hope or ambition of the queen and so puts that idea first.

*Interlocked Order or **Synchysis**: Gr., *pouring together*, an interlocked arrangement of related pairs of words in an ABAB pattern, often emphasizing the close connection between two thoughts or images, e.g., *Odes* 1.1.1, <u>Maecēnās</u> <u>atavīs</u> <u>ēdite</u> <u>rēgibus</u>.

*Irony: Gr., *pretended ignorance*, the use of language with a meaning opposite its literal meaning, e.g., the description of the duplicitous Pyrrha as **simplex munditiīs** (*Odes* 1.5.5a).

*Litotes: Gr., *plainness*, a form of deliberate understatement in which a quality is described by denying its opposite, usually intensifying the statement, e.g., *Odes* 1.23.3–4, **nōn sine vānō / . . . metū** = *with empty/groundless fear.*

*Metaphor: Gr., *carrying across, transference*, an implied comparison, using one word for another that it suggests, usually with a visual effect, e.g., *Odes* 1.5.6–7, the phrase **aspera / nigrīs aequora ventīs** is a metaphor for Pyrrha when roused to anger or for a love affair with Pyrrha who is prone to anger; cf. Allegory.

*Metonymy: Gr., *change of name*, a type of imagery in which one word, generally a noun, is employed to suggest another with which it is closely related, e.g., *Odes* 1.1.13, **trabe Cypriā**, where the word **trabe**, *tree-trunk*, is used in place of **nāvis**, *ship*; this figure is a hallmark of high poetic or epic style and allows the poet to avoid prosaic, commonplace words (such as **nāvis**); this example of metonymy is also an example of synecdoche (see below).

*Onomatopoeia (adjective, *onomatopoetic* or *onomatopoeic*): Gr., *the making of words*, use of words the sounds of which suggest their meaning or the general meaning of their immediate context, e.g., *Odes* 1.9.19, **lēnēsque sub noctem susurrī**; the sibilants suggest the soft whispering of voices.

*Oxymoron: Gr., *pointedly foolish*, the juxtaposition of incongruous or contradictory terms, e.g., *Odes* 1.22.16, **ārida nūtrīx**; a *dry wet nurse* is a contradiction in terms.

*Personification: Fr., *person making*, a type of imagery by which human traits are attributed to plants, animals, inanimate objects, or abstract ideas, e.g., *Odes* 1.1.15, **Lūctantem Īcariīs flūctibus Āfricum**, where the wind is described as performing the distinctly human action of wrestling.

Polyptoton: Gr., *many case endings*, repetition of the same word or of words from the same root but with different endings, e.g., *Odes* 3.1.5–6, **Rēgum . . . / rēgēs.**; cf. Homoioteleuton.

*Prolepsis: Gr., *taking beforehand, anticipation*, attribution of some characteristic to a person or thing before it is logically appropriate, especially application of a quality to a noun before the action of the verb has created that quality, e.g., *Odes* 3.9.12, **sī parcent animae fāta superstitī**, not *if the fates spare my surviving beloved* but *if the fates spare my beloved and grant that she may live.*

*Simile: Lat., *like*, an explicit comparison (often introduced by **ut**, **velut**, **quālis**, or **similis***)* between one person or thing and another, the latter generally something more familiar to the reader (frequently an animal or a scene from nature) and thus more easily visualized, e.g., *Odes* 1.23.1, **Vītās īnuleō mē similis, Chloē**; cf. Metaphor.

*Synchysis: Gr., *pouring together*, see Interlocked Order above.

*Synecdoche: Gr., *understanding one thing with another*, a type of metonymy in which a part is named in place of an entire object, or a material for a thing made of that material, or an individual in place of a class, e.g., *Odes* 1.37.17a, **rēmīs adurgēns**, *pursuing closely <u>with his oars</u>* [= with his ship]; cf. Metonymy.

*Tmesis: Gr., *cutting*, separation of a compound word into its constituent parts, generally for metrical convenience, e.g., *Odes* 1.9.14, **quem . . . cumque**.

*Transferred Epithet: application of an adjective to one noun when it properly applies to another, often involving personification and focusing special attention on the modified noun, e.g., *Odes* 1.37.7, **rēgīna dēmentīs ruīnās**, where it is strictly the queen and not the ruin(s) that is **dēmēns**, *insane*.

*Tricolon Crescens: see Ascending Tricolon above.

Word-Picture: a type of imagery in which the words of a phrase are arranged in an order that suggests the visual image being described, e.g., *Odes* 1.5.1, **Quis multā gracilis tē puer in rosā**; the word **tē**, referring to the addressee, Pyrrha, is surrounded by the words **gracilis . . . puer**, describing the boy who is embracing her, and all these words are surrounded by **multā . . . in rosā**, describing the ambience within which the boy is embracing Pyrrha.

Zeugma: Gr., *yoking*, use of a single word with a pair of others (e.g., a verb with two adverbial modifiers), when it logically applies to only one of them or applies to both of them, but with different meanings, e.g., *Odes* 3.1.20, **avium citharaeque <u>cantūs</u>**, *the <u>singing</u> of birds and the <u>music</u> of a lyre*.

THE METERS OF HORACE'S VERSE

Double vertical lines mark diaereses in the first six patterns below and caesuras in the Sapphic stanza. For the terms *diaeresis* and *caesura*, see "Metrical Terms" below.

First Asclepiadean (found in *Odes* 1.1 and 3.30)

This meter is based on the choriamb, _ ˘ ˘ _ . The pattern is:

　　　_ _ 　_ ˘ ˘ _ ‖ _ ˘ ˘ _ 　˘ ˘

Second Asclepiadean (found in *Odes* 1.13 and 3.9)

Glyconics alternate with the basic Asclepiadean pattern shown above:

　　　_ _ 　_ ˘ ˘ _ 　˘ ˘
　　　_ _ 　_ ˘ ˘ _ ‖ _ ˘ ˘ _ 　˘ ˘

Third Asclepiadean (found in *Odes* 1.24)

The basic Asclepiadean pattern shown above appears in the first three lines, and the last line of the stanza is a glyconic:

```
– –   – ˘ ˘ –  ‖  – ˘ ˘ –    ˘ ᴗ
– –   – ˘ ˘ –  ‖  – ˘ ˘ –    ˘ ᴗ
– –   – ˘ ˘ –  ‖  – ˘ ˘ –    ˘ ᴗ
      – –   – ˘ ˘ –    ˘ ᴗ
```

Fourth Asclepiadean (found in *Odes* 1.5, 1.23, and 3.13)

The basic Asclepiadean pattern shown above appears in the first two lines, the third line is a pherecratean, and the last line of the stanza is a glyconic:

```
– –   – ˘ ˘ –  ‖  – ˘ ˘ –    ˘ ᴗ
– –   – ˘ ˘ –  ‖  – ˘ ˘ –    ˘ ᴗ
      – –   – ˘ ˘   –    ᴗ
      – –   – ˘ ˘ –    ˘ ᴗ
```

Fifth Asclepiadean (found in *Odes* 1.11)

Three choriambs provide the core of this meter:

```
– –   – ˘ ˘ –  ‖  – ˘ ˘ –  ‖  – ˘ ˘ –    ˘ ᴗ
```

Alcaic (found in *Odes* 1.9, 1.37, 2.3, 2.7, 2.14, and 3.1)

```
ᴗ – ˘ – –  ‖  – ˘ ˘ –    ˘ ᴗ
ᴗ – ˘ – –  ‖  – ˘ ˘ –    ˘ ᴗ
ᴗ – ˘ – – –   ˘ – ᴗ
   – ˘ ˘   – ˘ ˘ –    ˘ – ᴗ
```

Sapphic (found in *Odes* 1.22, 1.25, 1.38, and 2.10)

In the first three lines, the caesura may come after the fifth or the sixth foot as follows:

```
– ˘ – –   – ‖ ˘ ˘ –    ˘ – ᴗ
```

or

```
– ˘ – –   – ˘ ‖ ˘ –    ˘ – ᴗ
```

The last line of the stanza is an adonic:

```
– ˘ ˘   – ᴗ
```

Archilochian (found in *Odes* 4.7)

A dactylic hexameter line followed by a hemiepes (half a dactylic pentameter). Single vertical lines indicate division between metrical feet:

‒ ◡◡ | ‒ ◡◡ | ‒ ◡◡ |‒ ◡◡ | ‒ ◡◡ | ‒ ◡

◡◡◡◡◡◡◡◡◡ ‒ ◡◡ | ‒ ◡◡ | ◡

Dactylic Hexameter (found in *Satires* 1.9)

Double vertical lines indicate where caesuras may occur:

‒ ◡◡ | ‒ ◡◡ | ‒ ‖ ◡◡ |‒ ◡◡ | ‒ ◡◡ | ‒ ◡

‒ ◡◡ | ‒ ◡◡ | ‒ ˘ ‖ ˘ |‒ ◡◡ | ‒ ◡◡ | ‒ ◡

‒ ◡◡ | ‒ ‖ ◡◡ | ‒ ◡◡ |‒ ‖ ◡◡ | ‒ ◡◡ | ‒ ◡

‒ ◡◡ | ‒ ‖ ◡◡ | ‒ ◡ | ‒ ˘ ‖ ˘ | ‒ ◡◡ | ‒ ◡

Spondees may be substituted for dactyls in the first five feet, but the substitution of a spondee in the fifth foot is rare.

Metrical Terms

Adonic Line: a line with the metrical pattern ‒ ˘ ˘ ‒ ◡ , named from the mythical figure Adonis.

Caesura: Lat., *cutting*, a division between words occurring within a metrical foot; cf. Diaeresis.

Choriamb: Gr., a metrical foot consisting of a chorius ‒ ˘ and an iambus ˘ ‒ = ‒ ˘ ˘ ‒ .

Dactyl: Gr., *finger*, a metrical foot with the pattern ‒ ˘ ˘ .

Dactylic Hexameter Line: a line with the metrical pattern

‒ ◡◡ | ‒ ◡◡ | ‒ ‖ ◡◡ |‒ ◡◡ | ‒ ◡◡ | ‒ ◡

Dactylic Pentameter Line: a line with the metrical pattern

‒ ◡◡ | ‒ ◡◡ | ‒ ‖ ‒ ˘ ˘ | ‒ ˘ ˘ | ◡

Diaeresis: Gr., *division*, a division between words at the end of a metrical foot; cf. Caesura.

Diastole: Gr., *expansion*, lengthening of an ordinarily short vowel (and hence the syllable containing it), usually when it occurs under the ictus and before a caesura; sometimes reflecting an archaic pronunciation; e.g., *Satires* 1.9.21, **subiit**, with the third syllable, **-it**, counted as long or heavy.

Elision: Lat., *bruising*, the partial suppression of a vowel or diphthong at the end of a word when the following word begins with a vowel or with *h*. A final *m* does not block elision.

Glyconic Line: a line with the metrical pattern - -   - ˘ ˘ -   ˘ ≍ , named from its inventor Glycon.

Hemiepes: a line with the metrical pattern

- ᷍ | - ᷍ | ≍

Hexameter: Gr., *six measures*, a line of poetry consisting of six metrical feet.

Hiatus: Lat., *gaping*, omission of elision; this is generally avoided, but when it does occur it emphasizes the word that is not elided or coincides with a pause in the sense, e.g., *Odes* 1.1.2, **ō et praesidium et dulce decus meum** (**Ō** and **et** do not elide).

Hypermetric Line: a line containing an extra syllable, which elides with the word at the beginning of the next line, e.g., *Odes* 2.3.27–28, **aeternum / exsilium**; **aeternum** elides with **exsilium**. Elision of this sort is called synapheia (see below).

Iambic Shortening: words with a metrical pattern of a short syllable followed by a long syllable, e.g., **volō**, could be pronounced as two short syllables in ordinary speech. See *Satires* 1.9.17, **volo**, with the second syllable counted as short or light, instead of the usual **volō**.

Iambus (Iamb): Gr., *lampoon*, a metrical foot with the pattern ˘ - .

Ictus: Lat., *stroke*, the verse accent or beat, falling on the first long syllable in each foot.

Pherecratean Line: a line with the metrical pattern - -   - ˘ ˘ -   ≍ , used by Pherecrates.

Spondee: a metrical foot with the pattern - - , used in songs accompanying libations (Gr., σπονδή, spondē, *libation*).

Synapheia or **Synaphaea**: Gr., *binding*, elision at the end of one line with a word at the beginning of the next, e.g., *Odes* 2.3.27–28, **aeternum / exsilium**; **aeternum** elides with **exsilium**; cf Hypermetric Line.

Syncope or **syncopation**: Gr., *striking together, cutting short*, omission of a letter or a syllable from the middle of a word, e.g., *Satires* 1.9.7a, **nōris** = **nōveris**.

Synizesis: Gr., *settling together, collapsing*, the pronunciation of two vowels as one syllable without full contraction, e.g., *Odes* 2.7.5, **Pompēī**, scanned as two syllables without full contraction of the two adjoining vowels.

LEXICAL AND GRAMMATICAL TERMS

Archaism: deliberate use of old-fashioned words or forms no longer in common currency.

Diminutives: the suffixes **-ulus, -olus** (after a vowel), **-culus, -ellus**, and **-illus** form diminutive adjectives and nouns, often expressing endearment and affection, sometimes pity, but sometimes conveying no special force, e.g., *Satires* 1.9.20, **auricula** [dim. of **auris, auris**, f., *ear*], **-ae**, f., *ear*.

Inceptive/InchoativeVerbs: inceptive or inchoative verbs are formed with the suffix **-scō** added to the present stem only. See *Odes* 1.23.5, **inhorrēscō, inhorrēscere, inhorruī**, *to begin to shake/tremble.* Such verbs in the present and imperfect tenses may denote the beginning of an action, though sometimes no special sense is perceptible.

Iterative/Intensive Verbs: iterative or intensive verbs are formed with the suffix **-sō** or **-tō** or **-itō**. See *Odes* 1.9.12, **agitō [agō, agere, ēgī, āc-tus**, *to do; to drive* + **-itō**, iterative or intensive suffix], **-āre, -āvī, -ātus**, *to toss, shake, stir.* Such verbs may express repeated or forcible action, though sometimes no special sense is perceptible.

SELECTIONS FROM HORACE

"A Difficult Line from Horace"
Lawrence Alma-Tadema, British (1836–1912)
Corcoran Gallery, Washington, DC.; William A. Clark Collection

Meter: First Asclepiadean

1   **Maecēnās, Maecēnātis**, m., *Maecenas* (C. Cilnius Maecenas, Roman knight,
      advisor to Augustus, and patron of Horace. Maecenas was the most impor-
      tant patron of literature in the Augustan era. In addition to being Horace's
      patron, he was the patron of Vergil and Propertius as well).
      atavus [**atta, -ae**, m., child language, *father* + **avus, -ī**, m., *grandfather*], **-ī**, m.,
      great-great-great grandfather; ancestor.
      ēdō [**ex-, ē-**, *from, out of* + **dō, dare, dedī, datus**, *to give*], **ēdere, ēdidī, ēditus**,
      to bring forth, bear (a child).
          ēdite: vocative, modifying **Maecēnās.**
      rēgibus: adjectival here, modifying **atavīs**, *kingly ancestors;* or take **atavīs** in
      apposition to **rēgibus**, *kings [as] ancestors.*
          atavīs ēdite rēgibus: Maecenas traced his lineage back to Etruscan
          kings.
2   **ō et**: hiatus; elision does not take place.
      praesidium, -ī, n., *guard, protection.*
          praesidium: both the abstract *protection* and the concrete *protector* are in-
          tended.
      dulcis, -is, -e, *sweet; dear.*
      decus, decoris, n., *honor.*
          decus: again abstract for concrete, here used of a person (i.e., Maecenas)
          who confers distinction on someone by his association with that person.
      meum: take with both **praesidium** and **dulce decus.**

ODES 1.1

The poet addresses his patron Maecenas and defines his vocation.

The speaker describes how people pursue many different ways of life. His own life as a poet stands apart from all others and has its own pleasures and rewards.

1   Maecēnās atavīs ēdite rēgibus,
2   ō et praesidium et dulce decus meum,

continued

Explorations

1. What is the speaker's intention in referring to Maecenas's kingly ancestry in the first line?
2. What do the words **praesidium** and **dulce decus** say about the relationship between Maecenas and the speaker?
3. Analyze the arrangement of words in each of these two lines.
4. Find examples of effective patterns of sounds in these lines.

"C. Cilnius Maecenas"
Palazzo dei Conservatori, Rome, Italy

3   **sunt quōs . . . iuvat** (4): Olympic charioteers are the first of three different
     types of people in lines 3–10 who receive apparent reward for what they
     do.
     sunt quōs: *there are [those] whom.*
     curriculum, -ī, n., *chariot.*
     curriculō: = **in curriculō.**
     pulvis, pulveris, m., *dust* (of a race track).
     Olympicus, -a, -um, *Olympic* (that is, having to do with the famous games
     held at Olympia in Greece every four years).
4   **colligō** [**con-,** *together,* + **legō, legere, lēgī, lēctus,** *to gather*], **colligere, col-**
     lēgī, collēctus, *to collect, gather.*
     iuvō, iuvāre, iūvī, iūtus, *to help; to please.*
     iuvat: impersonal, X *pleases,* with **collēgisse** as its subject and **quōs** (3) as
     its object.
     mēta, -ae, f., *turning post* (ancient race tracks had a wall, called a **spīna,** *spine,*
     in the middle, around which the chariots raced; the ends of this wall were
     called **mētae,** *turning posts*).
     mēta . . . / . . . palmaque (5) **. . . / . . . ēvehit** (6): the speaker offers two
     further thoughts on the Olympic charioteer: his skillful handling of
     the chariot around the turning post (**mēta**) and his receiving the
     wreath of victory (**palma**). Both **mēta** and **palma** are subjects of **ēvehit**
     (6); repeat **quōs** (3) as its object.
     fervidus, -a, -um, *burning, blazing.*
5   **ēvītō** [**ē-** *away; thoroughly* + **vītō, -āre, -āvī, -ātus,** *to avoid*], **-āre, -āvī, -ātus,** *to*
     avoid, clear.
     ēvītāta: modifying **mēta,** equivalent to *the clearing of the turning post.*
     Chariots raced around the turning posts at each end of the track; the
     chariot on the inside had the advantage if it could cut the inside corner
     and miss the post by inches.
     rota, -ae, f., *wheel.*
     palma, -ae, f., *palm; palm branch* (placed in the hands of a victor in the races or
     made into a crown for him to wear on his head).
     nōbilis, -is, -e, *distinguished, famous, celebrated;* here, perhaps, *ennobling.*
6   **dominus, -ī,** m., *master; lord.*
     terrārum dominōs: this phrase may function as predicate to **quōs** (3) **. . .**
     ēvehit (6), *whom X raises up as lords of the earth,* and it may also function in
     apposition to **deōs:** *the gods, lords of the earth.*
     ēvehō [**ex-, ē-,** *away,* + **vehō, vehere, vexī, vectus,** *to carry, bear*], **ēvehere,**
     ēvexī, ēvectus, *to carry away; to raise up.*

3   sunt quōs curriculō pulverem Olympicum
4   collēgisse iuvat, mētaque fervidīs
5   ēvītāta rotīs palmaque nōbilis
6   terrārum dominōs ēvehit ad deōs;

continued

Explorations

5. To what three aspects of chariot racing does the speaker refer in lines 3–6? Why does he arrange them in this order?

6. What three words are emblematic of the three stages of the race, and what is significant about their placement in their lines?

7. Locate an example of interlocked word order or synchysis and examples of effective repetition of sounds in these lines.

8. Line 6 can be read two ways, depending on whether we take the phrase **terrārum dominōs** as predicate to **quōs** (3) . . . **ēvehit** (6), *whom X raises up as lords of the earth,* or in apposition to **deōs** (6), *the gods, lords of the earth.* What is implied in each of these two readings? Are they necessarily mutually exclusive?

9. What is the tone of the portrayal of the Olympic victor in these lines? Is the speaker completely serious? Is he adulatory? Are there any hints of playfulness, humor, or mockery? Is there any ambiguity?

"The Charioteer of Delphi"
A votive offering from Polyzalos, prince of Syracuse,
after victory in the races of 474 or 478 B.C.
Archaeological Museum, Delphi, Greece

7   **hunc**: supply **iuvat** from line 4: *it pleases this man*; the second type is the successful politician, who is pleased *if . . .*, **sī** *. . .*
    mōbilis, -is, -e, *active, lively; shifting, changeable; fickle.*
    turba, -ae, f., *crowd; mob.*
    Quirītēs, Quirītium, m. pl., *Quirites* (a formal name, perhaps of Sabine origin, used of the citizens of Rome); *Roman citizens.*
       Quirītium: the distinguished word **Quirītēs** is used of the entire Roman citizen body when it is acting in a political manner, as it is here in electing the politician.

8   **certō, -āre, -āvī, -ātūrus** + infin., *to fight, compete.*
    tergeminus [**ter-**, *three times* + **geminus, -a, -um**, *born at the same time, twin*], **-a, -um**, *threefold, triple.*
    tollere: supply **eum** as object of the infinitive.
    honor, honōris, m., *honor; political office.*
       tergeminīs . . . honōribus: ablative of means, *by [conferring] triple offices*; the offices are those that a Roman politician would seek as he ascended the **cursus honōrum**, those of **aedīlis, praetor**, and **cōnsul**.

9   **illum**: repeat the grammatical pattern of line 7, i.e., supply **iuvat**: *it pleases that man*; the third type is the grain contractor, whose business would normally consist of acquiring grain from North Africa (**Libya**) and selling it in Rome at as high a price as he could get.
    proprius, -a, -um, *one's own.*
    propriō: referring to the grain contractor, *his own.*
    condō [**con-**, *together* + **dō, dare, dedī, datus**, *to give*], **condere, condidī, conditus**, *to found, establish; to put away; to hide; to store up.*
       condidit: the subject is the grain contractor referred to with the word **illum**.
    horreum, -ī, m., *barn, granary.*
    horreō: = **in horreō**.

10   **quisquis, quisquis, quidquid**, indefinite pronoun, *whoever, whatever.*
    quidquid: subject of **verritur**; the entire clause (**quidquid . . . āreīs**) is the object of **condidit** (9).
    Libycus, -a, -um, *Libyan; North African; African* (North Africa was an important producer of grain in Roman times; the adjective **Libycus** sometimes refers to North Africa or more generally to Africa).
    verrō, verrere, *to sweep.*
       verritur: after wheat was harvested in Roman agriculture, it was taken to the **ārea**, *threshing floor*, where the stalks were beaten with flails to separate them from the grains of wheat with their encasing chaff. The grains of wheat were then winnowed by throwing them up in the air so that the wind would separate the grain from the chaff, which would blow away. The grain fell to the floor and was swept up to be stored away in a granary.

7   hunc, sī mōbilium turba Quirītium

8   certat tergeminīs tollere honōribus;

9   illum, sī propriō condidit horreō,

10   quidquid dē Libycīs verritur āreīs.

continued

Explorations

10.   What pleases the politician (7–8)?
11.   What is the tone of the speaker's portrayal of the politician in these lines?
12.   What pleases the grain contractor (9–10)?
13.   To what specifically does the pronoun **quidquid** refer?
14.   How does the speaker characterize the grain contractor?
15.   What do you notice about the placement of the adjective/noun pairs in lines
      7–10?

11   **gaudeō, gaudēre, gavīsus sum**, *to be glad, rejoice;* + infin., *to delight in* (doing), *enjoy* (doing).

         Gaudentem . . . dēmoveās (13): the grammar changes here as the speaker continues his survey of different activities with an example of a farmer. The verb is no longer **iuvat**. **Gaudentem** is the direct object of **dēmoveās** and functions as a noun, *[the man] enjoying/who enjoys* + infin.; translate the infinitive as a participle.

     patrius [pater, patris, m., *father*], **-a, -um**, *ancestral.*

     findō, findere, fīdī, fissus, *to split, cleave* (used of cleaving the earth with a hoe or plow and of cleaving the sea in sailing).

     sarculum, -ī, n., *hoe.*

12   **Attalicus, -a, -um**, *of/belonging to/typical of Attalus* (king of Pergamum in Asia Minor and known for his great wealth and support of the Romans; he left his entire kingdom to the Roman people at his death in 133 B.C.).

     condiciō, condiciōnis, f., *contract, agreement; terms presented for acceptance, proposal, offer.*

         Attalicīs condiciōnibus: *on terms that an Attalus might offer*, i.e., with an offer of great wealth.

13   **dēmoveō [dē-**, *down, away* + **moveō, movēre, mōvī, mōtus**, *to move*], **dē-movēre, dēmōvī, dēmōtus**, *to remove; to divert, turn aside;* + **ut** + subjunctive, *to induce* X (to do something).

         numquam dēmoveās: potential subjunctive: *you would never induce.* Note that the second person here is a generalized "you," not specifically Maecenas, the nominal addressee of the poem.

     trabs, trabis, f., *tree-trunk* (or a length of a tree-trunk cut for some specific purpose); by metonymy, since a beam formed from a tree-trunk served as a ship's keel, *ship.*

     Cyprius, -a, -um, *Cyprian* (Cyprus was a center of shipbuilding in the ancient world).

         trabe Cypriā: ablative of means or instrument with **secet** (14).

14   **Myrtōus, -a, -um**, *Myrtoan.*

         Myrtōum . . . mare: i.e., the western Aegean Sea, situated between the islands of the Cyclades and mainland Greece, named after the Greek island of Myrtos, and known as a difficult area of the Aegean to navigate.

     pavidus, -a, -um, *fearful, frightened.*

     nauta, -ae, m., *sailor.*

         pavidus nauta: *as a . . .* , in apposition to the subject of **secet**.

     secō, secāre, secuī, sectus, *to cut* (sometimes used of cutting the earth in plowing); of water, *to cut, cleave.*

11 Gaudentem patriōs findere sarculō
12 agrōs Attalicīs condiciōnibus
13 numquam dēmoveās ut trabe Cypriā
14 Myrtōum pavidus nauta secet mare.

continued

Text

13 **dēmoveās**: the Oxford Classical Text reads **dīmoveās**, from **dīmovēre**, *to divert*, but this verb was not used in classical Latin in the sense needed here (Nisbet and Hubbard, p. 9); Rudd (Loeb Classical Library, 2004, p. 22) reads **dēmoveās**.

Explorations

16. What does the speaker's use of the word **sarculō** (11) tell us about the size of the farmer's land?
17. What is the farmer's emotional connection to his fields?
18. What would it be impossible to induce the farmer to do?
19. What contrasts, correspondences, and oppositions can you find between words in lines 11–12 and words in lines 13–14?
20. What is striking about the embedded phrasing of line 14?
21. How do you respond to the portrayal of the farmer, and how does the hypothetical alternative life of the sailor affect your response to the farmer?

15　　lūctor, -ārī, -ātus sum, *to wrestle;* + dat., *to wrestle* (with).

　　　　Lūctantem . . . Āfricum / mercātor metuēns (16): the next on Horace's
　　　　　list is the merchant, whose income is from shipping and foreign trade.

　　　Īcarius, -a, -um, *Icarian* (referring to the stormy Icarian Sea, part of the east-
　　　　ern Aegean Sea off the coast of Turkey; it was named after the mythologi-
　　　　cal character Icarus, who tried to fly too high on the wings that his father
　　　　made for him and plunged into the sea when the wax that held the feath-
　　　　ers of his wings in place melted under the heat of the sun. The story is told
　　　　by the Roman poet Ovid in his *Metamorphoses* 8.183–235).

　　　fluctus, -ūs, m., *wave.*

　　　Āfricus, -ī, m., *Africus* (the southwest wind, thought to bring storms).

16　　metuō, metuere, metuī, *to fear.*

　　　　metuēns: with Lūctantem . . . Āfricum (15) as object.

　　　ōtium, -ī, n., *leisure.*

17　　rūs, rūris, n., *country;* pl., *fields, farmlands.*

　　　　oppidī (16) . . . rūra: a reference to a typical Italian settlement (oppidum),
　　　　　where the farmlands extended to the town walls; oppidum refers to the
　　　　　village, and rūra refers to the surrounding farmlands.

　　　reficiō [re-, *back, again* + faciō, facere, fēcī, factus, *to make*], reficere, refēcī,
　　　　refectus, *to rebuild, repair.*

　　　ratis, ratis, f., *wooden beams joined together to make a raft;* by metonymy, *boat,*
　　　　ship.

18　　quatiō, quatere, quassus, *to shatter; to wreck.*

　　　indocilis [in-, *not, un-* + doceō, docēre, docuī, doctus, *to teach,* + -ilis, -ilis,
　　　　-ile, *being able to*], -is, -e, *unteachable;* + infin., *not able to be taught how* (to).

　　　pauperiēs, -ēī, f., *poverty; simple living.*

15   Lūctantem Īcariīs flūctibus Āfricum
16   mercātor metuēns ōtium et oppidī
17   laudat rūra suī; mox reficit ratīs
18   quassās, indocilis pauperiem patī.

continued

Explorations

22.   Of what is the merchant afraid? What two things does he praise? What, eventually, does he decide to do and why?
23.   Locate examples in lines 15–18 of the following poetic devices:
      a.   Personification
      b.   Embedded word order
      c.   Alliteration
      d.   Assonance
      e.   Interlocked word order or synchysis
      f.   Enjambment
      How does the word order in line 15 illustrate the meaning?
24.   What words in lines 11 and 15 suggest that the vignettes of the farmer and the merchant go together to form a distinct section of the poem?
25.   What parallels and contrasts does the poet create between the merchant here and the farmer in lines 11–14? Begin by identifying specific words and phrases here that echo the earlier portrayal.
26.   How do your responses to the farmer (11–14) and to the merchant (15–18) change as you read through these two passages and contrast these two representative individuals?

19   **Est quī nec . . . / . . . / spernit** (21): *There is [someone] who neither [refuses]* . . .
      nor refuses (to). . . . ; understand a pronoun complement of **Est** (which is
      translated *There is* when it is the first word in the sentence), such as **aliquis**,
      someone. In contrast to the merchant who can only dream of leisure, the
      speaker now presents the man who enjoys leisure.
      pōculum, -ī, n., *cup.*
          pōcula: object of **spernit** (21).
      Massicum, -ī, n., *Massic wine* (a fine wine grown in Campania south of
          Rome).
20   **solidus, -a, -um,** *unbroken, entire, whole.*
      dēmō [dē-, *from, away* + **emō, emere, ēmī, ēmptus,** *to take; to buy*], **dēmere,**
          dēmpsī, dēmptus, *to take away, remove; to take off.*
          dēmere: dependent on **spernit** (21).
21   **spernō, spernere, sprēvī, sprētus,** *to spurn, refuse.*
      viridis, -is, -e, *green.*
      membra, -ōrum, n. pl., *limbs; body.*
      arbutus, -ī, f., *arbutus tree* (a shady evergreen tree).
22   **sternō, sternere, strāvī, strātus,** *to spread out, stretch out.*
      membra . . . strātus: the perfect passive participle is here used in the
          sense of the Greek middle voice and governs the accusative **membra**
          (21) as its object: *having stretched out his limbs.*
      aquae: genitive with **caput.**
      lēnis, -is, -e, *moving slowly; gentle;* of sounds, *soft.*
      caput: here the *head* of a spring.
      sacer, sacra, sacrum, *sacred.*

Passage for Comparison

In *Odes* 2.3, the speaker encourages his friend Dellius to keep a level head in difficult circumstances and not to rejoice excessively in good times. After addressing
Dellius as **moritūre,** *soon to die* (4), the speaker continues:

5   seu maestus omnī tempore vīxeris,
6   seu tē in remōtō grāmine per diēs
7   fēstōs reclīnātum beāris
8   interiōre notā Falernī.

    whether you live gloomily all the time or whether you enjoy yourself
    during holidays stretched out on distant grass with a fine bottle of Faler-
    nian wine.

19   Est quī nec veteris pōcula Massicī
20   nec partem solidō dēmere dē diē
21   spernit, nunc viridī membra sub arbutō
22   strātus, nunc ad aquae lēne caput sacrae.

continued

Explorations

27.   How does the choice of words at the beginning of line 19 suggest that the
      speaker is making a new start in his list with this character?
28.   What does a man such as the one described here enjoy?
29.   What arrangements of words and what sounds are particularly striking in
      these lines?
30.   What similarities do you find between the scene described in lines 19–22 of
      this ode and the lines of *Odes* 2.3 in the passage for comparison on the oppo-
      site page? What similarities and differences do you find in the passage from
      Lucretius quoted below? How can these passages help you interpret lines
      19–22 of *Odes* 1.1?
31.   How do you respond to the type of person described in these lines? Does
      your response to this type of person differ from your responses to the lives
      and occupations of the men described earlier in the poem? How may this
      type of person serve as a touchstone against which to test and evaluate the
      lives and occupations of the other men?

Passage for Comparison

Lucretius, an Epicurean poet living in the first half of the first century B.C., in his
didactic epic poem on the nature of things presents the following idealized scene of
men relaxing in a pleasant natural setting, the so-called **locus amoenus** or *pleasant
place*:

Lucretius *De rerum natura* 2.29b–33:

29b   .   .   .   Inter sē prōstrātī in grāmine mollī
30   propter aquae rīvum sub rāmīs arboris altae
31   nōn magnīs opibus iūcundē corpora cūrant,
32   praesertim cum tempestās adrīdet et annī
33   tempora cōnspergunt viridantīs flōribus herbās.

Men, stretched out on soft grass in groups, near a stream of water beneath
the limbs of a tall tree pleasantly rest their bodies with no great efforts, especially when the weather smiles on them and the season of the year
sprinkles the green grass with flowers.

23   **Multōs**: *Many men*, adjective used as a substantive. The speaker now exam-
      ines the life of Roman soldiers.
      iuvant: the subjects are **castra** (23), **sonitus** (24), and **bella** (24); the direct ob-
      ject is **Multōs** (23).
      lituus, -ī, m., *curved bugle* (used by the cavalry).
      lituō: dative or ablative, dependent on **permixtus**.
      tuba, -ae, f., *war trumpet* (used by the infantry).
      tubae: genitive, dependent on **sonitus**.
24   **permixtus** [**per-**, *thoroughly* + **mixtus, -a, -um**, *mixed*], **-a, -um** + dat. or abl.,
      mixed with.
      sonitus, -ūs, m., *sound*.
25   **dētestor** [**dē-**, *thoroughly* + **testor, -ārī, -ātus sum**, *to swear*], **-arī, -ātus sum**,
      to curse; to detest.
          mātribus (24) **/ dētestāta**: **mātribus** is dative of agent with the perfect
          participle of the deponent verb, which is here passive in meaning.
      Manet: the next occupation is that of the hunter (**vēnātor**, 26).
          Manet . . . / . . . (26) **/ seu vīsa est** (27) **. . . / seu rūpit** (28): a present gen-
          eral condition, with the verb of the main clause in the present indicative
          and the verbs of the conditional clauses in the perfect indicative; trans-
          late all the verbs as present: *if [ever] . . . or if [ever] . . . , the hunter [always]
          remains.* General or habitual actions are being described here. The im-
          plication is that hunters always behave like this.
      Iuppiter, Iovis, m., *Jupiter/Jove* (king of the gods and god of the sky).
          sub Iove frīgidō: = **sub caelō frīgidō**; since Jupiter is the god of the sky,
          his name can be used by metonymy to mean the sky.
26   **vēnātor, vēnātōris**, m., *hunter*.
      tener, tenera, tenerum, *tender; loving; dear; young*.
      immemor, immemoris + gen., *forgetful* (of).
27   **seu . . . seu**, conj., *whether . . . or*.
      catulus, -ī, m., *puppy; young hound*.
          catulīs: dative of agent with **vīsa est**.
      cerva, -ae, f., *deer*.
28   **rumpō, rumpere, rūpī, ruptus**, *to break*.
      teres, teretis, *smooth and rounded; curved*.
      Marsus, -a, -um, *Marsian* (referring to a mountainous region in central
      Italy).
      aper, aprī, m., *wild boar*.
      plaga, -ae, f., *net* (used to capture animals in hunting).
          teretēs . . . plagās: the ends of hunting nets were tied to trees, and ani-
          mals would be caught in the billowing nets.

23   Multōs castra iuvant et lituō tubae
24   permixtus sonitus bellaque mātribus
25   dētestāta. Manet sub Iove frīgidō
26   vēnātor tenerae coniugis immemor,
27   seu vīsa est catulīs cerva fidēlibus,
28   seu rūpit teretēs Marsus aper plagās.

continued

Explorations

32.   How does line 23 recall the beginning of the catalogue in lines 3–4?
33.   What are the three things, according to the speaker (23–25a), that are enjoyed
      by soldiers?
34.   How might the sound suggested by the description of the spring in line 22 be
      different from the sound suggested by the phrase **lituō tubae / permixtus
      sonitus** here (23–24)?
35.   Of what or whom is the hunter forgetful (26)? What prompts his forgetful-
      ness (27–28)? What in the description of the hunter makes him seem obses-
      sive?
36.   Find examples of the following in lines 26–28:
      a.   Line-framing with embedded word order
      b.   Interlocked word order or synchysis
      c.   Two more examples of embedded word order
      d.   A chiasmus
37.   Identify the geographical location of the hunter's activity.
38.   How do the soldiers and the hunter form a pair of lifestyles? How do you re-
      spond to them?
39.   How are the soldiers and the hunter antithetical to the type of person de-
      scribed in the previous lines (19–22)?

29   **Mē**: adversative asyndeton; in the final and longest section (29–34), the
      speaker presents himself and his life as a poet.

   Mē: accusative, direct object of **miscent** (30); the subject is **hederae**.

doctus, -a, -um, *learned.*

   doctārum: here used, as in Catullus, of poetic learning and sophistication;
   take with **frontium**.

hedera, -ae, f., *ivy*; pl., *ivy vines; ivy wreath* (ivy wreaths were associated with
   Bacchus and Apollo as gods of poetry).

praemium, -ī, n., *payment; prize; reward.*

   praemia: plural for singular, *a reward* (for) + gen.; **praemia** is in apposition
   to **hederae**.

frōns, frontis, f., *forehead, brow.*

30   **dīs**: = **deīs**, dative or ablative.

misceō, miscēre, miscuī, mixtus, *to mix;* + dat. or abl., *to bring into association*
   (with).

superus, -a, -um, *above, upper; heavenly.*

gelidus, -a, -um, *cool.*

nemus, nemoris, n., *grove, sacred grove.*

31   **Nymphae, -ārum**, f., *Nymphs.*

levis, -is, -e, *light; graceful.*

Satyrī, -ōrum, m., *Satyrs.*

   Nymphārum ... Satyrīs: two sets of woodland divinities, who are often
   associated with Bacchus, god of wine, poetry, and music.

chorus [Gr., χορός], **-ī**, m., *dance.*

32   **sēcernō** [**sē-**, *apart, aside* + **cernō, cernere, crēvī, crētus**, *to distinguish, sepa-
      rate*], **sēcernere, sēcrēvī, sēcrētus**, *to separate.*

populō: ablative of separation: *from the people.*

tībia, -ae, f., *flute* (a musical instrument consisting of two pipes made of
   reeds—thus the plural—with holes for fingering; its Greek counterpart,
   the αὐλός, *aulos*, was used to accompany Greek choral lyric songs such as
   those written by Pindar).

33   **Euterpē** [Gr., Εὐτέρπη = εὖ, *well* + τέρπω, *I delight*], **Euterpēs**, f., *Euterpe* (one
      of the nine Muses, sometimes specifially the Muse of lyric poetry).

cohibeō [**con-**, *together* + **habeō, -ēre, -uī, -itus**, *to have; to hold*], **-ēre, -uī**, *to
   hold back, withhold.*

Polyhymnia [Gr., Πολύμνια = πολύς, *much* + ὕμνος, *song in praise of gods or
   heroes*; = *abounding in song*], **-ae**, f., *Polyhymnia* (one of the nine Muses).

34   **Lesbōus** [Gr., Λεσβόος], **-a, -um**, *Lesbian, from Lesbos* (an island near Asia Mi-
      nor, home of the archaic Greek lyric poets Alcaeus and Sappho and of lyric
      poetry generally).

refugiō [**re-**, *back* + **fugiō, fugere, fūgī, fugitus**, *to flee*], **refugere, refūgī**, *to
   shrink back, recoil;* + infin., *to refuse* (to).

tendō, tendere, tetendī, tentus, *to stretch; to tune* (a stringed instrument, such
   as the lyre).

barbitos [Gr., βάρβιτος, *a musical instrument with many strings*], **-ī**, Greek accusative, **barbiton**, m., *lyre* (a stringed instrument like a harp, used to accompany Greek solo lyric performances).

29   Mē doctārum hederae praemia frontium
30   dīs miscent superīs, mē gelidum nemus
31   Nymphārumque levēs cum Satyrīs chorī
32   sēcernunt populō, sī neque tībiās
33   Euterpē cohibet nec Polyhymnia
34   Lesbōum refugit tendere barbiton.

continued

Explorations

40. How does the first word in line 29 suggest that the speaker has come to a new stage in his list of characters?
41. What two words in particular in lines 29–30 tell us that the speaker is here presenting himself as a poet?
42. Find an embedded phrase in line 29. Does the embedding emphasize the meaning of the line or contradict it? What else is important about word order in this line?
43. How does the speaker's life as a poet situate him with respect to normal humanity on the one hand and the gods in heaven on the other?
44. The words **dīs miscent superīs** (30) recall the words **ēvehit ad deōs** (6) and invite a comparison between the poet and the charioteer. What are the similarities and what are the differences between the poet and the charioteer?

"Melpomene, Erato, and Polyhymnia"
Eustache Le Sueur (1617–1655)
Louvre, Paris, France

35   **quodsī**, conj., *but if.*

lyricus [Gr., λυρικός], **-a, -um,** *lyric* (i.e., associated with the lyre, a Greek musical instrument).

vātēs, vātis, m., *prophet, seer; poet* (as divinely inspired), *bard.*

The Latin word **vātēs** derives from an old Italo-Celtic word meaning variously *bard, song of praise, frenzied,* or *possessed,* with religious overtones. It
has different connotations from the Latin word **poēta,** which derives
from the Greek word ποιητής, meaning literally *maker* and then *poet* as
one who makes verses.

īnserō [**in-,** *in* + **serō, serere, sēvī, satus,** *to sow, plant*], **īnserere, īnseruī,**
īnsertus, *to insert;* + dat., *to put* (among), *include* (in), *insert* (in a class or cate-
gory).

īnserēs: the speaker is asking to be admitted to the ranks of the nine
Greek lyric poets, who centuries earlier set the standard for lyric composition. They were Alcaeus, Alcman, Anacreon, Bacchylides, Ibycus,
Pindar, Sappho, Simonides, and Stesichorus; the earliest was Alcman,
who was born around 654 B.C., and the last was Pindar, who lived from
518–438 B.C. Corinna was sometimes added as a tenth.

36   **sublīmis, -is, -e,** *lofty; raised high.*

sublīmī: proleptic, not *with my lofty head* but *with my head raised high.*

feriō, ferīre, *to strike.*

sīdus, sīderis, n., *star.*

vertex, verticis, m., *top of the head.*

35   Quodsī mē lyricīs vātibus īnserēs,
36   sublīmī feriam sīdera vertice.

Explorations

45.   How does the word **Quodsī** logically connect these last two lines to the
       statement made in the previous lines (29–34)?
46.   What does the speaker imply by using the verb **īnserēs** (35)?
47.   Is Maecenas the only possible person to whom these lines are addressed?
       Whom else might the speaker be addressing?
48.   Compare what the speaker says in line 36 with what he said in lines 29–30a.
       What are the similarities? What are the differences?
49.   What is the tone of the last line?

Odes 1.1

1   Maecēnās atavīs ēdite rēgibus,
2   ō et praesidium et dulce decus meum,
3   sunt quōs curriculō pulverem Olympicum
4   collēgisse iuvat, mētaque fervidīs
5   ēvītāta rotīs palmaque nōbilis
6   terrārum dominōs ēvehit ad deōs;
7   hunc, sī mōbilium turba Quirītium
8   certat tergeminīs tollere honōribus;
9   illum, sī propriō condidit horreō,
10   quidquid dē Libycīs verritur āreīs.
11   Gaudentem patriōs findere sarculō
12   agrōs Attalicīs condiciōnibus
13   numquam dēmoveās ut trabe Cypriā
14   Myrtōum pavidus nauta secet mare.
15   Lūctantem Īcariīs flūctibus Āfricum
16   mercātor metuēns ōtium et oppidī
17   laudat rūra suī; mox reficit ratīs
18   quassās, indocilis pauperiem patī.
19   Est quī nec veteris pōcula Massicī
20   nec partem solidō dēmere dē diē
21   spernit, nunc viridī membra sub arbutō
22   strātus, nunc ad aquae lēne caput sacrae.
23   Multōs castra iuvant et lituō tubae
24   permixtus sonitus bellaque mātribus
25   dētestāta. Manet sub Iove frīgidō
26   vēnātor tenerae coniugis immemor,
27   seu vīsa est catulīs cerva fidēlibus,
28   seu rūpit teretēs Marsus aper plagās.
29   Mē doctārum hederae praemia frontium
30   dīs miscent superīs, mē gelidum nemus
31   Nymphārumque levēs cum Satyrīs chorī
32   sēcernunt populō, sī neque tībiās
33   Euterpē cohibet nec Polyhymnia
34   Lesbōum refugit tendere barbiton.
35   Quodsī mē lyricīs vātibus īnserēs,
36   sublīmī feriam sīdera vertice.

Discussion

1. Divide the poem into sections. How is it structured?
2. What similarities can you find between the speaker's view of humanity in *Odes* 1.1 and Lucretius's view of humanity as revealed in the prologue to Book 2 of his *De rerum natura*, quoted in Passages for Comparison I following these questions?
3. Examine the speaker's portrayal of himself as poet (29–34):
   a. Find as many similarities as you can between the passages from Propertius quoted in Passages for Comparison II following these questions and lines 29–34 of *Odes* 1.1.
   b. What differences do you find between Propertius's description of himself as poet and the speaker's of himself as poet in lines 29–34 of *Odes* 1.1? With what poets does Propertius align himself? With what poetic tradition does the speaker of *Odes* 1.1 align himself?
   c. How do you respond to the speaker's presentation of himself as poet?
4. Compare the reference to the *gentle source of sacred water* (**aquae lēne caput sacrae**, 22b) with the lines from Callimachus's *Hymn to Apollo* quoted in Passages for Comparison III following these questions. These lines of Callimachus describe the *sacred spring* that serves as a metaphor for the source of his poetic inspiration. What do the *gentle source of sacred water* in *Odes* 1.1 and this echo of Callimachus add to the characterization of the wine drinker who enjoys leisure in Horace's *Ode*?
5. What does the phrase **lyricīs vātibus** (35), which combines the transliteration of a Greek word (λυρικός) with an Italo-Celtic-Latin word (**vātēs**) with religious and sacred overtones (as in the English word *bard*), reveal about the speaker's conception of himself as poet?
6. Compare *Odes* 1.1 to Catullus 1, quoted in Passages for Comparison IV following these questions. Both are dedications. What elements are similar, and what are different?

Passages for Comparison

I.

The following is from the prologue to Book 2 of Lucretius *De rerum natura*:

1   Suāve, marī magnō turbantibus aequora ventīs,
2   ē terrā magnum alterius spectāre labōrem;
3   nōn quia vexārī quemquamst iūcunda voluptās,
4   sed quibus ipse malīs careās quia cernere suāve est.
5   Suāve etiam bellī certāmina magna tuērī
6   per campōs īnstructa tuā sine parte perīclī.
7   Sed nīl dulcius est bene quam mūnīta tenēre
8   ēdita doctrīnā sapientum templa serēna,
9   dēspicere unde queās aliōs passimque vidēre
10   errāre atque viam palantīs quaerere vītae,
11   certāre ingeniō, contendere nōbilitāte,

12 noctēs atque diēs nītī praestante labōre
13 ad summās ēmergere opēs rērumque potīrī.
14 Ō miserās hominum mentēs, ō pectora caeca!
15 Quālibus in tenebrīs vītae quantīsque perīclīs
16 dēgitur hoc aevī quodcumquest! Nōnne vidēre
17 nīl aliud sibi nātūram lātrāre, nisi utquī
18 corpore sēiunctus dolor absit, mēnsque fruātur
19 iūcundō sēnsū cūrā sēmota metūque?

How pleasant, when winds are stirring up the waters on a great sea, to watch from the land the great struggle of someone else; not because it is a pleasing delight that someone is in trouble, but because it is pleasant to realize what ills you are yourself free from. It is likewise pleasant to view the great strife of armies drawn up on plains, without yourself having any part of the danger. But nothing is sweeter than to have peaceful, lofty temples, well defended by the teachings of the wise, from which you can look down upon others and see them wander here and there and, straying about, seek the path of life, as they compete with their wits, strive for precedence with their good birth, and night and day contend with outstanding effort to come out on top in wealth and to gain power. Oh, the pitiable minds of men! Oh, their blind hearts! In what darkness of life, in what great dangers is this poor span of life spent! Do you not see that nature cries out for nothing more than this, that pain should be absent, unyoked from the body, and that the mind should enjoy pleasant feelings remote from care and fear?

II.

In the first passage below, Propertius, a younger contemporary of Horace, describes the grove of poetry inhabited by Callimachus and Philitas, his Hellenistic Greek poetic models. In the second, Propertius describes the grotto of poetry where one of the Muses, Calliope, moistens his lips with the water of poetic inspiration that Philitas and Callimachus once drank:

Propertius 3.1.1–6:

1 Callimachī Mānēs et Cōī sacra Philītae,
2   in vestrum, quaesō, mē sinite īre nemus.
3 Prīmus ego ingredior pūrō dē fonte sacerdōs
4   Ītala per Graiōs orgia ferre chorōs.
5 Dīcite, quō pariter carmen tenuāstis in antrō
6   quōve pede ingressī? Quamve bibistis aquam?

Spirit of Callimachus and sacred rites of Philitas of Cos, allow me, I pray you, to enter into your grove. I enter as the first priest, from the pure spring, to bring Italian rites in Greek rhythms. Tell me, in what cave did you together make your song fine, or with what foot did you enter? And what water did you drink?

Propertius 3.3.27–36 and 51–52:

27 Hīc erat affīxīs viridis spēlunca lapillīs,
28   pendēbantque cavīs tympana pūmicibus,
29 orgia Mūsārum et Sīlēnī patris imāgō
30   fictilis et calamī, Pan Tegeaee, tuī;
31 et Veneris dominae volucrēs, mea turba, columbae
32   tingunt Gorgoneō pūnica rōstra lacū;
33 dīversaeque novem sortītae iūra Puellae
34   exercent tenerās in sua dōna manūs:
35 haec hederās legit in thyrsōs, haec carmina nervīs
36   aptat, at illa manū texit utrāque rosam.

51 Tālia Calliopē, lymphīsque ā fonte petītīs
52   ōra Philītēā nostra rigāvit aquā.

> Here was a green cave with mosaics decorating it, and tambourines, the sacred instruments of the Muses, were hanging from hollowed rocks, and the carved statue of father Silenus and your pipe, O Pan of Tegea [i.e., of Arcadia]. And the birds of the lady Venus, the doves, my own company, touch their purple beaks in the Gorgon's lake; the nine Maidens, having been given their own various duties, exercise their tender hands in their own gifts; this one picks ivy for her sacred wands, this one fits her songs to the lyre strings, but that one weaves a rose in either hand.

> This Calliope [said], and wet my lips with Philitas's water, having taken it from the spring.

III.

In Callimachus *Hymn to Apollo* 111–12, Apollo, the god of poetry, defines the ideal source of poetic inspiration as water

> which, pure and undefiled, rises up from a sacred spring, a small flow of water, the choicest flower of its kind.

IV.

Here is Catullus's dedication of his little book of verse to Cornelius Nepos:

Catullus 1:

1 Cui dōnō lepidum novum libellum
2 āridā modo pūmice expolītum?
3 Cornēlī, tibi: namque tū solēbās
4 meās esse aliquid putāre nūgās
5 iam tum, cum ausus es ūnus Ītalōrum
6 omne aevum tribus explicāre cartīs
7 doctīs, Iuppiter, et labōriōsīs.
8 Quārē habē tibi quidquid hoc libellī
9 quālecumque; quod, <ō> patrōna virgō,
10 plūs ūnō maneat perenne saeclō.

To whom do I give my charming, new little papyrus roll, freshly polished with dry pumice? To you, Cornelius: for already you used to think that my trifles were [worth] something at that time when you alone of Italians dared to unfold all recorded history in three volumes, learned—by Jupiter!—and laborious! So take for yourself whatever this [is] of a little papyrus roll such as it is; and, O patroness maiden, may it last/endure through the years for more than one generation/century.

Meter: Fourth Asclepiadean

1   **Quis**: = **Quī**; take the interrogative adjective with **gracilis . . . puer**.
    multā . . . in rosā: *amid many a rose;* some readers prefer to see a bed of roses,
      others, garlands of roses, and others, roses decorating the cave or grotto (3),
      where the encounter is taking place.
    gracilis, -is, -e, *slender*.
      gracilis: the word may be used scornfully here.
2   **perfundō** [**per-**, *thoroughly* + **fundō, fundere, fūdī, fūsus**, *to pour*], **perfun-**
    dere, perfūdī, perfūsus, *to soak, drench*.
    liquidus, -a, -um, *fluid, flowing*.
    urgeō, urgēre, ursī, *to press, squeeze; to push; to thrust oneself on*.
    odor, odōris, m., *smell; fragrance; perfume*.
3   **Pyrrha** [cf. Gr., πῦρ, *fire*, and πυρρός, *flame-colored, yellowish red;* of persons, *red-*
    headed], **-ae**, f., *Pyrrha* (the woman to whom the poem is addressed, probably
      to be thought of as a **meretrīx** or **scortum**, i.e., a courtesan; in mythology,
      Pyrrha is the name of the woman who with her husband Deucalion began
      to repopulate the earth after the flood).
    sub, prep. + abl., *under, beneath; under the cover of*.
    antrum [Gr., ἄντρον, *cave*], **-ī**, n., *cave, grotto*.
4   **Cui . . . ?**: *For whom . . . ?*
    flāvus, -a, -um, *yellow, golden-yellow;* of hair, *blonde*.
    religō [**re-**, *back* + **ligō, -āre, -āvī, -ātus**, *to tie*], **-āre, -āvī, -ātus**, *to tie back* (out
      of the way).
    coma, -ae, f., *hair*.
5a **simplex, simplicis**, *single, one-fold; straightforward; without artifice or deceit;*
      simple.
        simplex: compare **duplex, duplicis**, *double, two-fold;* of persons, *"two-*
          faced," deceitful.
    munditia, -ae, f., *cleanliness; neatness; elegance, refinement* (of appearance or
      manners).
        simplex munditiīs: Milton translated "plain in thy neatness."

ODES 1.5

To Pyrrha

The speaker addresses Pyrrha and predicts that a young man is about to experience a tempestuous love affair with her.

1   Quis multā gracilis tē puer in rosā
2   perfūsus liquidīs urget odōribus
3   grātō, Pyrrha, sub antrō?
4   Cui flāvam religās comam,

5a simplex munditiīs?

continued

Explorations

1. To what two actions do the two opening questions refer?
2. How does the arrangement of the words create a word picture in the first line?
3. How is the boy characterized?
4. How does the word order reflect the scene in the third line?
5. Why does the poet locate the scene in a cave or grotto (**antrō**, 3)?
6. How is Pyrrha characterized?

"Head of a Courtesan"
Drawn from a Pompeian fresco

5b **heu**, interj. expressing sorrow, regret, etc., *alas.*
    quotiēns, adv., *how often, how many times.*
    fidēs, fideī, f., *trust; promise; honesty; good faith; sincerity.*
      fidem: supply **mūtātam** from **mūtātōs** (6).
6   **mūtō, -āre, -āvī, -ātus**, *to change.*
    fidem mūtāre: idiom, *to transfer one's allegiance, change sides.*
      fidem [mūtātam]: = *faithlessness.*
    fleō, flēre, flēvī, flētus, *to weep, cry; to weep over.*
    asper, aspera, asperum, *rough* (to the touch); of the sea, *rough.*
7   **aequor, aequoris**, n., *a smooth, level surface;* by extension, *the sea* (either calm
    and flat or, as here, tossed by storms).
      aequora: plural for singular; object of **ēmīrābitur** (8).
        aspera . . . aequora: literally, *the rough sea,* but **aspera**, when used of
        persons, may also mean *roused to anger, raging;* in addition to its lit-
        eral sense, the phrase **aspera . . . aequora** is a metaphor for Pyrrha
        when roused to anger or for the love affair when Pyrrha is roused to
        anger.
8   **ēmīror** [apparently a Horatian coinage, found only here in extant Latin liter-
    ature; **ex-, ē-**, intensive + **mīror, -ārī, -ātus sum**, *to be surprised, amazed, be-*
    wildered; to marvel at], **-ārī, -ātus sum**, *to wonder at, be astonished at.*
    īnsolēns, īnsolentis [**in-**, *not* + **soleō, solēre, solitus sum**, *to be accustomed*],
    naive; unaccustomed (to a sight), *unfamiliar* (with); *excessive, unrestrained; ar-*
    rogant, insolent.
      īnsolēns: here, *naive* (as he is), *unaccustomed* (as he is to such sights). The
      other meanings of the word may also be applicable to the boy here.

Passage for Comparison

Semonides of Amorgos (mid seventh century B.C.) 7:

In the opening of the poem from which the excerpt (lines 27–42) on the facing page
is taken, Semonides states that in the beginning Zeus made women's minds to be
of various natures. In a highly misogynistic poem, he then lists the kinds of minds
Zeus took from animals or elements of nature and gave to women. He made the
mind of one type of woman from that of a fox, another from that of a dog, another
from earth, another from the sea, another from a donkey, another from a weasel,
another from a mare, another from a monkey, and the last from a bee (the only
good type of female mind). On the facing page is an English translation of
Semonides' description of the woman whose mind was made from the sea.

5b   Heu quotiēns fidem
6   mūtātōsque deōs flēbit et aspera
7   nigrīs aequora ventīs
8   ēmīrābitur īnsolēns,

continued

Explorations

7. Why will the boy cry? What discovery will he have made?
8. What is meant by the statement made in lines 6b–8, **et aspera / nigrīs ae-quora ventīs / ēmīrābitur īnsolēns**? How is the scene here different from that in lines 1–5a?
9. Consider the passage for comparison below. How is Pyrrha like the woman described by Semonides?
10. Locate an example of interlocked word order or synchysis in lines 6–7, and explain **nigrīs** (7) as a transferred epithet.
11. The vocabulary note distinguishes three sets of definitions for **īnsolēns** (8). Which of the three sets of definitions is most appropriate for the use of the word in line 8? How might the other definitions be appropriate for the boy as he is seen earlier in the poem?

Passage for Comparison (continued from the opposite page)

Semonides of Amorgos (mid seventh century B.C.) 7.27–42:

> One kind of woman is born from the sea and has two different dispositions. One day she laughs and is happy. A guest will praise her when he sees her in the house and will say, "There is no better or more beautiful woman than this in the whole world." But another day you couldn't stand to look her in the face or approach her, for then she rages terribly like a dog protecting her puppies. No one can calm her, and she is out of spirits with everyone, both friends and enemies. She is often like the sea, calm, harmless, a great joy for sailors in the season of summer, but often she rages like the sea when it heaves with loudly thundering waves. Such a woman seems exactly like this in her moods. Just like the sea, she has contradictory dispositions.

9   **fruor, fruī, fructus sum** + abl., *to enjoy; to delight* (in).
       crēdulus, -a, -um, *trusting; credulous; gullible.*
       aureus, -a, -um, *made of gold; of great excellence or beauty, splendid, golden.*
          tē ... aureā: *golden you* or *you, [as if you were] golden* (like Venus herself,
          often described as golden, as in Vergil, *Aeneid* 10.16, **Venus aurea**).
10   **quī ... / spērat** (11): supply **tē futūram esse** or **tē fore** to complete the in-
       direct statement.
       vacuus, -a, -um, *empty;* of the sky, *clear; free* (from other engagements), *avail-
       able.*
       amābilis, -is, -e, *able to be loved, lovable.*
11   **nescius, -a, -um** + gen., *unaware* (of), *ignorant* (of).
       aura, -ae, f., *breeze* (often found in nautical contexts, in which the "breeze" is
       regarded as changeable, unreliable, and dangerous to mariners);
       metaphorical, *breath* (of popular or political favor, regarded as fickle and
       unreliable); of a woman, *aura, charm, sex-appeal.*
          aurae: here, *breeze,* but keep the third definition given above in mind as
          well.
12   **fallāx, fallācis,** *false, deceitful, shifting, treacherous.*
       miser, misera, miserum, *to be pitied, pitiable; wretched.*
       Miserī: predicate adjective; supply **sunt.**
13   **intemptātus [in-,** *not* + **temptō, -āre, -āvī, -ātus,** *to test, try*], **-a, -um,** *untested,
       untried.*
       niteō, -ēre, *to shine.*
          intemptāta nitēs: Vessey (p. 467) suggests that **nitēs** may pick up the im-
          age of gold from **aureā** (9) and that "*intemptata* would then mean
          'unassayed,' 'untried' in a metallurgical sense." Thus, "all those who
          'assay' Pyrrha in the fire of love find her base metal, despite the superfi-
          cial sheen that captivates them."
       Mē ... / ... / suspendisse (15): indirect statement introduced by **sacer /
          ... pariēs indicat** (13–14); **vestīmenta** (16) is the object of **suspendisse**
          (15).
       tabulā: survivors of a shipwreck would place a votive tablet with a message
          written on it on a temple wall and hang up their wet clothes as dedications
          to Neptune, the god of the sea.
       sacer, sacra, sacrum, *sacred.*
14   **vōtīvus, -a, -um,** *promised, vowed, votive.*
       pariēs: here the wall of a shrine or temple.
       indicō, -āre, -āvī, -ātus, *to show.*
       ūvidus, -a, -um, *wet.*
15   **potēns, potentis,** *powerful;* + gen., *having power over.*
16   **maris**: usually taken with **potentī** (15), but may also be taken with **deō.**

Text

deō (16): some editors change this manuscript reading to **deae**, referring to Venus;
some commentators note that **deō** could be used of either a male or a female deity,
thus either Neptune or Venus.

9   quī nunc tē fruitur crēdulus aureā,

10   quī semper vacuam, semper amābilem

11   spērat, nescius aurae

12   fallācis. Miserī, quibus

13   intemptāta nitēs. Mē tabulā sacer

14   vōtīvā pariēs indicat ūvida

15   suspendisse potentī

16   vestīmenta maris deō.

Explorations

12.   How does the time frame change in lines 9–12a? To what scene earlier in the poem does the poet now revert?

13.   Compare the word order in the phrase **tē fruitur crēdulus aureā** (9) to that in **gracilis tē puer** (1). What reversal has taken place?

14.   Comment on the effectiveness of repetition in lines 9–10.

15.   How does the phrase **nescius aurae / fallācis** (11b–12a) comment on the three main elements of the poem: the boy, the sea, and Pyrrha?

16.   How do lines 12b–13a generalize what the speaker has been saying about Pyrrha and the boy? How can the words **intemptāta nitēs** (13a) be seen as continuing the metaphor of seafaring and the sea? In your answer, consider the passage from Lucretius below. Is the suggested allusion to metallurgy (see the vocabulary entry for **intemptāta nitēs**, 13) convincing?

17.   What is the speaker saying about himself in lines 13b–16?

18.   In lines 13b–16, what pattern do you find in the placement of nouns and adjectives? What is its effect?

19.   What arguments can you make for and against changing **deō** (16) to **deae**?

Passage for Comparison

Lucretius *De rerum natura* 5.1004–5:

Lucretius is speaking about the way things were in the remote past, before the advent of seafaring:

1004   nec poterat quemquam placidī pellācia pontī
1005   subdola pellicere in fraudem rīdentibus undīs.

> nor was the treacherous allure of the calm sea able to entice anyone into ruin with its smiling waves.

Odes 1.5

1 Quis multā gracilis tē puer in rosā
2 perfūsus liquidīs urget odōribus
3 　grātō, Pyrrha, sub antrō?
4 　　Cui flāvam religās comam,

5 simplex munditiīs? Heu quotiēns fidem
6 mūtātōsque deōs flēbit et aspera
7 　nigrīs aequora ventīs
8 　　ēmīrābitur īnsolēns,

9 quī nunc tē fruitur crēdulus aureā,
10 quī semper vacuam, semper amābilem
11 　spērat, nescius aurae
12 　　fallācis. Miserī, quibus

13 intemptāta nitēs. Mē tabulā sacer
14 vōtīvā pariēs indicat ūvida
15 　suspendisse potentī
16 　　vestīmenta maris deō.

Passage for Comparison

John Milton, 1608–74:

1 What slender youth bedew'd with liquid odours
2 Courts thee on roses in some pleasant cave,
3 　Pyrrha, for whom bind'st thou
4 　in wreaths thy golden hair,

5 Plain in thy neatness? O how oft shall he
6 On faith and changed Gods complain: and seas
7 　Rough with black winds and storms
8 　unwonted shall admire:

9 Who now enjoys thee, credulous, all-gold,
10 Who always vacant, always amiable
11 　Hopes thee; of flattering gales
12 　unmindful. Hapless they

13 To whom thou untry'd seem'st fair. Me in my vow'd
14 Picture the sacred wall declares t'have hung
15 　My dank and dripping weeds
16 　to the stern God of Sea.

Discussion

1. *Odes* 1.5 contains many words and phrases that respond to one another at a distance within the poem or are antithetical to one another. Locate the following examples and consider how they mark the difference between the present and the future of the boy and between the love affair of the boy and Pyrrha on the one hand and the figure of the speaker in the final sentence of the poem on the other:

    tē (1) : Mē (13)
    perfūsus liquidīs (2) : ūvida (14)
    urget (2) : flēbit (6) : fruitur (9)
    grātō . . . antrō (3) : aspera / . . . aequora (6–7)
    simplex munditiīs (5) : nitēs (13)
    quotiēns (5) : nunc (9)
    fidem (5) : fallācis (12)
    mūtātōs (6) : semper . . . semper (10)
    deōs (6) : deō (16)
    nigrīs (7) : aureā (9)
    ēmīrābitur (8) : crēdulus (9)
    īnsolēns (8) : nescius (11)
    crēdulus (9) : spērat (11)
    aureā (9) : aurae (11)

2. The scene in lines 5b–8 can be seen as a reversal of the scene that is described at the opening of the poem (1–5a) and that is explored further in lines 9–12a. The boy's enjoyment of Pyrrha in his present blissful ignorance in lines 1–5a and 9–12a is contrasted strongly with his future bewilderment and tears in lines 5b–8. The boy will repeatedly (cf. **quotiēns**, 5) suffer the storms of a tempestuous love affair.

    a. How do the adjectives **īnsolēns** (8), **crēdulus** (9), **nescius** (11), and **intemptāta** (13) suggest that the boy may one day escape from the inevitable storms of an affair with Pyrrha?

    b. To what does the speaker attribute his own salvation from the shipwreck of his affair with Pyrrha?

3. Ronald Storr spent many years collecting translations of *Odes* 1.5. The result: *Ad Pyrrham: A Polyglot Collection of Translations* (Oxford, 1959) with 144 versions in twenty-five languages. The most famous translation is that of John Milton, which is quoted on the facing page. Point out places in the translation where Milton has tried to imitate the Latin word order of the original. Point out places where he has used English words that derive from their Latin counterparts in the original. Where has Milton introduced original elements of his own? Overall, would you call Milton's translation successful? Why or why not?

4. If you have read the love poetry of Catullus, consider how the story of the boy and Pyrrha in this ode is similar to the story of Catullus and Lesbia as revealed in Catullus's poetry.

Meter: Alcaic

1   **ut**, interrogative adv., *how.*
     ut: introducing three indirect questions.
     altā . . . nive: may initially be taken as ablative of manner with **stet** but is
        usually taken as ablative of respect with **candidum.**
     stet: *stands out* or *looms up;* the subject is **Sōracte.**
     nix, nivis, f., *snow.*
     candidus, -a, -um, *bright, gleaming; white.*
2   **Sōracte, Sōractis,** n., *Mt. Soracte* (about 25 miles north of Rome).
     nec iam: *and [how] no longer.*
     sustineō [sub-, expressing movement from below + **teneō, tenēre, tenuī,**
        tentus, *to hold*], **-ēre, -uī,** *to support, hold up* (a load or burden).
3   **labōrō, -āre, -āvī, -ātus,** *to work; to labor* (from physical strain); *to be distressed,*
        to suffer.
           labōrantēs: i.e., "straining and bending under their load of snow"
              (Nisbet and Hubbard, p. 119).
     gelū, -ūs, n., *frosty weather; ice; cold.*
4   **flūmen, flūminis,** n., *river, stream.*
     cōnstō [con-, intensive + **stō, stāre, stetī, stātūrus,** *to stand*], **cōnstāre, cōn-**
        stitī, *to stand still.*
     acūtus, -a, -um, *pointed; piercing.*

ODES 1.9

To Thaliarchus, on Enjoying Youth

The speaker gives advice to a young man.

1   Vidēs ut altā stet nive candidum
2   Sōracte, nec iam sustineant onus
3   silvae labōrantēs, gelūque
4   flūmina cōnstiterint acūtō.

continued

Explorations

1. When one reads this stanza for the first time, who appears to be addressed with the second person singular verb **Vidēs**?
2. The addressee of the verb **Vidēs** is invited to see three things. What are they? What does the scene illustrate?
3. What is significant about the placement of words in the stanza?
4. What poetic figure is operative in the word **labōrantēs** (3), and what is its effect?

Mt. Soracte

5 **dissolvō** [dis-, *apart* + **solvō, solvere, solvī, solūtus,** *to loosen*], **dissolvere, dissolvī, dissolūtus,** *to undo; to melt, dissolve.*
frīgus, frīgoris, n., *cold.*
lignum, -ī, n., *wood; log.*
  ligna: object of **repōnēns** (6).
super, prep. + abl., *on, upon.*
focus, -ī, m., *hearth.*
6 **largē,** adv., *generously; abundantly.*
repōnō [re-, *back* + **pōnō, pōnere, posuī, positus,** *to put, place*], **repōnere, reposuī, repositus,** *to replace.*
  repōnēns: i.e., putting fresh logs on the fire to replace those that have already burned.
benignus, -a, -um, *kind; liberal; generous.*
  benignius: comparative adv., *more generously [than usual]*, modifying **dēprōme** (7).
7 **dēprōmō** [dē-, *down, away from* + **prōmō, prōmere, prōmpsī, prōmptus,** *to bring X out* (from where it is kept)], **dēprōmere, dēprōmpsī, dēprōmptus,** *to bring X out* (from where it is kept), *bring* (wine) *out* (from a wine cellar or storage jar).
quadrīmus [quadru-, *having four* + **hiems, hiemis,** f., *winter*], **-a, -um,** *four-winter-old.*
Sabīnus, -a, -um, *Sabine* (the Sabine region of Italy, where Horace had his estate, was northeast of Rome).
8 **Thaliarchus, -ī,** m., *Thaliarchus* (perhaps to be thought of as a young Greek slave or freedman; the name has been variously explained as meaning "Master of Festivities," "Master of the Feast," or "Prince of Good Cheer," from θαλία, *abundance, good cheer*; pl., *festivities; feast* + ἄρχω, *to rule,* or "In the Bloom of Youth," from θαλλία or θαλία, *foliage, leaf-buds, twigs,* especially of the olive + ἄρχω, *to begin*).
  ō Thaliarche: "The interjection [i.e., the word **ō**] sounds a Greek note" (Nisbet and Hubbard, p. 120).
merum, -ī, n., *undiluted wine; wine.*
diōta [Gr., δίωτος, *two-eared, two-handled*], **-ae,** f., *two-handled jar.*
  Sabīnā, (7) / ... **diōtā:** ablative of separation or ablative of instrument; the jar may be Sabine, but the epithet is also to be taken as transferred from the wine that the jar contains; Sabine wine was an ordinary wine.

5   Dissolve frīgus ligna super focō
6   largē repōnēns atque benignius
7   dēprōme quadrīmum Sabīnā,
8   ō Thaliarche, merum diōtā:

continued

Explorations

5. What word in the second stanza echoes a phrase in the first? In what specific ways does the second stanza contrast with the first? How are the orders given in the second stanza a fitting response to the scene described in the first?

6. Where is the scene of this second stanza set? Given that windows in Roman houses were usually small, high up, and generally shuttered in winter, is it likely that the speaker and Thaliarchus were actually looking at Mount Soracte in the first stanza?

7. What words and what prefix add a sense of urgency? What words add local color and a homely touch? Why does the speaker use a Greek word for the wine jar (note the etymological information in the word list for the word **diōta**)? What is ironic about calling the wine **quadrīmum** (7)?

8. How do the diaereses articulate the expression of thought in lines 5–6a? What pattern can you find in the order of the words **quadrīmum Sabīnā/ ... merum diōtā** (7–8)?

9   **permittō** [**per-**, *thoroughly* + **mittō, mittere, mīsī, missus**, *to send*], **permit-**
     tere, permīsī, permissus, *to allow to travel over a distance; to let go of; to give*
     (to another) *to do with as he wishes, to surrender, leave.*
     dīvus, -ī, m., *god.*
     simul: = **simul ac** or **simul atque**, *as soon as.*
10   **sternō, sternere, strāvī, strātus**, *to lay out on the ground; to spread; to lay flat; to*
     make (usually, waves) *subside.*
     aequor, aequoris, n., *a smooth, level surface;* by extension, *the sea* (either calm
     and flat or, as here, tossed by storms).
     fervidus, -a, -um, *extremely hot, blazing;* of the sea, *violently agitated, seething.*
        aequore fervidō: the ablative here could be of location, = **in aequore fer-**
        vidō, or it could be an ablative absolute, *while the.* . . .
11   **dēproeliāns** [the word appears only here in Latin literature; **dē-**, intensive
     + **proelior, -ārī, -ātus sum**, *to battle*], **dēproeliantis**, *struggling, battling*
     fiercely.
        dēproeliantīs: i.e., with one another.
     cupressus, -ī, f., *cypress* (an evergreen tree).
12   **agitō** [**agō, agere, ēgī, āctus**, *to do; to drive* + **-itō**, iterative or intensive suf-
     fix], **-āre, -āvī, -ātus**, *to toss, shake.*
        agitantur: sometimes the passive voice is used to make a transitive verb
           intransitive in sense; translate *shake.*
           quī simul (9) / **strāvēre** (10) . . . / . . . **nec** (11) . . . / **nec** . . . **agi-**
           tantur (12): the perfect indicative in the subordinate clause and
           the present indicative in the main clause create a present gen-
           eral structure; translate both verbs as present tense: *who, as soon*
           as they [ever] . . . *neither the X nor the Y [ever].* . . .
     ornus, -ī, f., *ash tree.*

9   permitte dīvīs cētera, quī simul

10   strāvēre ventōs aequore fervidō

11   dēproeliantīs, nec cupressī

12   nec veterēs agitantur ornī.

continued

Explorations

9. What is similar about the way that this stanza and the previous one open?
10. What, exactly, does the speaker mean when he says **permitte dīvīs cētera** (9a)?
11. Explain the phrase **aequore fervidō** (10) as an oxymoron.
12. What is striking about the word order of **ventōs aequore fervidō / dēproeliantīs** (10–11a)?
13. What is the speaker's point as he describes the activities of the gods in lines 9b–12?

13   **Quid ... crās:** indirect question dependent on **quaerere**.
        sit futūrum: *is going to be, is going to happen.*
        fuge: = **nōlī** + infin., *don't. ...*
14   **quīcumque, quaecumque, quodcumque,** indefinite pronoun, *whoever,*
            whatever.
            quem ... dabit: this clause is the object of **appōne**.
                quem ... cumque: tmesis; translate as one word with **diērum** depen-
                    dent on it, *whatever (of) days.*
        Fors, Fortis, f., *Luck, Chance.*
        lucrum, -ī, n., *profit, gain.*
15   **appōnō** [**ad-**, *to, toward* + **pōnō, pōnere, posuī, positus**, *to put, place*], **ap-**
            pōnere, apposuī, appositus, *to apply; to reckon, count; to put down* (in a
            ledger).
                lucrō (14) **/ appōne:** i.e., "credit to your account" (Nisbet and Hubbard, p.
                    122); the dative **lucrō** expresses purpose, *for profit, as gain.*
        nec, conj., = **nēve** or **neu,** *and don't.*
        dulcis, -is -e, *sweet.*
        amor, amōris, m., *love; love affair.*
16   **spernō, spernere, sprēvī, sprētus,** *to scorn, reject.*
        puer: nominative, not vocative; take as adjectival, *while a boy, in your youth.*
        chorēa [Gr., χορεία], **-ae,** f., *dance.*
            chorēās: i.e., "formal group dancing at parties" (Quinn, p. 142); see the
                passage for comparison below.

Passage for Comparison

With **nec ... / sperne ... chorēās** (15b–16), compare *Odes* 4.1.25–28, where
Horace describes the dancing at a party celebrating the successful love affair of a
young man; the speaker is addressing Venus:

25   Illīc bis puerī diē
26   nūmen cum tenerīs virginibus tuum
27   laudantēs pede candidō
28   in mōrem Salium ter quatient humum.

        There twice each day boys with tender maidens, praising your divine
        power, will thrice shake the ground with white foot in the Salian manner.

13   Quid sit futūrum crās fuge quaerere et
14   quem Fors diērum cumque dabit lucrō
15   appōne, nec dulcīs amōrēs
16   sperne puer neque tū chorēās,

continued

Explorations

14. The repetition of what verb form links the second, third, and fourth stanzas?
15. How does the exhortation expressed in the words **Quid sit futūrum crās fuge quaerere** (13) reinforce the message of the words **permitte dīvīs cētera** (9a)?
16. How do the words **Quid sit futūrum crās** (13) also move the poem forward?
17. How do lines 14–16 focus on future time?
18. What is meant by **quem Fors diērum cumque dabit lucrō / appōne** (14–15a)?
19. What initial consonant sounds in lines 13 and 14 make these lines stand out in the poem?
20. What does the speaker's use of the word **puer** (16) imply about the relative ages of the speaker and Thaliarchus? What seems to be the relationship between the speaker and Thaliarchus?
21. The passages from Theognis and from the *Anacreontea* quoted below are often cited as background for the speaker's thoughts in the third and fourth stanzas, especially for the clauses **permitte dīvīs cētera** (9a) and **Quid sit futūrum crās fuge quaerere** (13). What similarities are there? How does Horace move his poem in a different direction?

Passages for Comparison

I.

With **permitte dīvīs cētera** (9a), compare Theognis (seventh or sixth century B.C.) 1047–48:

> Now let us delight in drinking, speaking fair words: but whatever will be tomorrow, that is in the care of the gods.

II.

With **Quid sit futūrum crās fuge quaerere** (13), compare *Anacreontea* (poems written by various hands between the first century B.C. and the sixth century A.D. in the meters and manner of the Greek poet Anacreon of the sixth century B.C.) 8.9–10:

> I care about today, who knows tomorrow?

17   **dōnec**, conj. + indicative, *while, as long as.*
      vireō, -ēre, -uī, *to be green with vegetation;* generally, *to be green;* figuratively,
          to be in a vigorous condition; to be in youthful bloom.
          virentī: the participle here modifies an understood **tibi** (dative of separa-
              tion with **abest**) referring to Thaliarchus, *from you in the green of your
              youth.*
      cānitiēs, -ēī, f., *white/gray color; grayness* (of hair); *white-old-age.*
      virentī cānitiēs: a striking juxtaposition.
18   **mōrōsus, -a, -um,** *set in one's ways; hard to please; difficult, exacting; gloomy.*
      campus: = **Campus Mārtius,** the large field outside the old walls of Rome
          used for military practice and assemblies of citizens; it came to be filled
          with temples, porticoes, and commemorative monuments; in *Odes* 1.8 the
          Campus Martius is the site of athletic and military exercise; in the elegiac
          love poets its colonnades are places where courtesans stroll about hoping to
          attract men (see Catullus 55.6–8, Propertius 2.31.11–12 and 4.8.75, and Ovid
          Ars amatoria 1.67 and 3.387).
      ārea, -ae, f., *open area; open space* (in front of buildings).
19   **lēnis, -is, -e,** *gentle;* of sounds, *soft.*
      -que: joining **lēnēs . . . susurrī** closely with **āreae** (18).
      sub, prep. + acc., *at the approach of.*
      susurrus, -ī, m., *sigh, whisper.*
20   **compositus, -a, -um,** *arranged, appointed.*
      repetō [re-, *back, again* + **petō, petere, petīvī, petītus,** *to seek*], **repetere,**
          repetīvī, repetītus, *to return to; to seek again.*
21   **nunc . . . / . . . rīsus** (22) **. . . / pignusque** (23): supply **repetantur** (20).
      prōditor, prōditōris, m., *betrayer.*
          latentis prōditor: *betrayer of the one hiding;* the word **rīsus** in the next line is
              in apposition to **prōditor.**
      intimus, -a, -um, *inmost; the inmost part of.*
22   **rīsus, -ūs,** m., *laughter.*
      angulus, -ī, m., *corner.*
          intimō (21) **/ . . . ab angulō:** i.e., "from the depth of her hiding place"
              (Edmunds, p. 20).
23   **pignus, pignoris,** n., *pledge.*
          pignus . . . / . . . pertinācī (24): Horace is describing a rite of youthful ro-
              mance in which a boy tries to take a bracelet from a girl's arm or a ring
              from her finger as a pledge (**pignus**) that she will become his love. She
              will put up only a minimum of resistance.
      dēripiō [dē-, *away* + **rapiō, rapere, rapuī, raptus,** *to snatch; to take away by
          force*], **dēripere, dēripuī, dēreptus,** *to tear off, snatch away.*
      lacertus, -ī, m., *upper arm.*
          lacertīs / . . . digitō (24): dative or ablative of separation; **lacertīs** is poetic
              plural for singular.
24   **male,** adv., *badly;* here, idiomatic, *scarcely, barely.*
      pertināx [per-, *thoroughly* + **teneō, tenēre, tenuī, tentus,** *to hold*], **pertinācis,**
          having a firm grip, holding on tightly.
          male pertinacī: *feebly/faintly resisting.*

17 dōnec virentī cānitiēs abest
18 mōrōsa. Nunc et campus et āreae
19   lēnēsque sub noctem susurrī
20   compositā repetantur hōrā,

21 nunc et latentis prōditor intimō
22 grātus puellae rīsus ab angulō
23   pignusque dēreptum lacertīs
24   aut digitō male pertinācī.

Explorations

22. Within what time frame defined in lines 17–18a is Thaliarchus urged to seek the pleasures of *sweet love affairs* (**dulcīs amōrēs**, 15) and *dancing* (**chorēās**, 16)?

23. Why does the speaker refer to **cānitiēs . . . / mōrōsa** (17–18a) when defining the time frame within which Thaliarchus is urged to seek the pleasures of *sweet love affairs* and *dancing*? How does **cānitiēs** echo the first line of the poem, and how is this significant? What does the phrase **cānitiēs . . . / mōrōsa** suggest about the age of the speaker?

24. What places should be sought again (**repetantur**, 20)? What activities already mentioned in the poem might be found in these places?

25. What is significant about the placement of the words **lēnēs . . . susurrī** and **compositā . . . hōrā** (19–20)? How does sound reinforce sense in line 19?

26. What is significant about the word order in lines 21 and 22?

27. Six nouns serve as the subjects of **repetantur** (20). Identify these nouns. What is the ultimate goal of the actions in these two stanzas? What sequence of events could be imagined that would lead from activity in the **campus** to the snatching of the **pignus**?

28. Note that the passive verb **repetantur** (20) does not have an ablative of agent to accompany it. By whom is the action of this verb to be carried out?

29. Why does the speaker use the compound verb **repetantur** (20) instead of the simple verb **petantur**?

30. When are the actions described by the verb **repetantur** (20) to be carried out?

Odes 1.9

1   Vidēs ut altā stet nive candidum
2   Sōracte, nec iam sustineant onus
3   silvae labōrantēs, gelūque
4   flūmina cōnstiterint acūtō.

5   Dissolve frīgus ligna super focō
6   largē repōnēns atque benignius
7   dēprōme quadrīmum Sabīnā,
8   ō Thaliarche, merum diōtā:

9   permitte dīvīs cētera, quī simul
10   strāvēre ventōs aequore fervidō
11   dēproeliantīs, nec cupressī
12   nec veterēs agitantur ornī.

13   Quid sit futūrum crās fuge quaerere et
14   quem Fors diērum cumque dabit lucrō
15   appōne, nec dulcīs amōrēs
16   sperne puer neque tū chorēās,

17   dōnec virentī cānitiēs abest
18   mōrōsa. Nunc et campus et āreae
19   lēnēsque sub noctem susurrī
20   compositā repetantur hōrā,

21   nunc et latentis prōditor intimō
22   grātus puellae rīsus ab angulō
23   pignusque dēreptum lacertīs
24   aut digitō male pertinācī.

Discussion

1. How is this poem structured?
2. Horace's poem alludes to a poem of Alcaeus, a Greek lyric poet of the seventh century B.C. Alcaeus's poem is now only partially preserved. Compare the few remaining fragments of Alcaeus's poem quoted in Passage for Comparison below with Horace's ode.
3. How does the speaker present himself in this poem? What is his relationship to Thaliarchus?
4. How is the reader drawn into the poem, and what are the speaker's messages for Thaliarchus, for himself, and for the reader?

Passage for Comparison

Alcaeus 338:

```
1    ὕει μὲν ὁ Ζεῦς, ἐκ δ᾽ ὀράνω μέγας
2    χείμων, πεπάγαισιν δ᾽ ὑδάτων 'ρόαι
3    .   .   .   .   .   .   .   .   .
4    .   .   .   .   .   .   .   .   .
5    κάββαλλε τὸν χείμων᾽, ἐπὶ μὲν τίθεις
6    πῦρ, ἐν δὲ κέρναις οἶνον ἀφειδέως
7    μέλιχρον, αὐτὰρ ἀμφὶ κόρσα
8    μόλθακον ἀμφιβάλων γνόφαλλον.
```

Zeus (i.e., by metonymy, the sky) rains, and from the sky comes a great storm; the streams of water are frozen. . . . Defy the storm, building up the fire, and mixing honey-sweetened wine unsparingly, but putting a soft fillet around your brows.

Meter: Fifth Asclepiadean

1   **quaerō, quaerere, quaesiī** or **quaesīvī, quaesītus**, *to seek; to seek to know*
     about; to try to discover.
         Tū nē quaesieris: *Don't you try to discover;* the perfect subjunctive with
         nē is a more personal and demanding way of making a negative
         command than **nōlī** + infinitive. Horace is addressing Leuconoe (2).
         Use of the personal pronoun, **Tū**, suggests "earnest admonition"
         (Nisbet and Hubbard, p. 136).
     nefās [**ne-**, *not* + **fās**, n. indecl., (that which is) *in accord with divine or natural*
         law; (that which is) *possible or allowable*], n. indecl., (that which is) *not in ac-*
         cord with divine or natural law; (that which is) *not possible or allowable;* (that
         which is) *forbidden* (by divine or natural law).
         nefās: predicate; supply **est**; the subject is **scīre**; the expression is paren-
         thetical, set off by the metrical pauses.
     quem . . . / fīnem (2): = **quem mihi [fīnem], quem tibi fīnem**.
         fīnem: some commentators suggest supplying **vītae**, but **fīnis** by itself
         may mean *the end of a person's life,* or simply *death.*
2   **Leuconoē** [Gr., λευκός, *light, bright, clear;* of color, *white;* of special days, *bright,*
         fortunate, happy + voῦς, *mind*], **Leuconoēs**, f., *Leuconoe* (a fictitious name of
         uncertain meaning, perhaps "Clear-Minded," "White-Minded," or
         "Happy-Minded." The name fills a choriamb, - ˇ ˇ -).
     nec, conj., = **nēve** or **neu**, *and don't.*
     Babylōnius, -a, -um, *Babylonian* (here referring specifically to the
         Chaldaeans: "The Chaldaei were, strictly speaking, the inhabitants of lower
         Mesopotamia, then the Babylonian priesthood, finally astrologers in gen-
         eral," Nisbet and Hubbard, p. 138).
         Babylōniōs / . . . numerōs (3): Babylonian astrologers were well
         known for their numerical calculations based on astronomical tables
         and their predictions of the outcomes (**fīnēs**) of human affairs. As-
         trologers were, in fact, called **mathēmaticī**. Despite official expulsion
         from Rome in 139 B.C., astrologers had many followers among the
         Romans, including Maecenas and Livia.
3   **temptāris**: = **temptāveris**: parallel in construction to **quaesieris** (1).
     Ut melius: *How much better* (+ infinitive).
     quisquis, quisquis, quidquid, indefinite pronoun, *whoever, whatever.*
         quidquid erit: object of **patī**.
     patior, patī, passus sum, *to suffer; to endure, accept.*
4   **seu . . . seu**: *whether . . . or.*
     tribuō, tribuere, tribuī, tribūtus, *to assign, allot.*
         tribuit: note that this verb may be taken as present or perfect.
     Iuppiter, Iovis, m., *Jupiter, Jove* ("the weather god as much as the deity who
         presides over men's destinies," Quinn, p. 144).
     ultimus, -a, -um, *final, last.*
         ultimam: supply **hiemem**.

ODES 1.11

Carpe diem.

The following poem expresses a popular request in Western literature, that a girl or woman indulge in pleasures now with as little concern as possible for the future.

1 Tū nē quaesieris, scīre nefās, quem mihi, quem tibi
2 fīnem dī dederint, Leuconoē, nec Babylōniōs
3 temptāris numerōs. Ut melius, quidquid erit, patī,
4 seu plūrīs hiemēs seu tribuit Iuppiter ultimam,

continued

Explorations

1. What two things does the speaker urge Leuconoe not to do in lines 1–3a?
2. Which meaning of **nefās** is most appropriate in this context? Why?
3. Why does the speaker use the parallel construction **quem mihi, quem tibi** in line 1? What do these words suggest about the dramatic situation? What is the relationship between the speaker and Leuconoe?
4. What does the speaker encourage Leuconoe to do instead of seeking to know the future through astrology or other means (3b–4)?
5. What does the verb **patī** (3) imply about the human condition?
6. The word **hiemēs** (4) is an example of what poetic device?
7. The verb **tribuit** (4) may be present or perfect. Should the reader choose one or the other, or are both tenses appropriate to the context? If so, how?

"The Casting of a Child's Horoscope"
Drawing based on a 2nd century A.D. Roman relief sculpture

5   **quae**: the antecedent is **ultimam [hiemem]** (4).
     oppōnō [ob-, *against* + **pōnō, pōnere, posuī, positus**, *to put, place*], **op-**
        pōnere, opposuī, oppositus, *to place over/against; to place in the way of; to*
        station/array (troops or military installations against an enemy).
            oppositus, -a, -um, *opposing.*
                oppositīs . . . pūmicibus: *by means of/upon . . .* , instrumental ablative.
     dēbilitō [**dēbilis, -is, -e**, *weak, impaired, enfeebled* + **-itō**, verbal suffix], **-āre,**
        -āvī, -ātus, *to weaken, disable, incapacitate, enfeeble.*
     pūmex, pūmicis, m., *pumice* (a soft, porous volcanic rock).
6   **Tyrrhēnus, -a, -um**, *Tyrrhenian* (referring to the sea west of Italy, also called
        the Etruscan or Tuscan Sea).
     sapiō, sapere, sapīvī, *to have taste; to be intelligent, be sensible, be wise.*
        sapiās . . . liquēs . . . / . . . resecēs (7): jussive subjunctives.
     liquō, -āre, -āvī, -ātus, *to remove sediment from; to strain, purify.*
        liquēs: wine was poured through a cloth (**saccus**) or strainer (**colum**) or
            even snow to remove its sediment. This would be done right before
            drinking; if one had more time, the sediment could be allowed to settle to
            the bottom of the container by itself.
     spatium, -ī, n., *course, track* (for horse-racing or running); *space; length* (linear
        or temporal).
        spatiō brevī: *within short limits.*
7   **spēs, speī**, f., *hope.*
     resecō [re-, *back* + **secō, -āre, -āvī, -ātus**, *to cut* (e.g., crops)], **-āre, -āvī, -ātus**
        to cut back; to prune (trees or grape-vines).
     invidus [cf. **invideō, invidēre, invīdī, invīsus**, *to envy*], **-a, -um**, *hostile; jeal-*
        ous, envious, grudging.
8   **aetās, aetātis**, f., *age; time.*
     carpō, carpere, carpsī, carptus, *to pluck, pick* (fruit, flowers); figurative, *to*
        seize, pluck X (something thought to be desirable but transitory).
     quam minimum: *as little as possible.*
     crēdulus, -a, -um + dat., *believing* (in), *trusting* (in) (connoting foolish confi-
        dence).
        crēdula: cf. *Odes* 1.5.9, **quī nunc tē fruitur crēdulus aureā**.
     posterus, -a, -um, *later, future, coming hereafter.*
        posterō: supply **diēī** from **diem**.

5   quae nunc oppositīs dēbilitat pūmicibus mare

6   Tyrrhēnum: sapiās, vīna liquēs, et spatiō brevī

7   spem longam resecēs. Dum loquimur, fūgerit invida

8   aetās: carpe diem, quam minimum crēdula posterō.

Explorations

8.   Notice the relationship between individual words and metrical feet in line 5. How does this relationship enhance what Horace is saying in this line?

9.   What do lines 5–6a suggest as a possible scene for the dramatic monologue between the speaker and Leuconoe?

10. What is surprising about the action that the speaker is describing in lines 5–6a, **quae nunc oppositīs dēbilitat pūmicibus mare / Tyrrhēnum**? What might have been expected? Comment on possible military connotations present in the word **oppositīs**. How would they operate within the imagery?

11. Look at the three commands the speaker gives Leuconoe in lines 6b–7a. Explain the meaning of each command. What poetic device does the speaker use to suggest the relative importance of each of these commands?

12. Identify the tenses of **loquimur** and **fūgerit** in line 7b. How does the speaker use tenses effectively here to deliver his message?

13. How does the speaker personify time (7b–8a)? What is meant by the description of time as **invida** (7b)?

14. What metaphorical language earlier in the poem does the phrase **carpe diem** (8b) build on?

15. Some commentators suggest that the speaker has an amatory interest in Leuconoe. If so, what might the speaker be indirectly inviting Leuconoe to do by inviting her to seize the day? How would you then interpret the final phrase, **quam minimum crēdula posterō** (8b)? How would the echo in **crēdula** of **crēdulus** in *Odes* 1.5.9 influence your interpretation of the final phrase in *Odes* 1.11?

Odes 1.11

1   Tū nē quaesieris, scīre nefās, quem mihi, quem tibi
2   fīnem dī dederint, Leuconoē, nec Babylōniōs
3   temptāris numerōs. Ut melius, quidquid erit, patī,
4   seu plūrīs hiemēs seu tribuit Iuppiter ultimam,
5   quae nunc oppositīs dēbilitat pūmicibus mare
6   Tyrrhēnum: sapiās, vīna liquēs, et spatiō brevī
7   spem longam resecēs. Dum loquimur, fūgerit invida
8   aetās: carpe diem, quam minimum crēdula posterō.

Discussion

1. How is the poem structured?
2. The name Leuconoe is a compound noun made up of two Greek bases (see vocabulary entry). If the name is fictional, as it probably is, why would Horace have chosen it for the name of the young woman in this poem?
3. What is the message for humans of the imagery in lines 5–6a of this ode? What does the speaker intend to convey to Leuconoe by describing the workings of nature in these terms?
4. The clauses **spatiō brevī / spem longam resecēs** (6b–7a) and **carpe diem** (8) are usually interpreted as containing allusions to the pruning of grape vines and the harvesting of grapes. How would these allusions reinforce the positive message that the speaker conveys to Leuconoe in these lines as a human response to the vision of the vulnerability and transitoriness of nature displayed in lines 5–6a?
5. This poem's message is similar to that of *Odes* 1.9. What similarities do you find between the two odes? What major differences? Which poem do you prefer? Why?
6. Compare and contrast Horace's entreaty to Leuconoe here with Catullus's plea to Lesbia in his poem 5, quoted below. Which poem is more direct? How do you account for your answer?

Passage for Comparison

Catullus 5:

1   Vīvāmus, mea Lesbia, atque amēmus,
2   rūmōrēsque senum sevēriōrum
3   omnēs ūnius aestimēmus assis!
4   Sōlēs occidere et redīre possunt:
5   nōbīs cum semel occidit brevis lūx,
6   nox est perpetua ūna dormienda.
7   Dā mī bāsia mīlle, deinde centum,
8   dein mīlle altera, dein secunda centum,

9   deinde ūsque altera mīlle, deinde centum.
10 Dein, cum mīlia multa fēcerīmus,
11 conturbābimus illa, nē sciāmus,
12 aut nē quis malus invidēre possit,
13 cum tantum sciat esse bāsiōrum.

Let us live, my Lesbia, and let us love, and let us value all the gossip of those rather stern old men as worth just one cent. Suns can set and rise again; whenever [our] brief light has once set/once sets for us, one uninterrupted night must be slept by us. Give me a thousand kisses, then a hundred, then a second thousand, then a second hundred, then yet another thousand, then a hundred. Then, when we will have reached many thousands, we will confound them, so that we may not know [how many they are], or some evil person may not be able to cast a spell on us, once he knows there to be so great a number of kisses.

Meter: Second Asclepiadean

1 **Cum . . . / . . . / laudās** (3) **. . . / . . . tumet** (4): a present general grammatical structure; translate **cum** as *whenever*, and add *always* with **tumet**.

  Lȳdia [Gr., Λυδία], **-ae**, f., *Lydia* (a woman's name, from Lydia, a country in Asia Minor, on the Aegean Sea; it was a characteristic name of Greek women slaves and freedwomen in Rome at Horace's time. The name Lydia is given to women in three other poems of Horace, *Odes* 1.8, 1.25, and 3.9; *Odes* 1.8 is given in Passages for Comparison II at the end of the material for this ode, and *Odes* 1.25 and 3.9 appear later in this collection; whether these Lydias are meant to represent the same character is an open question).

  Tēlephus [Gr., Τήλεφος], **-ī**, m., *Telephus* (Horace also refers to a Telephus in two other poems, *Odes* 3.19.26 and 4.11.21, not included in this collection).

2 **cervīx, cervīcis**, f., *neck.*

  roseus, -a, -um, *made of roses; rose-colored, rosy.*

  cervīcem roseam: the adjective here implies youthfulness.

  cēreus, -a, -um, *made of wax, waxen; wax-colored, pale yellow; soft, delicate.*

3 **bracchium, -ī**, n., *arm.*

  vae, interj. expressing anguish, *alas.*

4 **fervēns, ferventis**, *intensely hot; boiling; inflamed.*

  difficilis, -is, -e, *hard to deal with, troublesome, difficult.*

  bīlis, bīlis, f., *fluid secreted from the liver, bile;* by extension, *anger.*

  tumeō, -ēre, -uī, *to swell.*

  iecur, iecoris, n., *liver* (considered the seat of deep emotions and passions).

ODES 1.13

Jealousy, Anger, and Love

Lydia's adoring praise of Telephus inflames the speaker.

1   Cum tū, Lȳdia, Tēlephī
2 cervīcem roseam, cērea Tēlephī
3   laudās bracchia, vae meum
4 fervēns difficilī bīle tumet iecur.

continued

Explorations

1.   What is the dramatic scene?
2.   What can you deduce about the present relationship of Lydia with Telephus, about the speaker's feelings about Telephus, and about the present and past relationship of the speaker with Lydia?
3.   What is it in particular that the speaker cannot stand about Lydia's praise of Telephus? How would this make the speaker envious? What might this suggest about the relative ages of Telephus and the speaker?
4.   The speaker's repetition of Telephus's name (**Tēlephī / . . . Tēlephī**, 1b–2b) as he recounts Lydia's praise of the boy suggests that he is echoing Lydia's repetition of Telephus's name when she praises him.
   a.   What reaction would such repetition provoke on the part of the speaker?
   b.   What would Lydia's repetition of Telephus's name reveal about her own feelings?
   c.   Why would Lydia be praising Telephus and repeating his name in the presence of the speaker?
5.   The speaker carefully arranges words and sounds as he repeats Lydia's praise of Telephus (1–3a). Locate examples of the following:
   a.   Initial *c*'s
   b.   Arrangement of initial consonants in the following sequences:
          a : b :: c :: b : a
          a : b : c :: d :: c : b : a
   c.   Asyndeton
   d.   Chiasmus
   e.   Effective juxtaposition
   f.   End of line repetition
6.   How does the speaker react in lines 3b–4 to Lydia's praise of Telephus?

5   **Tum**: i.e., on all the occasions referred to in the present general grammatical
     structure in lines 1–4.

     nec ... nec ... / ... manent (6a): although **nec ... nec** would normally
     require a singular verb in Latin and English, the use of the plural suggests
     that the wording is equivalent to *both ... and ... never remain. ...* The pre-
     sent general grammatical structure continues from lines 1–4; in translat-
     ing, add *ever* with **manent**.

     mēns, mentis, f., *mind.*

     color, colōris, m., *color; color of the skin, complexion.*

6   **certus, -a, -um**, *fixed, settled, regular.*

     sēdēs, sēdis, f., *seat; place; position.*

     ūmor, ūmōris, m., *moisture; tears; sweat, perspiration.*

     gena, -ae, f., *side of the face; cheek.*

7   **fūrtim**, adv., *secretly, imperceptibly, furtively.*

     lābor, lābī, lāpsus sum, *to glide, slip; to spread over* + **in** + acc.

        lābitur: *[always] spreads over*, present general.

     arguō, arguere, arguī, argūtus, *to show, reveal.*

8   **quam**, exclamatory adv., *how, with what.*

        quam: may be taken with **lentīs, penitus**, or **mācerer** or with all three.

     penitus, adv., *deep within.*

     mācerō, -āre, -āvī, -ātus, *to make wet, soak, steep, macerate; to soften; to weaken; to
     vex, torment.*

        mācerer: present subjunctive in an indirect question introduced by
        quam.

5   Tum nec mēns mihi nec color
6   certā sēde manent, ūmor et in genās
7   fūrtim lābitur, arguēns
8   quam lentīs penitus mācerer ignibus.

continued

Explorations

7.   What effective pattern of initial consonants can you find in lines 5–6a? What words in this stanza end in the same two or three letters?

8.   The speaker complains that when his liver becomes swollen and bilious in response to Lydia's praise of Telephus, he experiences three other things (5–7a). What are they?

9.   The participle **arguēns** (7b) introduces an explanation for the presence of **ūmor** on the speaker's face. How, according to line 8, should Lydia understand the cause of the moistening of the speaker's face?

9   **ūrō, ūrere, ūssī, ūstus**, *to destroy by fire; to cause to burn with intense emotion; to enrage, inflame.*

       Ūror . . . / turpārunt (10) **. . . / . . . / impressit** (12): this is the other form of present general structure in Latin, using the present indicative in the main clause and the perfect indicative in the conditional clauses; translate all three verbs as present and supply *always* with the main verb and *ever* with the subordinate verbs.

    seu . . . / . . . / . . . sīve (11): *whether . . . or* or *if . . . or if.*

    candidus, -a, -um, *white; fair-skinned;* by extension, *beautiful.*

10   **turpō, -āre, -āvī, -ātus**, *to make ugly; to bruise, disfigure.*

    umerus, -ī, m., *shoulder.*

    immodicus, -a, -um, *immoderate, unrestrained, excessive* (in size or number).

    merum, -ī, n., *pure wine* (i.e., wine that has not been diluted with water), *wine.*

11   **rixa, -ae**, f., *violent quarrel.*

    furō, -ere, *to be mad; to be out of one's mind with passion, rage.*

12   **imprimō [in-**, *into, against, on* + **premō, premere, pressī, pressus**, *to press*], **imprimere, impressī, impressus**, *to press one thing against another, imprint; to leave X* (accusative) *on Y* (dative).

    memor, memoris, *keeping in mind;* of marks, memorials, records, etc., *reminding, preserving the memory* (of something), *commemorative;* here translate, *telltale.*

    labrum, -ī, n., *lip.*

    nota, -ae, f., *mark.*

9   Ūror, seu tibi candidōs
10   turpārunt umerōs immodicae merō
11   rixae, sīve puer furēns
12   impressit memorem dente labrīs notam.

continued

Explorations

10. Lines 9b–11a allude to repeated violent quarreling (**rixae**, 11a). Why would
     Lydia and a lover quarrel? Why might a lover batter her?
11. What is the speaker's typical reaction whenever he sees that lovers' quarrels
     have bruised Lydia's beautiful shoulders ?
12. What repeated action is recorded in the second half of the sentence (11b–12)?
     Compare Lucretius's description of similar actions (see below). Why would
     the result of such an action inflame the speaker?
13. Why does the speaker describe the mark (**notam**, 12) as **memorem**?

Passage for Comparison

With lines 11b–12, compare Lucretius *De rerum natura* 4.1080b–83; Lucretius is talk-
ing about people in love:

1080b   .   .   .   et <u>dentēs inlīdunt saepe labellīs</u>
1081   <u>ōsculaque adflīgunt</u>, quia nōn est pūra voluptās
1082   et stimulī subsunt quī īnstīgant laedere id ipsum,
1083   quodcumque est, rabiēs unde illaec germina surgunt.

> and <u>often they dash teeth against lips and crush their mouths</u>, because
> their desire for pleasure is not pure and urges lie near the surface that
> compel them to hurt that very thing, whatever it is, from where those off-
> shoots of mad passion rise up.

13   **Nōn, sī mē . . . audiās, / spērēs** (14): future less vivid condition. Note that
      Nōn negates **spērēs**.
      satis audīre, *to heed.*
14   **perpetuus, -a, -um**, *continuous, uninterrupted; constant.*
      perpetuum: predicate in the indirect statement dependent on **spērēs**, with
          futūrum esse understood; the subject of the indirect statement is **laeden-
          tem**, substantive participle, *the one who/he who harms/disfigures.*
      dulcis, -is, -e, *sweet.*
      barbarus, -a, -um, *foreign; uncivilized; barbarous.*
15   **laedō, laedere, laesī, laesus**, *to injure, harm; to disfigure.*
      ōsculum, -ī, n., *kiss; mouth, lip.*
16   **nectar, nectaris**, n., *nectar* (the drink of the gods).
      quīntā parte suī nectaris: Lydia's lips or kisses are divine, but there are
          two schools of thought regarding the phrase here: it may allude to a the-
          ory widely held in the ancient world that there are four elements, earth,
          air, fire, and water, and a mysterious fifth element or essence more per-
          fect than the others, thus, *with the purest essence of her own* (i.e., Venus's)
          nectar, or it may mean simply *with a fifth part of her own* (i.e., Venus's) *nec-
          tar*, i.e., with nectar only a fifth as sweet as Venus's, yet supremely capti-
          vating for humans.
      imbuō, imbuere, imbuī, imbūtus, *to drench, wet, soak; to coat* (with a liquid).

13   Nōn, sī mē satis audiās,
14   spērēs perpetuum dulcia barbarē
15   laedentem ōscula quae Venus
16   quīntā parte suī nectaris imbuit.

continued

Explorations

14.   What rhetorical shift does the speaker make with the clause **sī mē satis au-dās** (13b)?
15.   What is the advice that the speaker wants Lydia to heed in lines 13–16?
16.   How does the speaker flatter Lydia? How does he indirectly appeal to her in this stanza?

"Aphrodite of Melos"
Hellenistic, ca. 130–120 B.C.
Louvre, Paris, France

17   Fēlīcēs: supply **sunt**.
      amplius, comparative adv., *more*.
18   **irruptus** [word found only here; **in-**, *not* + **rumpō, rumpere, rūpī, ruptus,** *to*
      break], **-a, -um,** *unbreakable; unbroken.*
      cōpula, -ae, f., *link, bond.*
      nec . . . / dīvulsus (19) **. . . / . . . solvet amor** (20): repeat **quōs** and take
      the negative meaning of **nec,** *and . . . not,* with both **dīvulsus** and **solvet,**
      and whom love, not . . . , will not. . . .
19   **dīvellō** [**dis-/dī-**, *apart* + **vellō, vellere, vellī, vulsus,** *to pull*], **dīvellere,**
      dīvellī, dīvulsus, *to tear apart; to break up, break apart.*
      querimōnia, -ae, f., *formal expression of a grievance; accusation, complaint.*
      nec malīs / dīvulsus querimōniīs: compare the phrase **immodicae merō**
      / rixae (10–11a); Garrison (p. 223) notes that "gravestones of married
      couples sometimes bore the abbreviation S. U. Q. for *sine ulla querella.*"
20   **suprēmus, -a, -um,** *highest; final.*
      suprēmā . . . diē: ablative of comparison; the phrase is a common expres-
      sion for *the final day of one's life;* the noun **diēs,** usually masculine, is fem-
      inine when it marks a specific day.
      citius: comparative adv., *more quickly; sooner.*
      solvō, solvere, solvī, solūtus, *to loosen, untie; to release, set free.*

17   Fēlīcēs ter et amplius
18 quōs irrupta tenet cōpula nec malīs
19   dīvulsus querimōniīs
20 suprēmā citius solvet amor diē.

Explorations

17. How does the thought expressed in the previous stanza prepare for this final stanza?
18. What does the speaker offer Lydia in this stanza?
19. How does the ideal love envisioned in the final stanza compare with the wished-for ideal loves envisioned in Catullus 109 and Propertius 2.15.25–26 and 36 quoted in Passages for Comparison I and II below?
20. The last stanza opens with a line that is reminiscent of famous words of Odysseus and Aeneas (see the passages for comparison on the next page). What tone does the allusion to the words of epic heroes give to the opening of this last stanza? Is that tone maintained?

Passages for Comparison

I.

Catullus 109:

1   Iūcundum, mea vīta, mihi prōpōnis: amōrem
2   hunc nostrum inter nōs <u>perpetuum</u> ūsque fore.
3   Dī magnī, facite ut vērē prōmittere possit,
4   atque id sincērē dīcat et ex animō,
5   <u>ut liceat nōbīs tōtā perdūcere vītā</u>
6   <u>aeternum hoc sānctae foedus amīcitiae.</u>

You propose a pleasant thing, my life: that this love of ours will be <u>everlasting</u> to the end between us. Great gods, cause her to be able to promise truly and to say this sincerely and from [her] heart, <u>so that it may be permitted to us to extend through all our life this eternal compact of sacred friendship.</u>

II.

Propertius 2.15.25–26 and 36; the speaker is addressing his beloved:

25   Atque utinam haerentīs sīc nōs <u>vincīre catēnā</u>
26   vellēs, ut numquam <u>solveret ūlla diēs!</u>

            .   .

36   Huius erō vīvus, <u>mortuus huius erō.</u>

If only you were willing <u>to bind us</u> in our embrace <u>with a chain</u> so that <u>no day might ever undo it</u>. . . . In life I would belong to her, <u>in death I would belong to her.</u>

more on next page

III.

Homer *Odyssey* 5.306–7; spoken by Odysseus as he is spun about on his raft in a terrible storm sent by Poseidon:

> "<u>Three times and four times blessed</u> are the Greeks who died back then in the wide land of Troy, bringing pleasure to the sons of Atreus."

IV.

Vergil *Aeneid* 1.94–96a; Aeneas is speaking when his ship is caught in a storm:

94   Talia vōce refert: "Ō <u>terque quaterque beātī,</u>
95   quīs ante ōra patrum Trōiae sub moenibus altīs
96a   contigit oppetere!

> He says the following aloud: "O <u>three times and four times blessed</u>, for whom it fell to meet death before the faces of their fathers beneath the high walls of Troy!"

Odes 1.13

1   Cum tū, Lȳdia, Tēlephī
2   cervīcem roseam, cērea Tēlephī
3   laudās bracchia, vae meum
4   fervēns difficilī bīle tumet iecur.

5   Tum nec mēns mihi nec color
6   certā sēde manent, ūmor et in genās
7   fūrtim lābitur, arguēns
8   quam lentīs penitus mācerer ignibus.

9   Ūror, seu tibi candidōs
10   turpārunt umerōs immodicae merō
11   rixae, sīve puer furēns
12   impressit memorem dente labrīs notam.

13   Nōn, sī mē satis audiās,
14   spērēs perpetuum dulcia barbarē
15   laedentem ōscula quae Venus
16   quīntā parte suī nectaris imbuit.

17   Fēlīcēs ter et amplius
18   quōs irrupta tenet cōpula nec malīs
19   dīvulsus querimōniīs
20   suprēmā citius solvet amor diē.

Discussion

1. Compare the first and second stanzas of *Odes* 1.13 with the poems of Sappho and Catullus quoted in Passages for Comparison I following these questions.
    a. How is the configuration of the three people involved in Sappho 31 and the configuration of the three in Catullus 51 similar, and how is the triangle of people involved in *Odes* 1.13 different?
    b. What symptoms does the speaker experience in *Odes* 1.13.3b–4 that recall those that the speakers in Sappho 31.5b–6 and Catullus 51.5b–6a experience?
    c. What symptoms does the speaker experience in *Odes* 1.13.5–8 that recall symptoms experienced by the speakers in Sappho 31.7b–16 and Catullus 51.7b–12?
    d. How does the speaker's description of his symptoms in *Odes* 1.13 differ in tone from the descriptions in Sappho and Catullus?
2. This poem may be viewed as an attempt on the part of the speaker to woo Lydia and to lure her away from Telephus and perhaps other lovers. Do you think he will be successful?
3. A woman named Lydia appears also in *Odes* 1.8, 1.25, and 3.9. Some readers think that the Lydia who appears in all these poems may be regarded as the same character; others are not so certain. *Odes* 1.25 and 3.9 are included later in this collection. *Odes* 1.8 is given in Latin and English translation in Passages for Comparison II following these questions. What does *Odes* 1.8 tell us about Lydia, her love life, and the speaker's interest in her?

Passages for Comparison

I.

Sappho 31:

1   Φαίνεταί μοι κῆνος ἴσος θέοισιν
2   ἔμμεν᾽ ὤνηρ, ὄττις ἐνάντιός τοι
3   ἰσδάνει καὶ πλάσιον ἆδυ φωνεί-
4   σας ὑπακούει

5   καὶ γελαίσας ἰμέροεν, τό μ᾽ ἦ μὰν
6   καρδίαν ἐν στήθεσιν ἐπτόαισεν·
7   ὡς γὰρ ἔς σ᾽ ἴδω βρόχε᾽, ὥς με φώναι-
8   σ᾽ οὐδ᾽ ἓν ἔτ᾽ εἴκει,

9   ἀλλὰ κὰμ μὲν γλῶσσά ⟨μ᾽⟩ ἔαγε, λέπτον
10   δ᾽ αὔτικα χρῷ πῦρ ὑπαδεδρόμηκεν,
11   ὀππάτεσσι δ᾽ οὐδ᾽ ἓν ὄρημμ᾽, ἐπιρρόμ-
12   βεισι δ᾽ ἄκουαι,

13   κὰδ δέ μ᾽ ἴδρως κακχέεται, τρόμος δὲ
14   παῖσαν ἄγρει, χλωροτέρα δὲ ποίας
15   ἔμμι, τεθνάκην δ᾽ ὀλίγω ᾽πιδεύης
16   φαίνομ᾽ ἔμ᾽ αὔτᾳ.

17   ἀλλὰ πὰν τόλματον. . . .

Catullus 51:

1   Ille mī pār esse deō vidētur,
2   ille, sī fās est, superāre dīvōs,
3   quī sedēns adversus identidem tē
4   spectat et audit

5   dulce rīdentem, miserō quod omnīs
6   ēripit sēnsūs mihi: nam simul tē,
7   Lesbia, aspexī, nihil est super mī
8   <vōcis in ōre,>

9   lingua sed torpet, tenuis sub artūs
10   flamma dēmānat, sonitū suōpte
11   tintinant aurēs, geminā teguntur
12   lūmina nocte.

13   Ōtium, Catulle, tibī molestum est:
14   ōtiō exsultās nimiumque gestīs:
15   ōtium et rēgēs prius et beātās
16   perdidit urbēs.

Sappho 31:

   1   That man appears to me to be equal
   2   to the gods, who sits opposite
   3   you and listens to [you] speaking sweetly
   4   close at hand

   5   and laughing in a lovely manner, [a thing] that truly sets
   6   the heart in my breast aflutter,
   7   for whenever I look at you for a moment, I can
   8   no longer speak,

   9   but my tongue is tied, a thin
 10   flame has at once run beneath my skin,
 11   I cannot see even one thing with my eyes, but
 12   my ears are buzzing,

 13   sweat pours down me, a trembling
 14   takes hold of all of me, I am paler
 15   than grass, and I seem to myself little
 16   short of being dead.

 17   But all must be endured/dared. . . .

Catullus 51:

   1   That man seems to me to be equal to a god,
   2   that man, if it is possible, [seems to me] to surpass the gods,
   3   who sitting opposite repeatedly
   4   looks at you and listens to you

   5   sweetly laughing, [a thing] that takes all sensation from me
   6   [and makes me] miserable: for as soon as [ever] I catch sight of you,
   7   Lesbia, there is nothing left to me
   8   <of voice on my lips,>

   9   but my tongue is paralyzed, a thin flame
 10   flows down through my limbs, my ears ring
 11   with their own ringing, my eyes are covered
 12   with a twofold night.

 13   Leisure, Catullus, is troublesome for you;
 14   in leisure you revel and exult too much;
 15   Leisure in the past has destroyed both kings
 16   and wealthy cities.

II.

Odes 1.8:

1   Lȳdia, dīc, per omnīs
2 hoc deōs vērē, Sybarin cūr properēs amandō
3   perdere, cūr aprīcum
4 ōderit campum, patiēns pulveris atque sōlis,
5   cūr neque mīlitāris
6 inter aequālīs equitet, Gallica nec lupātīs
7   temperet ōra frēnīs?
8 Cūr timet flāvum Tiberim tangere? Cūr olīvum
9   sanguine vīperīnō
10 cautius vītat neque iam līvida gestat armīs
11   bracchia, saepe discō,
12 saepe trāns fīnem iaculō nōbilis expedītō?
13   Quid latet, ut marīnae
14 fīlium dīcunt Thetidis sub lacrimōsa Trōiae
15   fūnera, nē virīlis
16 cultus in caedem et Lyciās prōriperet catervās?

Lydia, tell me the truth in the name of all the gods, why are you rushing to destroy Sybaris with love, why does he hate the sunny field, suffering dust and sun, why does he neither ride in military service among his peers nor hold back his Gallic horse's mouth with jagged bridle? Why does he fear to touch the yellow Tiber? Why does he avoid the wrestling oil more cautiously than the blood of a snake and no longer displays his arms bruised by weapons, known as he was for having often hurled the discus, often the javelin across the finish line? Why does he lie low, as they say the son of the sea-born Thetis did at the time of the tearful fall of Troy, for fear that his manly way might send him and his Lycian bands to their death?

Note on lines 13–16:

According to one version of the mythological biography of Achilles, his mother, Thetis, learned that her son was fated to die in the Trojan War. She therefore sent him away to the court of Lycomedes on the island of Scyrus in the Aegean Sea. Lycomedes dressed Achilles as a girl and had him live with his daughters so that he would not be detected and drafted into service for the expedition against Troy. While thus skulking on Scyrus, Achilles had an affair with one of Lycomedes' daughters, Deïdameia. In spite of his disguise, he was discovered and joined the expedition to Troy.

Meter: Sapphic

1   **integer, integra, integrum** [**in-**, *not* + **tangō, tangere, tetigī, tactus**, *to touch*], *untouched; whole; morally unblemished;* + **ab** + abl. or (poetic) + gen., *unsullied* (by), *blameless* (in).

    pūrus, -a, -um, *spotless, clean; pure; innocent;* + abl. or (poetic) + gen., *free* (*from*).

        integer . . . pūrus: adjectives used substantively; supply *a person.*

2   **egeō, -ēre, -uī** + abl., *to require, need.*

    Maurus, -a, -um, *belonging to the Mauri* (*of North Africa*), *Moorish, Moroccan.*

    iaculum, -ī, n., *javelin.*

    arcus, -ūs, m., *arch; bow.*

3   **venēnātus, -a, -um**, *poisoned, poison-tipped.*

    venēnātīs . . . sagittīs: dependent on **gravidā**, not on **eget**. There is evidence in both Greek and Roman authors of the popularity of **iacula** among the Moors of North Africa and of poison-tipped arrows among the Libyans.

    gravidus, -a, -um [**gravis, -is, -e**, *heavy*], *pregnant; filled, loaded.*

    sagitta, -ae, f., *arrow.*

4   **Fuscus** [**fuscus, -a, -um**, *dark-colored; dark-skinned, swarthy*], **-ī**, m., *Fuscus* (Aristius Fuscus, a friend of the poet's who makes a humorous cameo appearance in *Satires* 1.9; Lee 1969, p. 72, comments that in *Odes* 1.22 "Horace teases Fuscus about his cognomen by introducing Moorish javelins, the Hydaspes, and the torrid zones").

    pharetra, -ae, f., *quiver* (a cylindrical canister strapped over the shoulder for carrying arrows).

Passage for Comparison

William Shakespeare, *Titus Andronicus*, Act IV, Scene II, 18–23

    Demetrius: What's here? a scroll, and written round about.
                      Let's see:
                      [Reads.] *"Integer vitae scelerisque purus,*
                      Non eget Mauri jaculis, nec arcu."
    Chiron: O, 'tis a verse in Horace, I know it well,
                      I read it in the grammar long ago.

(Chiron is referring to William Lilly's *Latin Grammar*, the standard work on the subject in Elizabethan England.)

ODES 1.22

The Person Blameless in Life and Free from Wrongdoing and the Speaker as Poet

An unusual encounter in the Sabine woods emboldens the poet.

1   Integer vītae scelerisque pūrus
2   nōn eget Maurīs iaculīs neque arcū
3   nec venēnātīs gravidā sagittīs,
4   Fusce, pharetrā,

continued

Explorations

1. With what two special qualities does the speaker endow the hypothetical person being described in line 1?
2. What are the individual weapons that the person will not need? How are the weapons unusual?
3. Point out examples of chiasmus, tricolon, and interlocked word order or synchysis in lines 1–4. What tone do these devices create?

5   **sīve . . . / sīve** (6) **. . . / . . . vel** (7): *whether . . . or . . . or.*
      Syrtis, Syrtis, f., *Syrtis,* usually plural, *Syrtes* (the name given to the sandy
            shores of the gulfs of Sidra and Gabes between ancient Carthage and
            Cyrene on the northern coast of Africa and the seething tides they created,
            widely regarded as dangerous to sailors, also the name given to the desert
            behind these coastal regions.   The desert here was the site of a death-
            defying march of 10,000 soldiers around the gulf of Sidra in 47 B.C. led by
            Cato the Younger in the African war against Caesar.   Pliny in his *Natural
            History* 5.4.26 noted that the desert here was inhabited by serpents and the
            neighboring forest by a "multitude of wild beasts").
      iter: object of **factūrus** in the next line.
      aestuōsus, -a, -um, *hot, sweltering;* of sands, *burning;* of water, *raging,
            seething.*
6   **factūrus**: supply **est.**
      inhospitālis [in-, *not* + **hospes, hospitis,** m., *guest; host*]**, -is, -e,** *inhospitable.*
7   **Caucasus, -ī,** m., *Caucasus Mountains* (a range that runs north to south be-
            tween the Black Sea and the Caspian).
            inhospitālem Caucasum: Plutarch in his *Life of Pompey* 34 describes
                  great battles that Pompey fought against the Albanians and Iberians in
                  the region of the Caucasus Mountains in 63 B.C. in his pursuit of
                  Mithridates.   The passes through the mountains were treacherous,
                  and the area "was notorious for its wild beasts, particularly tigers"
                  (Nisbet and Hubbard, p. 266).
      quae loca: = [**per**] **loca quae**; note that in the plural **locus** is neuter when it
            means *regions.*
      fābulōsus, -a, -um, *celebrated in legends or stories, fabled.*
8   **lambō, lambere, lambī,** *to lick;* here used in an unusual and striking way, *to
            wash against.*
      Hydaspēs, Hydaspis, m., *Hydaspes* (the modern *Jhelum,* one of the rivers of
            the Punjab in India, which eventually flows into the Indus River; the
            Hydaspes was the site in 326 B.C. of Alexander the Great's victory over the
            native commander Porus).

5   sīve per Syrtīs iter aestuōsās
6   sīve factūrus per inhospitālem
7   Caucasum vel quae loca fābulōsus
8   lambit Hydaspēs.

continued

Explorations

4. Through what three places would the hypothetical person described in line 1
    be able to journey without weapons? Which two places are beyond the
    boundaries of the Roman Empire? What do the adjectives attached to the
    place names tell us about the places? What do they contribute to the tone of
    the stanza?
5. How does the third member of the ascending tricolon in lines 5–8 stand out?
6. What in the content and tone of the first two stanzas do you think made this
    one of the most famous Latin pieces for memorization and recitation over the
    centuries?
7. What do you expect to follow in the next stanza?

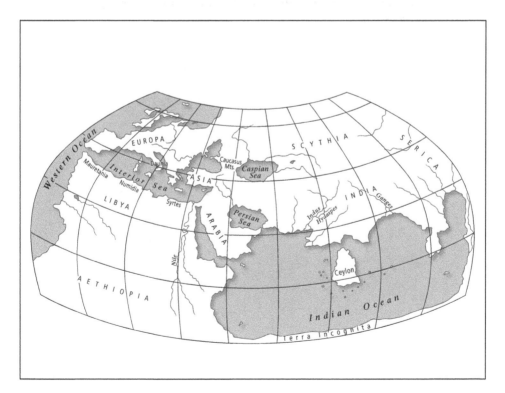

The World As the Romans Conceived It

9   **namque**, conj., *for; for instance, for once.*
     mē: direct object of **fūgit** (12), of which the subject is **lupus** (9).
     Sabīnus, -a, -um, *Sabine.*
          silvā . . . Sabīnā: i.e., the woods just beyond the Sabine farm that Maece-
          nas, advisor to Augustus and patron of Horace, gave the poet in 33 B.C.
10   **cantō, -āre, -āvī, -ātus**, *to sing; to sing* (a song); *to compose* (a poem); *to celebrate
     in song, sing of.*
          Lalagē [from the Greek verb, λαλαγέω, of people, *to speak; to chatter;* of birds,
          to chirp; of cicadas, *to produce a high-pitched song* (typical of this insect)],
          Lalagēs, f., *Lalage* (a name evocative of the song of the cicada, prized by
          Greek poets); often translated, *The Chatterer* or *The Prattler,* but these trans-
          lations do not catch the beauty of the name, which might better be ren-
          dered *Ms. Melodious.*
               Lalagēn: Greek accusative.
     ultrā, prep. + acc., *beyond.*
11   **terminus, -ī**, m., *boundary.*
     cūra, -ae, f., *care, anxiety.*
     vagor, -ārī, -ātus sum, *to travel without direction; to roam, wander.*
     expediō [**ex-**, *out of* + **pēs, pedis**, m., *foot*], **expedīre, expedīvī, expedītus**, *to
     set free; to extricate; to release; to solve, clear up, settle, put to rest.*
12   **inermis** [**in-**, *not* + **arma, -ōrum**, *weapons*], **-is, -e**, *unarmed.*
     inermem: modifying **mē** (9); translate the adjective as concessive,
          although. . . .

9   Namque mē silvā lupus in Sabīnā,

10   dum meam cantō Lalagēn et ultrā

11   terminum cūrīs vagor expedītīs,

12   fūgit inermem,

continued

Explorations

8.   What does the word **Namque** (9) indicate about the relationship of this stanza to what has come before?

9.   Who are the two figures in line 9? Where does the action take place? How does the word order effectively set up the scene?

10. What would the setting in the woods beyond the limits of the speaker's property and his absent-minded concentration on his singing lead the reader to expect to happen between the speaker and the wolf? What actually happens?

11. Locate a chiasmus formed by two words in line 9 and two in line 12. How does this rhetorical device underscore the point that is being made in this stanza?

12. How does the experience that the speaker describes here illustrate or prove the proposition stated in the first two stanzas?

13. The incident in the woods is adduced as proof of the initial proposition, and at the same time it introduces an image of the speaker himself. How is this significant? How does the speaker portray himself here? What elements of humor do you find?

13   **quālis, -is, -e,** *such as.*
      portentum, -ī, n., *portent; monster.*
        quāle portentum: = **portentum quāle,** *a portent such as,* object of **alit** (14)
        and **generat** (15). The word **portentum** conveyed several meanings to a
        Roman, as the word *portent* does to us. Originally it referred to a phe-
        nomenon that intimated an impending event of great importance, good
        or bad. Later, through a merger of the foreshadowing element with the
        subsequent event, a **portentum** also became an *unusual phenomenon,*
        strange creature, monster. At this point in the poem **portentum** would
        more likely have pointed to the *unusual event* that transpired in the pre-
        ceding stanza than to the **lupus,** common enough in the woods. The next
        three lines will revise this interpretation of the word.
      mīlitāris, -is, -e, *warring, martial.*
14   **Daunias,** f., adjective used as a substantive, *land of Daunus* (an early king of
        Horace's native Daunia/Apulia); *Daunia, Apulia.*
      lātus, -a, -um, *broad, wide.*
      alō, alere, aluī, altus, *to nourish.*
      aesculētum, -ī, n., *oak forest.*
        lātīs . . . aesculētīs: supply **in.**
15   **Iuba, -ae,** m., *Juba* (there were two kings by the name of Juba, a father and
        son. Juba I was king of Numidia during the civil wars in Rome. He
        sided with Pompey against Caesar, and after a stinging defeat at the bat-
        tle of Thapsus in 46 B.C. he committed suicide. His son, Juba II, to whom
        reference is made here in *Odes* 1.22, was brought to Rome under custody
        but later redeemed himself by fighting on Octavian's side at the battle of
        Actium in 31 B.C. He returned to northern Africa in 25 B.C. with
        sovereignty over the kingdom of Mauretania in parts of present-day
        Morocco and Algeria, where he researched and wrote widely, including
        a work on Africa containing stories about lions and other animals of the
        region).
      tellūs, tellūris, f., *earth, land.*
      generō, -āre, -āvī, -ātus, *to produce.*
16   **āridus, -a, -um,** *dry.*
      nūtrīx, nūtrīcis, f., *wet nurse* (for an infant).
        leōnum (15) **/ ārida nūtrīx**: in apposition to **tellūs** (15). In addition to the
        oxymoron (**ārida nūtrīx**) and transferred epithet (**ārida** properly belongs
        with **tellūs**), Horace is punning on the name Juba: the word **iuba** in Latin
        means *mane* or *hair on an animal's neck,* and is often used of lions.

13   quāle portentum neque mīlitāris
14   Daunias lātīs alit aesculētīs
15   nec Iubae tellūs generat, leōnum
16   ārida nūtrīx.

continued

Explorations

14.   What does this stanza add to the previous one to reinforce the proof of the proposition stated in the first two stanzas?
15.   What is the effect of the word **portentum** (13) as it is used to characterize the incident that the speaker has just described and the animal that he encountered?
16.   Explain the oxymoron in the phrase **ārida nūtrīx** (16).
17.   What is the tone of this stanza?
18.   Would *Odes* 1.22 be a satisfying whole if it ended with this stanza?

17   **piger, pigra, pigrum**, *sluggish, inactive; infertile, barren.*
      pigrīs . . . campīs: supply **in** and take these two words with **Pōne mē**.
         Cicero in *De republica* 6.20.21 and Vergil in *Georgics* 1.233–39 describe
         five geographical zones that were generally assumed to cover the earth:
         at the two poles were the frigid zones, next were two temperate zones,
         and at the equator was the desert belt. Horace has two of these zones in
         mind in the final stanzas of this ode.
18   **aestīvus, -a, -um**, *summer.*
      recreō [re-, *again* + **creō, -āre, -āvī, -ātus**, *to make, create*], **-āre, -āvī, -ātus**, *to*
         bring to life again, revive.
      aura, -ae, f., *breeze.*
19   **latus, lateris**, n., *side; edge; region.*
      mundus, -ī, m., *world.*
         quod latus mundī: = **latus mundī quod**. For the third time in the poem
         Horace has pulled the antecedent into its own relative clause; compare
         quae loca (7) and **quāle portentum** (13) above. The phrase **latus mundī**
         is in apposition to **ubi** (17).
      nebula, -ae, f., *mist, fog.*
20   **Iuppiter, Iovis**, m., *Jupiter;* by metonymy, *sky.*
         malus . . . (19) / Iuppiter: *an evil Jupiter*, i.e., a sullen or stormy sky.
      urgeō, urgēre, ursī, *to press; to push; to beset; to weigh heavily upon.*
         urget: the combined image of fog and sky dictates the use of the singular.
21   **pōne**: supply **mē**.
      currus, -ūs, m., *chariot.*
      nimium, adv., *very, too, exceedingly.*
      propinquus, -a, -um, *near, close.*
22   **domibus**: dative of purpose, *for/from having homes.*
      negō, -āre, -āvī, -ātus, *to deny; to forbid, ban, bar.*
23   **dulcis, -is, -e**, *sweet.*
      dulce: adverbial.
24   **dulce loquentem**: the Latin phrase reflects something of the meaning of the
         Greek name Lalage; see the vocabulary note on **Lalagē**, line 10.

17 Pōne mē pigrīs ubi nūlla campīs
18 arbor aestīvā recreātur aurā,
19 quod latus mundī nebulae malusque
20   Iuppiter urget;

21 pōne sub currū nimium propinquī
22 sōlis in terrā domibus negātā:
23 dulce rīdentem Lalagēn amābō,
24   dulce loquentem.

Explorations

19. In the first two stanzas the speaker describes a person **integer vītae scelerisque pūrus** who could apparently travel anywhere within or outside the Roman Empire safely with no need of weapons. In the central two stanzas he describes himself as wandering safely beyond the boundary of his Sabine estate and being left unscathed by a monstrous wolf. Where does he imagine himself being placed in the final two stanzas?

20. How do these two regions compare with the hypothetical destinations mentioned in the second stanza and with the places mentioned in the third and fourth stanzas?

21. The third and fourth stanzas are offered as proof that a person **integer vītae scelerisque pūrus** can go anywhere safely with no need of weapons. As a logical conclusion to the poem, what statement might the speaker be expected to make when he imagines himself placed in the regions of the world described in lines 17–22?

22. What statement, different from what one might expect (see the previous question), does the speaker actually make in the final two lines? How is it related to the speaker's presentation of himself as a love poet singing of Lalage and of his escape from the wolf in the third stanza?

23. With what tone of voice should the last two stanzas be recited?

24. Do the last two stanzas function more as proof of the proposition stated in the first two stanzas or as evidence of the speaker's love for Lalage?

25. What elements of humor and of the absurd are present in the final stanzas?

26. The final two lines are set off by anaphora and asyndeton and marked by assonance and consonance or alliteration. Note the occurrence of each of these devices.

Odes 1.22

1　Integer vītae scelerisque pūrus
2　nōn eget Maurīs iaculīs neque arcū
3　nec venēnātīs gravidā sagittīs,
4　　Fusce, pharetrā,

5　sīve per Syrtīs iter aestuōsās
6　sīve factūrus per inhospitālem
7　Caucasum vel quae loca fābulōsus
8　　lambit Hydaspēs.

9　Namque mē silvā lupus in Sabīnā,
10　dum meam cantō Lalagēn et ultrā
11　terminum cūrīs vagor expedītīs,
12　　fūgit inermem,

13　quāle portentum neque mīlitāris
14　Daunias lātīs alit aesculētīs
15　nec Iubae tellūs generat, leōnum
16　　ārida nūtrīx.

17　Pōne mē pigrīs ubi nūlla campīs
18　arbor aestīvā recreātur aurā,
19　quod latus mundī nebulae malusque
20　　Iuppiter urget;

21　pōne sub currū nimium propinquī
22　sōlis in terrā domibus negātā:
23　dulce rīdentem Lalagēn amābō,
24　　dulce loquentem.

Discussion

1. What mixture of seriousness and absurdity do you find in this poem?
2. How does the poem develop a contrast between the soldier/adventurer and the lover/poet?
3. Horace may have had lines 25–34 of Tibullus 1.2 in mind when writing *Odes* 1.22. These lines of the elegiac love poet Tibullus, Horace's younger contemporary by ten years, are quoted in Passages for Comparison I following these questions. What similarities and what differences do you find between *Odes* 1.22 and these lines of Tibullus? What would an allusion to this passage of Tibullus tell us about how Horace is defining his identity as a lover and a poet in *Odes* 1.22?
4. The first and second stanzas and the last stanza of *Odes* 1.22 recall two famous

poems of Catullus, numbers 11 and 51, the only two poems Catullus wrote in the Sapphic meter that Horace uses in *Odes* 1.22. The first and second stanzas of *Odes* 1.22 and the first three stanzas of Catullus 11 are quoted in Passages for Comparison II following these questions. What similarities can you find between these passages?

5. The hypothetical journeys of Catullus with Furius and Aurelius in Catullus 11 attest to the loyalty of the latter to Catullus, who entrusts them in this poem with a nasty message for Lesbia, bidding her farewell forever. In *Odes* 1.22, by way of contrast, the description of travels in the second stanza does not preface a farewell to a failed love. What does it preface?

6. What similarities and what differences can you find among the underlined words in *Odes* 1.22.21–24, Catullus 51.1–8, and Sappho 31.1–8, which are quoted in Passages for Comparison III following these questions?

7. How do the allusions to Catullus 51 and Sappho 31 in *Odes* 1.22 define Horace's identity as a poet?

8. What is the relationship between the name Lalage and the phrase **dulce loquentem** with which the poem ends? How does the name Lalage help to define Horace's identity as a poet?

9. In the tenth and last of Vergil's pastoral poems, the *Eclogues*, published in 37 B.C., the elegiac love poet Gallus talks about his inability to cure himself of his passionate and all-consuming love for his mistress Lycoris. What similarities and differences are there between the last two stanzas of *Odes* 1.22 and lines 64–69 of *Eclogues* 10, both of which passages are quoted in Passages for Comparison IV below? What does the passage from Vergil add to your understanding of Horace's ode?

10. How does Horace in *Odes* 1.22 set himself apart from Sappho, Catullus, Gallus, and Tibullus?

Passages for Comparison

I.

Tibullus 1.2.25–34; line 26 is missing in the best manuscripts, and various supplements such as the one given below in italics have been made. The speaker, shut out from the house of his beloved Delia, addresses her in this poem. In these lines he describes how he wanders through the city at night seeking her door and protected by Venus (to whom reference was presumably made in the missing line 26, as in the supplement offered below):

25   Ēn ego cum tenebrīs tōtā vagor ānxius urbe,
26   *sēcūrum in tenebrīs mē facit esse Venus,*
27   nec sinit occurrat quisquam quī corpora ferrō
28   vulneret aut raptā praemia veste petat.
29   Quisquis amōre tenētur, eat tūtusque sacerque
30   quālibet; īnsidiās nōn timuisse decet.
31   Nōn mihi pigra nocent hībernae frīgora noctis,
32   nōn mihi cum multā dēcidit imber aquā.

33   Nōn labor hic laedit, reseret modo Dēlia postēs
34   et vocet ad digitī mē tacitūrna sonum.

See, when I wander nervously in the dark throughout the whole city,
Venus makes me feel safe in the dark, nor lets anyone cross my path who
could wound my body with a sword or profit from taking my clothes.
Whoever is possessed of love may go safely and under divine protection
wherever he pleases; he should have no fears of ambush. The numbing
cold of a winter's night does not harm me, a heavy downpour does not fall
on me. This struggle does not hurt me provided that Delia opens the door
and quietly invites me in at the sound of her finger.

II.

Odes 1.22.1–8:

1   Integer vītae scelerisque pūrus
2   nōn eget Maurīs iaculīs neque arcū
3   nec venēnātīs gravidā sagittīs,
4   Fusce, pharetrā,

5   sīve per Syrtīs iter aestuōsās
6   sīve factūrus per inhospitālem
7   Caucasum vel quae loca fābulōsus
8   lambit Hydaspēs.

Catullus 11.1–12:

1 Fūrī et Aurēlī, comitēs Catullī,	Furius and Aurelius, comrades of Catullus, whether
2 sīve in extrēmōs penetrābit Indōs,	he will enter among the Indians at the end of the world,
3 lītus ut longē resonante Eōā	where the shore is beaten by the far resounding eastern wave,
4 tunditur undā,	
5 sīve in Hyrcānōs Arabasve mollēs,	or among the Hyrcanians or the soft Arabs, or [among]
6 seu Sagās sagittiferōsve Parthōs,	the Sagae or the arrow-bearing Parthians, or [at] the sea that the seven-mouthed Nile colors,
7 sīve quae septemgeminus colōrat	
8 aequora Nīlus,	
9 sīve trāns altās gradiētur Alpēs,	or whether he will cross the high Alps viewing the memorials of great Caesar, the Gallic Rhine, the rough sea, and the distant Britons....
10 Caesaris vīsēns monimenta magnī,	
11 Gallicum Rhēnum horribile aequor ulti-	
12 mōsque Britannōs....	

III.

Odes 1.22.21–24:

21 pōne sub currū nimium propinquī
22 sōlis in terrā domibus negātā:
23 <u>dulce rīdentem</u> Lalagēn amābō,
24   <u>dulce loquentem</u>.

Catullus 51.1–8:

1 Ille mī pār esse deō vidētur,

2 ille, sī fās est, superāre dīvōs,

3 quī sedēns adversus identidem tē

4   spectat et audit

5 <u>dulce rīdentem</u>, miserō quod omnīs

6 ēripit sēnsūs mihi: nam simul tē,

7 Lesbia, aspexī, nihil est super mī

8   <vōcis in ōre,>

That man seems to me to be equal to a god, that man, if it is possible, [seems to me] to surpass the gods, who sitting opposite repeatedly looks at you and listens to you

<u>sweetly laughing</u>, [a thing] that takes all sensation from me [and makes me] miserable/lovesick: for as soon as [ever] I catch sight of you, Lesbia, there is nothing left to me <of voice on my lips,>

Sappho 31.1–8; Catullus 51 is an adaptation of poem 31 by the Greek poet Sappho, which begins as follows:

1 Φαίνεταί μοι κῆνος ἴσος θέοισιν

2 ἔμμεν' ὤνηρ, ὄττις ἐνάντιός τοι

3 ἰσδάνει καὶ πλάσιον <u>ἆδυ φωνεί-</u>

4   <u>σας</u> ὑπακούει

5 καὶ <u>γελαίσας ἰμέροεν</u>, τό μ' ἦ μὰν

6 καρδίαν ἐν στήθεσιν ἐπτόαισεν·

7 ὡς γὰρ ἔς σ' ἴδω βρόχε', ὡς με φώναι-

8   σ' οὐδ' ἓν ἔτ' εἴκει.

That man appears to me to be equal to the gods, who sits opposite you and listens to you <u>sweetly speaking</u> close at hand

and <u>laughing in a lovely manner</u>, which truly sets the heart in my breast aflutter, for when I look at you for a moment, I can no longer speak.

IV.

Odes 1.22.17–24:

17   Pōne mē pigrīs ubi nūlla campīs
18   arbor aestīvā recreātur aurā,
19   quod latus mundī nebulae malusque
20   Iuppiter urget;

21   pōne sub currū nimium propinquī
22   sōlis in terrā domibus negātā:
23   dulce rīdentem Lalagēn amābō,
24   dulce loquentem.

Vergil *Eclogues* 10.64–69; Gallus, the elegiac love poet, unable to cure himself of his passionate and all-consuming love for his mistress Lycoris, speaks:

64   Nōn illum [= Amōrem] nostrī possunt mūtāre labōrēs,
65   nec sī frīgoribus mediīs Hebrumque bibāmus
66   Sithoniāsque nivēs hiemis subeāmus aquōsae,
67   nec sī, cum moriēns altā liber āret in ulmō,
68   Aethiopum versēmus ovīs sub sīdere Cancrī.
69   Omnia vincit Amor: et nōs cēdāmus Amōrī.

> Our labors cannot change that god [= Love], neither if in the middle of the frigid season we were to drink from the Hebrus River and endure the Thracian snows of a wet winter, nor if, when the bark dies and withers on the tall elm tree, we were to lead Ethiopian sheep here and there under the constellation of Cancer. Love conquers all; let us too yield to Love.

> (The Hebrus is a river in Thrace, and the constellation Cancer is associated with the heat of midsummer.)

Further Comparisons

With Horace's confidence in his inviolability as a poet in *Odes* 1.22, we may compare his confidence in *Odes* 1.17.13–14a that he and his Sabine farm are under divine protection:

13   Dī mē tuentur, dīs pietās mea
14a   et mūsa cordī est.

> The gods protect me, my piety and my muse are dear to the gods.

Horace's linkage here of his virtue (**pietās**) and his role as poet prefigures his appearance in *Odes* 1.22 as a person both **integer vītae scelerisque pūrus** and totally committed to poetry. He is assured of his safety in both poems.

Later, in *Odes* 3.4.21–36, Horace expresses confidence that the Muses have protected him in the past and will protect him in the future no matter where he might journey:

21   Vester, Camēnae, vester in arduōs
22   tollor Sabīnōs, seu mihi frīgidum
23   Praeneste seu Tībur supīnum
24   seu liquidae placuēre Bāiae.

25   Vestrīs amīcum fontibus et chorīs
26   nōn mē Philippīs versa aciēs retrō,
27   dēvōta nōn extīnxit arbōs,
28   nec Siculā Palinūrus undā.

29   Utcumque mēcum vōs eritis, libēns
30   īnsanientem nāvita Bosphorum
31   temptābō et ūrentīs harēnās
32   lītoris Assyriī viātor,

33   vīsam Britannōs hospitibus ferōs
34   et laetum equīnō sanguine Concanum,
35   vīsam pharetrātōs Gelōnōs
36   et Scythicum inviolātus amnem.

As one of your very own, Muses, I ascend the steep Sabine hills, or will go to cool Praeneste or low-lying Tibur or clear Baiae as it pleases me. Neither the military formation that was turned back at Philippi nor the accursed tree nor Cape Palinurus swept by waves from Sicily has destroyed me, a friend of your springs and dancing bands. Whenever you are with me, I will gladly try sailing the wild Bosphorus and try crossing the burning sands of the Syrian shore; I will visit the inhabitants of Britain, who are fierce to their guests, and visit the Concanian, who is delighted by horse's blood; I will visit unharmed the Geloni, who wear quivers, and the Scythian waters.

The second and third of the stanzas quoted above are reminiscent of the second stanza of *Odes* 1.22. In that stanza of *Odes* 1.22 it is the person **integer vītae scelerisque pūrus** who can travel safely anywhere in the world; in *Odes* 3.4 the Muses would accompany him and protect him. Horace's persona both as a person **integer vītae scelerisque pūrus** and as a poet dear to the Muses assure his inviolability wherever he may go.

Meter: Fourth Asclepiadean

1   **īnuleus** or **hinnuleus** [cf. Greek ἔνελος, *fawn*], **-ī**, m., *fawn*.
    īnuleō: dative, depending on **similis**, which modifies the subject of **vītās**.
    Chloē [Gr., χλόη, *the first green shoot of plants in spring*, especially the young
    green shoots of grass and wheat; cf. Χλόη, *The Verdant One*, an epithet of
    Demeter as the goddess of the young, growing grain; note the related verb
    χλοάζω, meaning *to be bright green*], **Chloēs**, f., *Chloe*, (the young woman
    whom the speaker addresses).
2   **pavidus, -a, -um**, of certain animals, *fearful, timorous* (by nature); more gen-
    erally, *panic-stricken, frightened*.
    āvius [**ā-**, *without* + **via, -ae**, f., *road, path*], **-a, -um**, *pathless*.
    montibus āviīs: ablative of place where without a preposition; take with
    quaerentī.
3   **nōn sine**: litotes.
    vānus, -a, -um, *empty; illusory; groundless*.
4   **aura, -ae**, f., *breeze*.
    siluae: = **silvae**, trisyllabic here to accommodate the meter.
    aurārum et siluae: perhaps hendiadys, *of breezes of the forest*.

"A Fawn"
*Drawing based on a 5th century B.C. bronze statuette from the sanctuary of Apollo,
Kourion, Cyprus, and now in the University Museum, Philadelphia*

Odes 1.23

Wooing a Young Girl Named Chloe

The speaker addresses a girl's fears about moving into womanhood.

1 Vītās īnuleō mē similis, Chloē,
2 quaerentī pavidam montibus āviīs
3   mātrem nōn sine vānō
4   aurārum et siluae metū.

continued

Explorations

1. Whom does Chloe avoid? What is the relationship between the speaker and Chloe? To what does Horace compare Chloe?
2. How does word order reinforce the sense of the first line?
3. What does the fawn seek? Why might its mother be described as *timorous/ frightened* (**pavidam**, 2)?
4. Comment on the effectiveness of the placement of each word or phrase in lines 2–3a.
5. Is the fawn's *fear of breezes and the forest* or *of breezes of the forest* (**aurārum et siluae metū**, 4) grounded in reality, according to the speaker? What figures of speech enhance the poet's description of the fawn's inexperience or naiveté?
6. What do the terms of the simile tell us about Chloe? What does the simile suggest about Chloe's mother and about Chloe's relationship to her mother? What does it suggest about Chloe's comfort when alone in the world apart from her mother?
7. What does the simile suggest about the reasons for which Chloe avoids (**vītās**, 1) the speaker?

5   **seu... seu**, conj., *whether ... or.*
        seu ... / ... seu (6): introducing the protases of a present general condi-
           tion, *if [ever] ... or if [ever].*
        seu ... / ... seu (6) ... / ... / **et** (8) ... **et**: notice the balance in this
           stanza, articulated by the conjunctions.
     mōbilis, -is, -e, *moveable; moving; fluttering.*
     vēr, vēris, n., *spring.*
     inhorrēscō, inhorrēscere, inhorruī, inceptive in the present and imperfect
        tenses only, *to begin to shake/tremble.*
        inhorruit: perfect tense used in the protasis of a present general condi-
           tional sentence; translate as present, *if ... [ever]. ...* The idea of shaking
           or trembling expressed in the verb **inhorruit** is transferred from the
           leaves (**mōbilibus ... / ... foliīs**, 6) to the approach of spring (**vēris
           ... / adventus**, 6); it is properly the leaves that shake or tremble, not
           the approach of spring.
6   **adventus, -ūs**, m., *arrival, approach.*
     folium, -ī, n., *leaf.*
        mōbilibus (5) **... / ... foliīs**: supply **in**.
     viridis, -is, -e, *green.*
     rubus [possibly related to **ruber, rubra, rubrum**, *red*], **-ī**, m., *bramble bush.*
7   **dīmoveō** [dis-/dī-, *apart* + **moveō, movēre, mōvī, mōtus**, *to move*], **dī-
        movēre, dīmōvī, dīmōtus**, *to move apart; to cleave; to part.*
        dīmōvēre: a second protasis of the present general conditional sentence;
           translate as present, *or if [ever]. ...*
     lacerta, -ae, f., *lizard.*
8   **genū, -ūs**, n., *knee.*
     tremō, tremere, tremuī, *to quake, tremble* (with fear or excitement).
        tremit: the subject is the fawn; since the verb is in the apodosis of a present
           general condition, one may add the word *always* in the translation.
9   **atquī**, conj., *but; and yet.*
     ut: *like.*
     asper, aspera, asperum, *rough; harsh; wild.*
10   **Gaetūlus, -a, -um**, *Gaetulian, of Gaetulia* (a region in the northwest of Africa
        known for its lions).
     frangere: infinitive used to express purpose.
     persequor [per-, *thoroughly* + **sequor, sequī, secūtus sum**, *to follow*], **perse-
        quī, persecūtus sum**, *to follow; to chase, pursue.*
11   **tandem**, adv., *at last, at length;* used to emphasize a command, with a strong
        sense of impatience, *Really, I ask you, after all.*
12   **tempestīvus, -a, -um**, of fruits, *ready, seasonable, ripe;* of women, *mature;* + dat.,
        ripe (for).
        tempestīva: causal, *since [you are]. ...*

5   Nam seu mōbilibus vēris inhorruit
6   adventus foliīs seu viridēs rubum
7   dīmōvēre lacertae,
8   et corde et genibus tremit.

9   Atquī nōn ego tē tigris ut aspera
10 Gaetūlusve leō frangere persequor:
11   tandem dēsine mātrem
12   tempestīva sequī virō.

Explorations

8. How does the second stanza expand upon lines 3b–4 of the first?
9. State in your own words what is being described in the words **mōbilibus vēris inhorruit / adventus foliīs** (5–6).
10. What is it about the approach of spring and the lizards that would make the fawn tremble?
11. Does the fawn have anything to fear from the rustling leaves and the lizards?
12. Where is the fawn's trembling localized? Is there any ambiguity in the verb **tremit** (8)?
13. Explain why **atquī** is an appropriate conjunction to introduce the statement made in lines 9–10.
14. The images of the wild tiger and the Gaetulian lion are humorously hyperbolic. Where did the speaker use humorous exaggeration earlier in this poem?
15. What is important about the word order in lines 9–10? In your answer, comment on significant juxtaposition of words, chiasmus, and hyperbaton.
16. How does the simile that the speaker develops in the first two stanzas already show that he does not wish to be like a tiger or lion or even to appear to be?
17. How are the last two lines a fitting conclusion for the poem? Comment on the significance of the following:
    a. **tandem** (11)
    b. **dēsine mātrem / . . . sequī** (11–12)
    c. **tempestīva . . . virō** (12)
    d. **tandem** (11) and **tempestīva** (12) as line-opening words
    e. **mātrem / tempestīva sequī virō** (11–12)
    f. **mātrem** (11) and **virō** (12) as line-closing words

Odes 1.23

1   Vītās īnuleō mē similis, Chloē,
2   quaerentī pavidam montibus āviīs
3   mātrem nōn sine vānō
4   aurārum et siluae metū.

5   Nam seu mōbilibus vēris inhorruit
6   adventus foliīs seu viridēs rubum
7   dīmōvēre lacertae,
8   et corde et genibus tremit.

9   Atquī nōn ego tē tigris ut aspera
10 Gaetūlusve leō frangere persequor:
11   tandem dēsine mātrem
12   tempestīva sequī virō.

Discussion

1. The first stanza of *Odes* 1.23 alludes to a fragment of Anacreon quoted in Passages for Comparison I following these questions. What similarities are there? What differences? We do not know anything about the rest of Anacreon's poem, which is lost. Why would Horace allude to this poem of Anacreon?
2. The coming of spring is often associated with Venus, love, and procreation; see lines 6–20 from the prologue to Book 1 of Lucretius's *De rerum natura*, quoted in Passages for Comparison II following these questions.
   a. How does the fawn's response to signs of the coming of spring in the second stanza of *Odes* 1.23 appear to be different from that of the birds and animals described by Lucretius?
   b. Why do the fawn and, by extension, Chloe have different or more complex responses to the coming of spring than do the birds and animals in the passage from Lucretius?
3. Of what must the speaker of *Odes* 1.23 convince Chloe if he is to be successful in his wooing of her?
4. The ferocity of lions and tigers was commonly used in poetry to symbolize the ferocity and savagery of people, particularly of warriors. The passage from Homer in Passages for Comparison III following these questions contains a simile in which Agamemnon is compared to a lion as he strips the armor from two sons of Priam whom he has just slain in battle. What similarities to and differences from elements in Horace's ode can you find? How would this passage from Homer help a reader understand Horace's poem?
5. How does Chloe's name contribute to the theme of *Odes* 1.23?
6. To what extent do the natural world and the human world parallel one another in *Odes* 1.23? How is the former a model for or a guide to humans?

Passages for Comparison

I.

Anacreon 408:

1   ἀγανῶς οἷά τε νεβρὸν νεοθηλέα
2   γαλαθηνὸν ὅς τ᾽ ἐν ὕλῃ κεροέσσης
3   ἀπολειφθεὶς ἀπὸ μητρὸς ἐπτοήθη.

Gently, like a new-born sucking fawn, that is frightened, abandoned in the woods away from its horned mother.

II.

Lucretius *De rerum natura* 1.6–20; the poet addresses Venus:

6   Tē, dea, tē fugiunt ventī, tē nūbila caelī
7   adventumque tuum, tibi suāvīs daedala tellūs
8   summittit flōrēs, tibi rīdent aequora pontī
9   plācātumque nitet diffūsō lūmine caelum.
10   Nam simul ac speciēs patefactast verna diēī
11   et reserāta viget genitābilis aura favōnī,
12   āeriae prīmum volucrēs tē, dīva, tuumque
13   significant initum perculsae corda tuā vī.
14   Inde ferae, pecudēs persultant pābula laeta
15   et rapidōs trānant amnīs: ita capta lepōre
16   tē sequitur cupidē quō quamque inducere pergis.
17   Dēnique, per maria ac montīs fluviōsque rapācīs
18   frondiferāsque domōs avium campōsque virentīs,
19   omnibus incutiēns blandum per pectora amōrem,
20   efficis ut cupidē generātim saecla propāgent.

O goddess, from you the winds flee, from you and your arrival the clouds of the heavens flee; for you the dappled earth puts forth delightful blossoms; for you the open stretches of sea smile, and the quieted sky shines with outpoured light. For as soon as the vernal appearance of the day is disclosed and the unbolted breeze of the productive/nourishing west wind flourishes, first the birds of the air, pierced in their hearts by your might, proclaim you and your advent. Next, the wild beasts and the farm animals dance over the rich pasture lands and swim across the rushing rivers: thus captured by your charm, each one greedily follows you wherever you continue to lead them. Finally, through the seas and the mountains and the grasping rivers and leafy dwellings of birds and the blooming plains, inspiring your coaxing love in the hearts of all creatures, you cause them greedily to beget their generations species by species.

III.

Homer *Iliad* 11.113–19:

> And as a lion easily broke into pieces the infant offspring of a swift hind, seizing them with its mighty teeth, having come into their lair, and took away their tender life. Although the hind happens to be very near, she is not able to defend them, for a terrible trembling comes upon her, and she rushes through the dense thicket and woods, hurrying and sweating over the attack of the terrible beast.

"A Lion"
Drawing based on a 6th–5th century B.C. bronze statuette from Southern Italy
now in The Art Museum, Princeton University

Meter: Third Asclepiadean

1   **Quis**: here functioning as an interrogative adjective, modifying **pudor** and
     modus.
     dēsīderium, -ī, n., *regret for loss; yearning, desire* (for something lost, for some-
     one absent, or for a dead person).
         dēsīderiō: dative dependent on **pudor** and **modus**, *shame for the desire,*
         limit to the desire.
     sit: *should there be*, deliberative subjunctive, or *can there be*, potential subjunc-
     tive.
     pudor, pudōris, m., *modesty; a sense of what is proper; shame.*
         pudor: = Greek αἰδώς, *shame, restraint*, a word that refers to the fear or in-
         hibition that holds one back from doing what one would be ashamed of.
     modus, -ī, m., *manner; limit.*
2   **capitis**: objective genitive dependent on **dēsīderiō** (1); by a metonymy
     common in Greek and Latin the "head" stands for the person; the tone is
     affectionate and emotional.
         tam cārī capitis: *for one so dear.*
     praecipiō [prae-, *before, in front* + **capiō, capere, cēpī, captus**, *to take*],
     praecipere, praecēpī, praeceptus, *to take beforehand; to advise, teach.*
     lūgubris, -is, -e, *sorrowful, mournful, of mourning.*
3   **cantus, -ūs**, m., *singing; song.*
     Melpomenē [Gr., Μελπομένη, participle of μέλπομαι, *to sing, dance*],
         Melpomenēs, f., *Melpomene* (one of the nine Muses; she is at times associ-
         ated particularly with tragedy, but here and in *Odes* 3.30.16, she is invoked
         in a general way as the source of inspiration of Horace's lyrics).
     liquidus, -a, -um, *flowing; clear.*
     pater: i.e., Jupiter, the father of the Muses by Mnemosyne, the goddess of
     memory.

ODES 1.24

Dear Quintilius is dead.

What limit to our grief?

1 Quis dēsīderiō sit pudor aut modus
2 tam cārī capitis? Praecipe lūgubrīs
3 cantūs, Melpomenē, cui liquidam pater
4   vōcem cum citharā dedit.

continued

Explorations

1. How are the two alternatives **pudor** and **modus** different? What is the implied answer to the question with which the poem begins (1–2a)?
2. What sort of relationship between the poet and the Muse is created by the imperative **praecipe** (2)? How does this affect our understanding of the verses that follow this address to Melpomene?
3. What kind of song does the speaker ask Melpomene to teach? How is this type of song appropriate to the setting?
4. Why does the poet mention that Jupiter has given Melpomene a clear voice and a lyre (3c–4)?

5   **ergō**, conj., *therefore; then, now; and so.*
        Ergō: "an exclamation of surprise and grief" (Garrison, p. 237); according
            to Nisbet and Hubbard (p. 283), who translate *and so*, the word here
            "expresses rueful realization that something has turned out the way it
            has."
     Quīntilius, -ī, m., *Quintilius* (the identity of this Quintilius is not certain, but
        a literary critic who was a friend of Horace and Vergil named Quintilius is
        reported to have died in 23/22 B.C.; Horace refers to the literary critic
        Quintilius in the passage printed below, written a number of years later).
     sopor, sopōris, m., *deep sleep.*
6   **urgeō, urgēre, ursī, ursus**, *to press; to weigh down on.*
     Cui: connecting relative, dative with **parem** (8), *equal to him.*
     Pudor: cf. above, line 1. In Greek Αἰδώς, *Shame*, is a common personification
        and a goddess; in Latin the personification **Pudor** is more unusual and
        does not bear any relationship to actual religious practice.
     Iūstitia, -ae, f., *Justice.*
        Iūstitia: like **Pudor**, not a goddess known among the Romans, though the
            Greeks worshiped Δίκη, *Justice.*
            Iūstitiae soror: to call Faithfulness (7) the *sister of Justice* implies that
                Quintilius possessed both virtues.
7   **incorruptus, -a, -um**, *unspoiled, uncorrupted; incorruptible.*
     nūdus, -a, -um, *nude, bare, naked.*
     Vēritās, Vēritātis, f., *Truth.*
8   **inveniet**: singular verb agreeing with plural subject.
     pār, paris + dat., *equal (to).*

Passage for Comparison

In *Ars poetica* 438–44, Horace pays Quintilius tribute as an honest and frank literary
critic:

438   Quīntiliō sī quid recitārēs, "Corrige sōdēs
439   hoc," āiēbat, "et hoc": melius tē posse negārēs,
440   bis terque expertum frūstrā, dēlēre iubēbat
441   et male tornātōs incūdī reddere versūs.
442   Sī dēfendere dēlictum quam vertere māllēs,
443   nūllum ultrā verbum aut operam īnsūmēbat inānem,
444   quīn sine rīvālī tēque et tua sōlus amārēs.

    If you would recite anything to Quintilius, he used to say, "Correct this,
    please, and this": if you denied that you were capable of better, he would
    order you to delete what you had tried two or three times without suc-
    cess and to send your improperly turned verses back to the anvil. If you
    preferred to defend a fault, rather than alter it, he would not waste a sin-
    gle word more in pointless effort to stop you unrivaled and alone from
    loving yourself and your own work.

5   Ergō Quīntilium perpetuus sopor

6   urget. Cui Pudor et Iūstitiae soror,

7   incorrupta Fidēs, nūdaque Vēritās

8   quandō ūllum inveniet parem?

continued

Explorations

5.   How does the word **Ergō** (5) make an appropriate transition from the first stanza to the second?

6.   How do the words **perpetuus sopor / urget** (5–6a) offer consolation to the bereaved in this song of mourning?

7.   What is distinctive about the placement of the words in line 5 with respect to the meter, and what is significant about the placement of the word **urget** (6a)? What similarly sounding words frame lines 5 and 6?

8.   How are lines 6b–8 relevant to a song of mourning?

9.   What does the modifier **nūda** add to the description of the virtues in lines 6b–7?

10. How does the portrayal of Quintilius in the eulogy in lines 6b–8 compare with the portrayal of the honest and frank critic in Horace's *Ars poetica* 438–44 (quoted on the opposite page)?

11. What has the Muse helped the poet to accomplish in this stanza?

Passage for Comparison

With **Cui . . . parem?** (6–8), compare the following lines from Milton's *Lycidas:*

8   For Lycidas is dead, dead ere his prime,

9   Young Lycidas, and hath not left his peer.

9   **bonīs**: substantive = *good men*, i.e., men of substance and social standing.
    Multīs ... bonīs: dative of agent with **flēbilis** in accordance with the
        passive sense of the adjective.
    flēbilis, -is, -e, *tearful; worthy of tears; to be wept over*.
        flēbilis: a common word in Latin funerary inscriptions.
    occidō [**ob-**, *in front of* + **cadō, cadere, cecidī, cāsūrus**, *to fall*], **occidere, oc-
        cidī, occāsūrus**, *to fall; of heavenly bodies, to set; to perish, die*.
10 **nūllī ... tibi**: for the dative, see above on **bonīs** (9).
    Vergilius, -ī, m., *Vergilius, Vergil* (presumably the Roman poet, 70–19 B.C.,
        with whom Horace was associated from the beginning of his poetic career.
        In *Satires* 1.6.54–55 Horace tells us that Vergil—together with the poet
        Varius—introduced him to Maecenas. Two other *Odes*, 1.3 and 4.12, are
        addressed to Vergil; in *Odes* 1.3.8, Horace refers to Vergil as **animae dīmi-
        dium meae**, *the half of my own soul*.
        Vergilī: vocative; the name comes at the end of the tenth line of the
            twenty-line poem, that is, at the center, a common point for emphasis
            in Horace.
11 **frūstrā**: modifying **pius** but in sense attaching equally to the verb **poscis**
        (12); Vergil's piety is in vain, and his request of the gods, even if made
        with the utmost correctness, is equally in vain.
    heu, interj. expressing sorrow, regret, etc., *alas*.
    nōn ita crēditum: this phrase has been thought to mean either *entrusted* (by
        you) (to the gods) *not with the provision* (that he might be returned to you
        upon demand) or *entrusted/loaned* (by the gods) (to us, i.e., to life) *not with
        the provision* (that he might after death be returned to us upon demand).
12 **poscō, poscere, poposcī** + double accusative, *to ask* someone *insistently* for
        something or someone; *to demand* something or someone from someone.
        crēditum / poscis: the metaphor is financial: **crēditum** = *entrusted* (i.e.,
            deposited) and **poscis** = *you demand* (back); cf. *Odes* 1.3.5–7 (quoted on
            the opposite page).

9   Multīs ille bonīs flēbilis occidit,
10 nūllī flēbilior quam tibi, Vergilī.
11 Tū frūstrā pius heu nōn ita crēditum
12   poscis Quīntilium deōs.

continued

Explorations

12. How do the statements made in lines 9–10 relate to what was said in the previous stanza? How at the same time do these statements move to a different focus or a different plane?
13. Compare the verb meaning *to die* in line 9 with the description of death in lines 5–6a. How are they different? How are the different expressions of death appropriate to their contexts?
14. What are we to assume is the reason that the dead Quintilius is lamented by Vergil more than by anyone else? What is the attitude of the speaker toward Vergil as the speaker addresses him for the first time in line 10?
15. How do the references to the tearful responses of the **multī bonī** and of Vergil relate to the rhetorical question that was asked at the beginning of the ode?
16. How does the address to Vergil (**tibi, Vergilī. / Tū . . .** , 10–11) move the poem in a new direction?
17. What adjective characterizes Vergil in line 11? What is he represented as doing in lines 11–12?
18. What does the adjective characterizing Vergil in line 11 tell about his relations with men and gods? What might he expect in return?
19. What attitude do the adverb **frūstrā** (11) and the interjection **heu** (11) suggest on the part of the speaker toward Vergil and toward what he is described as doing in lines 11–12?
20. Does either of the two interpretations of the phrase **nōn ita crēditum** (11) given in the vocabulary note make better sense? Consider the passage from *Odes* 1.3 given below. What does the interjection **heu** (11) add to the phrase **nōn ita crēditum**?

Passage for Comparison

With **crēditum** (11), compare *Odes* 1.3.5–7; the speaker is addressing a ship that is taking Vergil from Italy to Greece:

5   nāvis, quae tibi crēditum   ship, Vergil has been entrusted to you,
6   dēbēs Vergilium, fīnibus Atticīs   and you owe him back; I pray that you
7   reddās incolumem precor.   deliver him safe to the Attic land.

13   **Quid sī**: *What [would be the case] if . . . ? Supposing . . . ?*
      Thrēicius, -a, -um, *Thracian* (Thrace was traditionally the home of Orpheus
          and regarded as a semi-wild region just beyond the limits of the Greco-
          Roman world).
      blandus, -a, -um, *pleasing; flattering; coaxing; persuasive.*
          blandius: comparative adv., *more persuasively, more winningly.*
      Orpheus, -ī, m., *Orpheus* (the mythical poet whose music had the power to
          charm wild animals and even trees; see line 14. After his wife Eurydice
          was killed by a snakebite, Orpheus descended into the underworld to re-
          cover her. Orpheus's music charmed the gods of the underworld so much
          that they agreed to release Eurydice on the condition that Orpheus not
          look back at her until he had led her all the way out of the underworld.
          When Orpheus did look back prematurely, he lost Eurydice a second time,
          and he subsequently devoted himself to weeping and singing until he
          was killed by a group of Maenads. The story is told in, among other places,
          Vergil *Georgics* 4.453–527, published approximately six years before this
          poem).
14   **moderor [modus, -ī**, m., *manner; limit]*, **-ārī, -ātus sum**, *to set a measure; to
          moderate; to manipulate, handle, control;* only here of "controlling" a musical
          instrument, *to play.*
          moderēre: = **moderēris**, second person singular, present subjunctive.
              moderēre arboribus: there is an unusual elision here over the
                  diaeresis.
      arboribus: dative of agent with the perfect passive participle **audītam**.
      fidēs, fidis, f., *chord, string;* by metonymy, *stringed instrument, lyre.*
15   **vānus, -a, -um**, *empty.*
      imāgō, imāginis, f., *a representation; funeral mask* (aristocratic Roman families
          kept masks of their ancestors and displayed them at funerals); *image; ghost,
          shade.*
16   **semel**, adv., *once; once and for all.*
      horridus, -a, -um, *rough, bristly; horrid, frightening, terrible.*
          virgā . . . horridā: referring to the wand, or caduceus, of Mercury.

13 Quid sī Thrēiciō blandius Orpheō
14 audītam moderēre arboribus fidem,
15 num vānae redeat sanguis imāginī,
16   quam virgā semel horridā,

continued

Explorations

21. How are allusions to the story of Orpheus and Eurydice (13–15) appropriate after the statement in lines 11–12 that Vergil demands Quintilius back from the gods?
22. What are some of the implications of the phrase **vānae . . . imāginī** (15)?
23. How is Mercury's wand described in line 16? How does this description affect the reader's reaction to Mercury? Compare the description here with the scene in *Odes* 1.10, quoted below, where Mercury escorts souls to the underworld.

Passage for Comparison

With the phrase **virgā . . . horridā** (16) compare the phrase **virgā . . . / aureā** in *Odes* 1.10.17–20; the poet addresses Mercury:

17 Tū piās laetīs animās repōnis
18 sēdibus <u>virgā</u>que levem coercēs
19 <u>aureā</u> turbam, superīs deōrum
20   grātus et īmīs.

> You deliver pious spirits to their pleasant abodes, and <u>with your golden rod</u> you control the insubstantial throng, [you who are] pleasing both to the gods above and to those below.

"Orpheus"
Mosaic (3rd century A.D.)
Museo Archeologico, Palermo, Sicily

17   **lēnis, -is, -e**, *soft; gentle, lenient, mild;* + infin., *agreeable* (to doing something);
      easily persuaded (to do something).
          lēnis: masculine nominative singular, agreeing with **Mercurius** (18).
          nōn lēnis: *not easily persuaded:* litotes = *refusing* + infinitive.
      prex, precis [only used in the dative and ablative singular and in the plu-
      ral], f., *prayer.*
          precibus: "equally with *lenis* and *recludere*" (Quinn, p. 169); translate *in
          answer to our prayers.*
      fāta: accusative direct object of **reclūdere**.
      reclūdō [re-, expressing reversal + **claudō, claudere, clausī, clausus**, *to
      close*], **reclūdere, reclūsī, reclūsus**, *to unclose; to open.*
18   **nigrō . . . gregī**: dative of the goal of motion with **compulerit**.
          nigrō: transferred epithet; it is not the shades in the underworld that are
          black, but death or the underworld itself, devoid of light as it is.
      compellō [con-, *with*, also expressing intensity and completeness of action
      + **pellō, pellere, pepulī, pulsus**, *to push, drive*], **compellere, compulī,
      compulsus**, *to drive together, collect.*
      Mercurius, -ī, m., *Mercury* (here invoked in his guise as Psychopompus
      [Gr., Ψυχοπομπός = ψυχή, *soul* + πέμπειν, *to send*], the god who escorts the
      souls of the dead to the underworld).
      grex, gregis, m., *flock.*
19   **dūrus, -a, -um**, *hard.*
          dūrum: neuter singular nominative substantive; supply **est**, *[it is] a hard
          thing.*
      levius: neuter nominative singular comparative adjective, predicate to the
      clause introduced by **quidquid** (20).
      patientia, -ae, f., *patience; endurance.*
      patientiā: *through endurance*, ablative of means or cause.
20   **quisquis, quisquis, quidquid**, indefinite pronoun, *whoever, whatever.*
      corrigō [con-, expressing completeness of action + **regō, regere, rēxī, rēc-
      tus**, *to rule; to direct*], **corrigere, corrēxī, corrēctus**, *to set right, improve, cor-
      rect.*
      nefās [ne-, *not* + **fās**, n. indecl., (that which is) *right or permissible by or in ac-
      cord with divine or natural law;* (that which is) *possible or allowable*], n. indecl.,
      (that which is) *not right or permissible by or in accord with divine law or natural
      law;* (that which is) *not possible or allowable;* (that which is) *forbidden* (by di-
      vine or natural law).
          quidquid corrigere est nefās: this clause is the subject of **fit** (19).
          nefās: cf. *Odes* 1.11.1, **scīre nefās**.

17 nōn lēnis precibus fāta reclūdere,
18 nigrō compulerit Mercurius gregī?
19 Dūrum: sed levius fit patientiā
20   quidquid corrigere est nefās.

Explorations

24. What ideas associated with the underworld can you see combined in the phrase **fāta reclūdere** (17)?
25. How are the dead described in line 18? How is the image chosen here to describe the dead complemented by the verb **compulerit**?
26. What is metrically notable about line 18? Where else does this pattern appear in this poem?
27. Lines 13–18 make up a single rhetorical question in the form of a future less vivid condition. Review how this question (the longest sentence in the ode) relates to the statement made in lines 11–12. What is its message for Vergil?
28. How is the clause contained in the single word **Dūrum** (19), *[It is] a hard thing*, a fitting characterization to what is said in lines 11–18?
29. What has the speaker demonstrated to Vergil in the course of his address to him in lines 11–18? What is his final advice in lines 19b–20? What similar ideas do you find in the passages from Archilochus, Vergil, and Donatus quoted on the next page?
30. In the final stanza identify elements that contribute to a play on words for *soft*, *light*, and *hard*. How is **patientia** paradoxically appropriate as a response to something that is **dūrum**?
31. How does the final clause of the poem, **quidquid corrigere est nefās** (20), sum up the problem that Vergil faces in his response to the death of Quintilius in lines 11–18?

Passages for Comparison

I.

With **nōn lēnis precibus fāta reclūdere** (17), compare Vergil *Georgics* 4.469b–70:

469b ... Mānīsque adiit [i.e., Orpheus] rēgemque tremendum
470   nesciaque hūmānīs precibus mānsuēscere corda.

> ... and he [Orpheus] approached the shades of the dead, their fearsome king, and hearts that do not know the meaning of softening to human prayers.

more on next page

II.

With **sed levius fit <u>patientiā</u> / quidquid corrigere est nefās** (19b–20), compare
the passages below:

Archilochus 13.5b–7a:

> But, my friend, the gods have placed mighty <u>endurance</u> over incurable woes
> as an antidote [for them].

III.

Vergil *Aeneid* 5.709–10; the wise Nautes addresses Aeneas, distressed by loss of four
of his ships to fire after the games in Sicily in honor of Aeneas's deceased father
Anchises :

> 709   "Nāte deā, quō fāta trahunt retrahuntque sequāmur;
> 710   quidquid erit, superanda omnis fortūna <u>ferendō</u> est."

> > "Son of the goddess, let us follow where the fates draw us and draw us
> > again; whatever will be, we must overcome every misfortune <u>by bearing
> > it</u>."

IV.

Donatus *Life of Vergil* 18:

> > [Vergilius] solitus erat dīcere: "Nūllam virtūtem commodiōrem hominī
> > esse <u>patientiā</u>; ac nūllam adeō asperam esse fortūnam quam prūdenter <u>pa-
> > tiendō</u> vir fortis nōn vincat."

> > [Vergil] was accustomed to say: "No virtue is more suitable for a human
> > than <u>endurance</u>; and no misfortune is so harsh that a brave man cannot
> > overcome it by wisely <u>enduring it</u>."

Odes 1.24

1   Quis dēsīderiō sit pudor aut modus
2   tam cārī capitis? Praecipe lūgubrīs
3   cantūs, Melpomenē, cui liquidam pater
4   vōcem cum citharā dedit.

5   Ergō Quīntilium perpetuus sopor
6   urget. Cui Pudor et Iūstitiae soror,
7   incorrupta Fidēs, nūdaque Vēritās
8   quandō ūllum inveniet parem?

9   Multīs ille bonīs flēbilis occidit,
10   nūllī flēbilior quam tibi, Vergilī.
11   Tū frūstrā pius heu nōn ita crēditum
12   poscis Quīntilium deōs.

13   Quid sī Thrēiciō blandius Orpheō
14   audītam moderēre arboribus fidem,
15   num vānae redeat sanguis imāginī,
16   quam virgā semel horridā,

17   nōn lēnis precibus fāta reclūdere,
18   nigrō compulerit Mercurius gregī?
19   Dūrum: sed levius fit patientiā
20   quidquid corrigere est nefās.

Discussion

1. How is this poem structured?
2. Lines 5–6a of *Odes* 1.24 and the word **semel** in line 16 echo words and ideas in Catullus 5, which is quoted in Passages for Comparison I following these questions. What are the similarities and differences in the way death is represented in the two poems? What response to death does each of the poems offer? How does knowledge of Catullus's poem affect our understanding of Horace's poem?
3. Compare *Odes* 1.24 with Catullus 96, which is quoted in Passages for Comparison II following these questions. How are the two poems alike and different in their response to death?

Passages for Comparison

I.

Catullus 5:

```
 1   Vīvāmus, mea Lesbia, atque amēmus,
 2   rūmōrēsque senum sevēriōrum
 3   omnēs ūnius aestimēmus assis!
 4   Sōlēs occidere et redīre possunt:
 5   nōbīs cum semel occidit brevis lūx,
 6   nox est perpetua ūna dormienda.
 7   Dā mī bāsia mīlle, deinde centum,
 8   dein mīlle altera, dein secunda centum,
 9   deinde ūsque altera mīlle, deinde centum.
10   Dein, cum mīlia multa fēcerīmus,
11   conturbābimus illa, nē sciāmus,
12   aut nē quis malus invidēre possit,
13   cum tantum sciat esse bāsiōrum.
```

Let us live, my Lesbia, and let us love, and let us value all the gossip of those rather stern old men as worth just one cent. Suns can set and rise again; whenever [our] brief light has once set/once sets for us, one uninterrupted night must be slept by us. Give me a thousand kisses, then a hundred, then a second thousand, then a second hundred, then yet another thousand, then a hundred. Then, when we will have reached many thousands, we will confound them, so that we may not know [how many they are], or some evil person may not be able to cast a spell on us, once he knows there to be so great a number of kisses.

II.

Catullus 96; in elegiac couplets Catullus wrote a consolation to his fellow poet and friend Calvus, on the death of his wife Quintilia:

```
1   Sī quicquam mūtīs grātum acceptumve sepulcrīs
2      accidere ā nostrō, Calve, dolōre potest,
3   quō dēsīderiō veterēs renovāmus amōrēs
4      atque ōlim missās flēmus amīcitiās,
5   certē nōn tantō mors immātūra dolōrī est
6      Quīntiliae, quantum gaudet amōre tuō.
```

If anything pleasing or welcome to silent graves/to the silent dead in their graves can come, Calvus, from our grief, by means of which desire we renew old loves and [because of which desire] we weep for long-departed friendships, surely untimely death is not of such great grief to Quintilia, as she rejoices in your love.

Meter: Sapphic

1   **parcē**, adv., *sparingly; moderately; infrequently.*
     parcius: comparative adv., *less frequently* (i.e., than in the past).
     iūnctās … fenestrās: the windows of ancient houses in the Mediterranean
       world did not have glass panes but rather two shutters, which would be
       open to the air relatively infrequently; at night, as a rule, the shutters
       would be closed (**iūnctās**, *joined; closed*). The windows here are to be
       thought of as on a second or higher story of an **īnsula** or *tenement*, and they
       would face onto an alleyway at the side or the back of the tenement.
         iūnctās: the word may have erotic overtones suggesting lovers joined in
           love.
     quatiō, quatere, quassus, *to shake; to make X shake.*
2   **iactus, -ūs**, m., *a throw, a throwing.*
     iactibus: i.e., of sticks or stones to attract the attention of someone inside the
       house.
     crēber, crēbra, crēbrum, *repeated; frequent.*
     protervus, -a, -um, *bold, violent, boisterous; forward, shameless, impudent.*
         iuvenēs protervī: the young men of Greece and Rome would often go out
           during the night after dinner parties and drinking bouts in search of
           other kinds of fun. The Greeks called this reveling in the streets a κῶμος
           (*kōmos*), and for the Romans it was part of the **cōmissātiō**, the *drinking
           bout.* The revelers were called **cōmissātōrēs**, and as they reveled
           through the streets to the dwellings of courtesans they kept on their
           heads the garlands that they wore at the dinner party and drinking
           bout.
3   **tibī**: dative of separation with the compound verb **adimunt**.
     adimō [ad-, *to, toward* + **emō, emere, ēmī, ēmptus**, *to take; to buy*], **adimere,
       adēmī, adēmptus**, *to take away.*
         nec tibī somnōs adimunt: perhaps supply *as frequently as in the past*,
           continuing the comparative idea expressed by **Parcius** (1).
     amat: the verb has a wide range of meanings, including *to make love to; to hold
       on to, cling to, hug*; for the latter meaning, see Vergil *Aeneid* 5.163, **lītus amā**,
       hug the shore; here the door is shut and *hugs* the threshold.
         amatque iānua līmen: perhaps supply *more than in the past*, again con-
           tinuing the comparative idea expressed by **Parcius** (1).

A Shuttered Window

ODES 1.25

An Admonition to Lydia: "Carpe diem."

The speaker warns the arrogant Lydia that the tables will be turned on her.

1 Parcius iūnctās quatiunt fenestrās
2 iactibus crēbrīs iuvenēs protervī,
3 nec tibī somnōs adimunt, amatque
4   iānua līmen,

continued

Explorations

1. What happens *less frequently*, according to lines 1–2?
2. What would **iuvenēs protervī** (2) want when they throw sticks or stones at the woman's shuttered window? Why would their throwing of sticks or stones normally be *repeated* or *frequent* (**crēbrīs**, 2)?
3. Three actions are mentioned in the clauses containing the verbs **quatiunt** (1), **adimunt** (3), and **amat** (3). How does each of these clauses refer to part of the process of young men wooing a courtesan?
4. How is the present contrasted with the past in this stanza?
5. What is ironic about the use of the word **iūnctās** (1) with its possible erotic overtones and the use of the word **amat** (3)?

"Revelers"
Attic Greek red-figure drinking cup (ca. 490 B.C.)
Antikensammlung, Staatliche Museen zu Berlin, Berlin, Germany

5   **multum**: adverbial, with **facilis**, but its force may also be felt with **prius** and
     movēbat.
     facilis, -is, -e, *easy; easily moving;* of persons, *compliant, accommodating.*
     facilis: nominative singular modifying **quae**, referring to the **iānua** (4);
         translate as an adverb. Alternatively, one could print **facilīs**, accusative
         plural, modifying **cardinēs** (6), *compliant hinges.*
6   **cardō, cardinis**, f., *hinge* (Nisbet and Hubbard, pp. 294–95, comment: "The
     ancient *cardines* were vertical poles to which the door-panels . . . were at-
     tached; they were made of hard wood . . . and often turned in sockets set in
     the thresold and lintel").
7   **Mē tuō**: these words go together and join with **pereunte** in an ablative abso-
     lute; the adjective **tuō** means *your [devoted lover].*
     "Mē . . . / . . . dormīs?" (8): a snippet of a serenade sung by a lover
         locked out of Lydia's dwelling. The serenade sung by such an ex-
         cluded lover (**exclūsus amātor**) was called in Greek a παρακλαυσί
         θυρον, which transliterates into English as "paraclausithyron": Gr.,
         παρα , *by* + κλαυσ , *closed* + θυρ , *door.*
     longās . . . noctēs: accusative of duration of time; take with both **pereunte**
         and with **dormīs** (8).
     pereunte: *perishing; languishing, pining away* (with desire).
8   **Lȳdia** [Gr., Λυδία], **-ae**, f., *Lydia* (see the vocabulary note on the name at *Odes*
     1.13.1).

5   quae prius multum facilis movēbat
6   cardinēs. Audīs minus et minus iam
7   "Mē tuō longās pereunte noctēs,
8   Lȳdia, dormīs?"

continued

Explorations

6. Would you prefer **facilis** or **facilīs** in line 5? Why? Explain how personifica-
    tion continues in lines 5–6a from lines 3b–4. How would **multum** (5) be trans-
    lated differently with **prius**, **facilis**, **facilīs**, and **movēbat**?
7. How do the comparative adverbs **prius** (5) and **minus et minus** (6) connect
    this stanza with the first stanza?
8. Are the words of the paraclausithyron to be thought of as those of the speaker
    of the poem or as a generic example of this type of song? What is notable
    about the placement of the words **mē** and **tuō** in line 7?
9. How do lines 6b–8 echo lines 1–2 to form a ring around the first two stanzas?

9 **invicem** [in-, *in*, + **vicem**, adv., *turn*], adv., *in turn, in your turn*.
  Invicem: "Your turn will come to be out in the cold" (Garrison, p. 239).
  moechus [Gr., μοιχός, *adulterer*], **-ī**, m., *adulterer*.
  anus, -ūs, f., *old woman; old hag*.
  arrogāns, arrogantis, *insolent, overbearing, arrogant*.

> **moechōs ... arrogantīs**: **arrogantīs** is predicate: translate, *who are ...* or
> *that they are ...* or, turning the phrase around, *the arrogance of ...* "The
> phrase contrasts with *iuvenes protervi*; **moechos ...** implies that the cus-
> tomers she will miss after becoming an *anus levis* are dirty old men
> rather than exuberant youths" (Garrison, p. 239).

>> **arrogantīs**: usually it is the courtesan who is **arrogāns**, at least in the
>> eyes of her rejected lovers; in the future even "dirty old men" out
>> looking for love will be **arrogantēs**, i.e., will not make themselves
>> available to Lydia. She will lament their arrogance, just as lovers
>> would weep over her arrogance in the past and present, when she
>> would not make herself available to them.

10 **flēbis**: + acc. = *you will cry over/weep over/lament*.
  sōlō: *deserted*.
  levis: *light*; here meaning *inconsequential, unimportant, trivial, worthless*, modifying **anus** (9); but the basic meaning of *light* should be kept in mind in the
  context of the fierce wind blowing here (**Thrāciō bacchante ... / ...
  ventō**, 11–12) and when reading the last two lines of the poem.
  angiportus, -ūs, m., *alley, alleyway* (along the side and back of an **īnsula** or
  tenement block).

> **in sōlō ... angiportū**: "Her lovers no longer frequent the *angiportus*"
> (Bennett and Rolfe, p. 202); **sōlō** may be felt as a transferred epithet—
> Lydia will be as *lonely* as the alleyway is *deserted*.

11 **Thrācius, -a, -um**, *Thracian* (Thrace, a country in northern Greece, had the
  reputation of being cold and of being the source of cold winds that blow
  over Greece in the winter).
  bacchor [Gr., βακχεύω, *to celebrate the mysteries of Bacchus*], **-ārī, -ātus sum**, *to
  celebrate the mysteries of Bacchus; to act like a Bacchante; to rave, rage*.

> **Thrāciō bacchante ... / ... ventō** (12): the wind is pictured as a Thra-
> cian Bacchante dancing wildly under the influence of Bacchus
> (Dionysus).

  magis: = **magis [solitō]**, *more [than usual(ly)]*.

12 **interlūnium, -ī**, n., *the interlunar interval* (the four-day period between the
  old moon and the new moon when the moon is not visible; thought of as a
  time of unsettled weather).

> **sub interlūnia**: *under the dark of the moon*.

9   Invicem moechōs anus arrogantīs
10   flēbis in sōlō levis angiportū,
11   Thrāciō bacchante magis sub inter-
12   lūnia ventō,

continued

Explorations

10. The first two stanzas talked about the past and the present. What is the tense of the verb in this stanza? What noun and adjective describe Lydia here?
11. The first word of this stanza, **Invicem**, suggests that Lydia will suffer *in her turn*. For whose suffering will she suffer *in turn*?
12. What reason do lines 9–10 suggest for Lydia's presence in the alleyway? Will she find what she is looking for? Why or why not? How is she similar to and how is she different from the Lesbia that Catullus describes in his poem 58 quoted below?
13. How will the tables be turned on Lydia? That is, how will she suffer in the future what the **exclūsus amātor** has suffered in the past and still suffers in the present?

Passage for Comparison

Catullus 58:

1   Caelī, Lesbia nostra, Lesbia illa,
2   illa Lesbia, quam Catullus ūnam
3   plūs quam sē atque suōs amāvit omnēs,
4   nunc in quadriviīs et angiportīs
5   glūbit magnanimī Remī nepōtēs.

Caelius, our Lesbia, that [great] Lesbia, that very Lesbia, whom Catullus loved uniquely, more than himself and all his friends, now in crossroads and alleyways peels the skins off the greathearted sons of Remus.

13   **tibī**: dative of reference with **saeviet** (15); with this prominently placed
      dative, "Horace says, 'you will suffer then as others have done in the past'"
      (Nisbet and Hubbard, p. 297).
      flagrō, -āre, -āvī, *to be ablaze; to blaze.*
      libīdō, libīdinis, f., *desire, lust.*
14   **mātrēs . . . equōrum**: i.e., *mares;* **mātrēs** is accusative.
      furiō [probably a Horatian coinage], **-āre, -āvī, -ātus**, *to put into a state of mad-*
      ness; to drive X wild.
15   **saeviō** [**saevus, -a, -um**, *fierce, wild*], **saevīre, saeviī, saevītūrus**, *to be fierce,*
      be furious; to rage.
      circā, prep. + acc., *around.*
      iecur, iecoris, n., *liver* (considered the seat of deep emotions and passions).
         iecur: cf. *Odes* 1.13.3–4: **meum / fervēns difficilī bīle tumet iecur**.
      ulcerōsus [probably a Horatian coinage], **-a, -um**, *ulcerated; inflamed.*
         ulcerōsum: ulcers on the liver were thought to be caused by excessive pas-
         sion.
16   **questus, -ūs**, m., *complaint.*

Passage for Comparison

Vergil *Georgics* 3.266 and 269–77a:

266   Scīlicet ante omnīs **furor** est īnsignis equārum.

       .   .
              .   .

269   Illās dūcit **amor** trāns Gargara trānsque sonantem
270   Ascanium; superant montīs et flūmina trānant.
271   Continuōque <u>avidīs</u> ubi subdita **flamma** <u>medullīs</u>
272   (vēre magis, quia vēre calor redit ossibus), illae
273   ōre omnēs versae in Zephyrum stant rūpibus altīs
274   exceptantque levīs aurās, et saepe sine ūllīs
275   coniugiīs ventō gravidae (mīrābile dictū)
276   saxa per et scopulōs et dēpressās convallīs
277a   diffugiunt.

          But certainly the **madness** of mares is most notable of all. . . . **Lust** drives
          them across Gargarus [mountains in Asia Minor] and across the re-
          sounding Ascanius River [also in Asia Minor]; they climb across moun-
          tains and swim across rivers. Immediately when the **flame** has slipped
          into their <u>lustful marrow</u> (mostly in spring, since in spring heat returns
          to the bones), they all stand on high rocky crags with their faces turned
          toward the Zephyr wind, and they receive the gentle breezes, and often
          without any sexual activity, they become pregnant from the winds
          (strange to say) and they scatter through the rocks and crags and low
          valleys.

13 cum tibī flagrāns amor et libīdō,
14 quae solet mātrēs furiāre equōrum,
15 saeviet circā iecur ulcerōsum,
16   nōn sine questū

continued

Explorations

14. How will the tables be turned on Lydia emotionally?
15. How does the allusion to the passage in Vergil's *Georgics* quoted on the opposite page contribute to the portrayal of Lydia's emotional state? If the future emotional state of Lydia is projected by the speaker as a requital for the emotional state of the **exclūsus amātor**, with what animal would it be appropriate to compare the latter?
16. In *Odes* 1.13 (see below), the speaker suffers from a troubled liver. How is the future Lydia's *ulcerated/inflamed liver* (**iecur ulcerōsum**, 15) another example of how the tables will be turned on her?
17. The last line contains an example of litotes. Does the litotes indicate a lessened or increased emotional torment for Lydia arising from the complaint that she harbors and that is expressed in the final stanza?

Passage for Comparison

Odes 1.13.1–4:

1   Cum tū, Lȳdia, Tēlephī
2 cervīcem roseam, cērea Tēlephī
3   laudās bracchia, vae meum
4 fervēns difficilī bīle tumet iecur.

17   laeta: *happy, merry*, ironically not referring to Lydia or her libīdō, as one
      might expect at first glance, but modifying pūbēs later in the line; the
      happiness of the young men contrasts strongly with the angry indignation
      that prompts Lydia's complaint; thus questū (16) and laeta (17) are in strik-
      ing and ironic juxtaposition with each other.

      quod: delayed conjunction after nōn sine questū (16), "'because (as you will
      say regretfully to yourself) . . . youth rejoices'" (Page, p. 79); the verbs
      gaudeat (18) and dēdicet (20) are subjunctive because the reasons are not
      given on the authority of the speaker but are attributed to Lydia.

      pūbēs, pubis, f., *the state of being in puberty;* collective noun, *the youth.*

      pūbēs: = iuvenēs (cf. line 2) but with emphasis on youth as the time of sex-
      ual maturity.

            laeta . . . pūbēs: in strong contrast to Lydia as portrayed in the previ-
            ous stanza, the young men are *happy* or *merry*, but other meanings of
            the word laeta may be felt here too: *flourishing, luxuriant, fertile,* still
            in stark contrast with Lydia as an anus levis.

      hedera, -ae, f., *ivy* (associated with Bacchus as the god of wine).

      vireō, -ēre, -uī, *to be green with vegetation;* generally, *to be green;* figuratively,
      to be in a vigorous condition, to be full of youthful vigor; to be fresh.

            hederā virentī: ablative with gaudeat (18), *takes pleasure* (in); the
            phrase hederā virentī refers literally to wreaths made of ivy, which
            were worn by young men at dinner parties, at drinking bouts, and
            during reveling in the streets in front of the houses of courtesans (see
            note to line 2); here it also refers metaphorically to young women
            (such as Lydia used to be).

18   pullus, -a, -um, *dark-colored.*

      pullā: take with myrtō.

      atque: *and,* connecting hederā virentī (17) with pullā . . . myrtō (18), abla-
      tives with gaudeat, *takes pleasure* (in). Both phrases in the ablative would
      refer metaphorically to young women (such as Lydia used to be). Alterna-
      tively, atque may be taken to mean *than,* i.e., *takes pleasure in fresh green ivy
      more* than *in dusky myrtle.* The former phrase in the ablative would refer
      metaphorically to young women (such as Lydia used to be) and the latter
      to middle-aged women (such as Lydia is now).

      myrtō: associated with Venus as the goddess of love.

19   āridus, -a, -um, *dry, dried-out.*

      frōns, frondis, f., *foliage, leafy branches, leaves.*

            āridās frondīs: referring literally to ivy and myrtle used in wreaths and
            metaphorically to aged women like Lydia as she will be in the future.

      sodālis, sodālis, m., *companion.*

      sodālī: dative, in apposition to Hebrō (20).

20   dēdicet: asyndeton, *[and] dedicate;* ironic here in that revelers or excluded
      lovers would *dedicate* their wreaths on the doors of courtesans who do not
      admit them as a sign that they were there; here the young men *dedicate* or
      consign dried-out foliage, i.e., old women such as Lydia will be in the fu-
      ture, to the Hebrus River.

      Hebrus, -ī, m., *Hebrus River* (in Thrace; now the Maritza River).

17 laeta quod pūbēs hederā virentī

18 gaudeat pullā magis atque myrtō,

19 āridās frondīs hiemis sodālī

20   dēdicet Hebrō.

Explorations

18. Note that **atque** (18) can be interpreted as meaning either *and* or *than*. If it is interpreted to mean *and*, what will Lydia's complaint in lines 17–20 be? If it is interpreted to mean *than*, what will her complaint be?
19. In the third and fourth stanzas the speaker has turned the tables on Lydia; she will suffer in the future what the **exclūsus amātor** has suffered in the past and is still suffering in the present. If the suffering of which she is envisioned as complaining in the last stanza represents a final turning of the tables on Lydia, what might it imply about the present age of the speaker?
20. Locate a chiasmus in lines 17–18. The references to ivy and myrtle may be suggestive of wreaths worn by young men at dinner parties, drinking bouts, and reveling. How do these allusions here bring the poem full circle?
21. Can you see any reason for preferring either **Hebrō** or **Eurō** (see below) in line 20?

Text

Some editors print **Eurō**, *the East Wind*, instead of the manuscript reading **Hebrō** in line 20.

Odes 1.25

1   Parcius iūnctās quatiunt fenestrās
2   iactibus crēbrīs iuvenēs protervī,
3   nec tibī somnōs adimunt, amatque
4   iānua līmen,

5   quae prius multum facilis movēbat
6   cardinēs. Audīs minus et minus iam
7   "Mē tuō longās pereunte noctēs,
8   Lȳdia, dormīs?"

9   Invicem moechōs anus arrogantīs
10 flēbis in sōlō levis angiportū,
11 Thrāciō bacchante magis sub inter-
12   lūnia ventō,

13 cum tibī flagrāns amor et libīdō,
14 quae solet mātrēs furiāre equōrum,
15 saeviet circā iecur ulcerōsum,
16   nōn sine questū

17 laeta quod pūbēs hederā virentī
18 gaudeat pullā magis atque myrtō,
19 āridās frondīs hiemis sodālī
20   dēdicet Hebrō.

Discussion

1. How does this ode develop a **carpe diem** theme?
2. Compare *Odes* 1.25 with *Odes* 1.23. Can you see any way in which the two poems form a pair?
3. Why might Horace have placed *Odes* 1.24 in between *Odes* 1.23 and 1.25?

Meter: Alcaic

1   **est bibendum**: *drinking must be done, it is necessary to drink,* passive peri-
     phrastic.
     līber, lībera, līberum, *free.*
     pede līberō: i.e., with free and unrestrained dancing.
2   **pulsō, -āre, -āvī, -ātus,** *to strike.*
     pulsanda: supply **est.**
     tellūs, tellūris, f., *earth.*
     Saliāris, -is, -e, *of/belonging to the Salii, Salian* (the Salii were Roman priests
     associated with the worship of Mars as the ancestor and protector of Rome
     and were known for their sumptuous banquets and their elaborate ritual
     dances); of banquets, *sumptuous* (like those of the Salii).
        Saliāribus: take with **dapibus** (4), ablative of means with **ōrnāre** (3).
3   **pulvīnar, pulvīnāris,** n., *couch.*
        ōrnāre pulvīnar: Horace is referring to a Roman ritual of supplication (a
     supplicātiō), a religious ceremony of prayer or thanksgiving intended
     to propitiate the gods or to offer thanks for a great military victory. Im-
     ages of gods were placed on couches (**pulvīnāria**) and served banquets.
     This ritual was called **lectisternium** (**lectus, -ī,** m., *bed; couch* + **sternō,**
     sternere, strāvī, strātus, *to spread,* e.g., with blankets or coverings).
     Cicero in his third Catilinarian oration, addressing the citizens of Rome
     after the expulsion of Catiline from the city, says, "Therefore since a
     thanksgiving (**supplicātiō**) has been decreed at all the sacred couches
     (**ad omnia pulvīnāria**), you should celebrate these days with your wives
     and children" (*In Catilinam* 3.23). Augustus (*Res gestae* 4) reports that for
     victories won under his auspices the Senate decreed that thanks should
     be given to the gods (**supplicandum esse dīs immortālibus**) fifty-five
     times over a total of 890 days during his rule.
4   **tempus erat**: this is a Greek use of the imperfect to express a fact that has just
     been recognized but was true before, as if to say, *It's high time, and we didn't*
     realize it!
     daps, dapis, f., *banquet, feast.*
     sodālis, sodālis, m., *fellow* (i.e., a member of an association or fellowship such
     as that of the Salii); more generally, *comrade, companion; mate; crony; drink-*
     ing companion.

ODES 1.37

Now's the time to celebrate!

Why does the speaker call for celebration in this poem? What is to be celebrated?

1   Nunc est bibendum, nunc pede lībero
2   pulsanda tellūs, nunc Saliāribus
3   ōrnāre pulvīnar deōrum
4   tempus erat dapibus, sodālēs.

continued

Explorations

1. Identify an ascending tricolon. What rhetorical device articulates the three clauses?
2. What kind of occasion would call for drinking and unrestrained dancing (1–2a)?
3. What does the repeated grammatical construction (the passive periphrastic) add to the tone of the first two clauses?
4. What new dimension is added to the occasion in the third clause (2b–4)?
5. Whom is the speaker addressing with the word **sodālēs** (4)? What kind of setting is implied by the speaker's use of this word?
6. Is there any hint so far as to what the special occasion is that calls for celebration?

5   **antehāc**, adv., *previously, before.*

     antehāc: pronounced and scanned as two syllables, equivalent to **ant(eh)āc**.

     nefās [**ne-**, *not* + **fās**, n. indecl., (that which is) *right or permissible by or in accord with divine or natural law;* (that which is) *possible or allowable*], n. indecl., (that which is) *not right or permissible by or in accord with divine law or natural law;* (that which is) *not possible or allowable;* (that which is) *forbidden* (by divine or natural law); *act of impiety, sacrilege; sin.*

     nefās: supply **erat**; the metrical pause after **nefās** highlights the word.

     dēprōmō [**dē-**, *down, from* + **prōmō, prōmere, prōmpsī, prōmptus**, *to bring forth, produce*], **dēprōmere, dēprōmpsī, dēprōmptus**, *to take down, bring out.*

     Caecubum, -ī, n., *Caecuban wine* (a prized vintage produced in Latium).

6   **cella, -ae**, f., *storeroom; wine-cellar.*

     avītus, -a, -um, *ancestral.*

     Capitōlium, -ī, n., *the Capitol.*

     Capitōliō: the two peaks of the Capitoline Hill were the Arx on the northern side, where, according to legend, the sacred geese of Juno warned the Romans of a night raid by the Gauls in 390 (387) B.C., and the Capitol to the south. On the Capitol was Rome's most sacred temple, dedicated to Jupiter Optimus Maximus, Juno, and Minerva. It was here that consuls took their vows of office and generals concluded their triumphal processions with an offering of thanks.

        Capitōliō: dative of reference, *for . . .* , to be translated after **ruīnās**; so also **imperiō** is to be translated after **fūnus** in line 8.

7   **rēgīna**: i.e., Cleopatra; Horace does not name her in this poem.

     dēmēns [**dē-**, here suggesting removal or reversal + **mēns, mentis**, f., *mind*], **dēmentis**, *mad, insane.*

     ruīna [**ruō, ruere, ruī, rutūrus**, *to tumble down; to come to ruin*], **-ae**, f., *a tumbling down; a fall; destruction, ruin.*

8   **fūnus, fūneris**, n., *funeral;* metaphorical, *death, destruction.*

     fūnus et: delayed conjunction, = **et fūnus**.

"Head of Cleopatra"
Michelangelo (1475–1564)
Gabinetto dei Disegni e delle Stampe
Uffizi, Florence, Italy

5   Antehāc nefās dēprōmere Caecubum

6   cellīs avītīs, dum Capitōliō

7   rēgīna dēmentīs ruīnās

8   fūnus et imperiō parābat

continued

Explorations

7.   What do lines 5–6a add that was not said in the first stanza?

8.   What is special about the wine and the place where it is stored (5–6a)? What does its use now tell us about the present occasion?

9.   How is suspense built up in the first five and a half lines of the poem?

10. How does the **dum** clause (6b–8) narrow the time frame of the main clause (**Antehāc . . . / . . . avītīs,** 5–6a)?

11. Do lines 6b–8 resolve the suspense created in lines 1–6a?

12. Does the speaker now explicitly inform the reader of the occasion for celebration? Compare the passage from Alcaeus below. Or does the speaker move his poem in some other direction? If so, in what direction?

13. What is the tone of the description of the actions of the queen (6b–8)?

14. Find examples in this stanza of:

    a. Alliteration

    b. Effective juxtaposition of words

    c. Transferred epithet

    d. Metaphor

    e. Chiasmus

Passage for Comparison

The archaic Greek poet Alcaeus of Mytilene, the chief city of Lesbos, in a poem of which we have only the first two lines (fragment 332) called for heavy drinking to celebrate the death of the hated tyrant Myrsilus in a civil war:

1   νῦν χρῆ μεθύσθην καί τινα πὲρ βίαν

2   πώνην, ἐπειδὴ κάτθανε Μύρσιλος.

   Now men must get drunk and drink with all their might, since Myrsilus is dead (literally, "died," "was killed").

9   contāminātus [con-, expressing connection or completeness + tangō, tan-
     gere, tetigī, tactus, *to touch*], -a, -um, *befouled; infected with disease; morally
     debased; guilt-ridden; ritually unclean; desecrated, polluted.*
         contāminātō: with grege.
     grex, gregis, m., *flock, herd; gang* (a derogatory term when used of men).
     turpis, -is, -e, *filthy, foul.*
         turpium . . . virōrum: i.e., the perverted (according to the Romans) men of
         Cleopatra's court, which would have included eunuchs, rendering
         virōrum ironic.
10   morbus, -ī, m., *illness; disease.*
         morbō: ablative of cause with turpium; Horace leaves it up to the reader to
         imagine what kind of morbus is involved, whether physical or psycho-
         logical.
     quīlibet, quaelibet, quodlibet or quidlibet, *anyone/anything you please; any-
     one/anything at all.*
         quidlibet: the object of spērāre (11).
     impotēns, impotentis, *powerless, impotent;* often in phrases such as impotēns
     suī or impotēns animī, *out of one's mind, deranged;* often used without a
     genitive to mean *lacking in self-control, headstrong, wild, violent, crazy.*
         impotēns / spērāre (11): *crazy [enough] to hope for.*
11   dulcis, -is, -e, *sweet.*
12   minuit: the subject is nāvis in line 13. In lines 12b–16a Horace is giving a
         very condensed account of the battle of Actium in September 31 B.C., in
         which Octavian defeated the fleets of Antony and Cleopatra.
13   vix: take with ūna.
     sōspes, sōspitis, *safe.*
         vix ūna sōspes nāvis: i.e., the fact that scarcely one of Cleopatra's ships es-
         caped being burned at the battle of Actium.
14   mēns, mentis, f., *mind.*
         mentem: i.e., Cleopatra's.
     lymphō, -āre, -āvī, -ātus, *to drive crazy, derange, craze.*
     Mareōticum, -ī, n., *Mareotic wine* (from the region of Lake Mareotis, near
     Alexandria in Egypt).
15   redigō [re-, *back;* also suggesting reversal or restoration + agō, agere, ēgī,
     āctus, *to do; to drive*], redigere, redēgī, redāctus, *to bring back, restore; to
     bring down, reduce.*
16   Caesar: this refers to Octavian, the subject of redēgit (15), adurgēns (17), and
         daret (20).
     Ītaliā: the initial *I* of this word is usually short but is often lengthened in po-
     etry.
     volō, -āre, -āvī, -ātūrus, *to fly.*
         volantem: supply eam or rēgīnam.

9   contāminātō cum grege turpium
10   morbō virōrum, quidlibet impotēns
11   spērāre fortūnāque dulcī
12   ēbria. Sed minuit furōrem

13   vix ūna sōspes nāvis ab ignibus,
14   mentemque lymphātam Mareōticō
15   redēgit in vērōs timōrēs
16   Caesar ab Ītaliā volantem

continued

Explorations

15. What impression does the speaker create of the queen's entourage in lines
     9–10a? What feelings is he evoking?
16. Lines 10b–12a shift focus from the queen's entourage to the queen herself.
     Identify an example of hysteron proteron. How does the speaker represent
     the queen in these lines?
17. The speaker gives only a very condensed account of the battle of Actium in
     lines 12b–16. What does he focus on instead in these lines?

Background

fortūnā . . . dulcī / ēbria (11b–12a)

Garrison (p. 255) explains the nature of Cleopatra's "sweet fortune": "She had an
affair with Julius Caesar in 48 B.C., and a son by him the following summer; she
lived two years in Rome by his invitation, 46–44 B.C." Nisbet and Hubbard (p. 407)
continue the story: "After the Ides of March she returned to the East, and in 41 met
Antony at Tarsus. Their liaison was interrupted by his marriage to Octavia in 40,
but was revived in 37. In the succeeding years they lived together in imperial
magnificence at Alexandria."

17   **rēmus, -ī**, m., *oar*.
      rēmīs: synecdoche for oared ships, triremes.
      adurgeō [ad-, *against* + **urgeō, urgēre**, *to press*], **adurgēre**, *to press hard upon; to
          pursue closely*.
      accipiter, accipitris, m., *hawk*.
18   **mollis, -is, -e**, *soft; mild, gentle*.
      columba, -ae, f., *dove*.
      accipiter velut (17) / **mollīs columbās**: supply **adurget**.
      citus, -a, -um, *swift*.
19   **vēnātor, vēnātōris**, m., *hunter*.
      leporem citus (18) / **vēnātor**: supply **adurget** again.
      nivālis, -is, -e, *snowy*.
      nivālis: hare-hunting season in Thessaly was during winter, when deep
          snow would make it difficult for hares to run and escape their pursuers.
20   **Haemonia, -ae**, f., *Haemonia* (an old name for Thessaly in northern Greece).
      daret ut: delayed conjunction, = **ut daret**.
      catēna, -ae, f., *chain*.
      catēnīs dare, *to put in chains*.

Passage for Comparison

With the simile contained in the words **accipiter velut / mollīs columbās
[adurget]** (17b–18a), compare the following passage from Homer's *Iliad* describing
the beginning of Achilles' pursuit of Hector, which ends with the former slaying
the latter:

Homer *Iliad* 22.131–38 and 143–44:

> Hector waited and pondered. And Achilles, the equal of Ares, the warrior with
> a waving plume on his helmet, came near to him, shaking his menacing
> Pelian spear made of Ash wood above his right shoulder. Around him his
> bronze armor shone with the gleam of burning fire or of the rising sun. Trem-
> bling seized Hector when he caught sight of him, nor did he still dare to re-
> main there but left the gates behind and went off in fear. The son of Peleus
> sprang after him, relying on his swift feet. . . . So Achilles in eager haste was fly-
> ing straight along, and Hector fled in fear beneath the wall of the Trojans, ply-
> ing his nimble knees.

17   rēmīs adurgēns, accipiter velut
18   mollīs columbās aut leporem citus
19   vēnātor in campīs nivālis
20   Haemoniae, daret ut catēnīs

continued

Explorations

18.   In lines 16–20a the speaker reports the immediate aftermath of the battle of
      Actium. While the queen was previously described as preparing ruin for
      the Capitoline Hill in Rome and the destruction of Rome's empire (6b–8), all
      this is now reversed as she is described as flying away from Italy and being
      pursued by Caesar (16–17a).
      a.   Look closely at the two similes with which the pursuit is described (17b–
           20a). Do the comparisons in the similes invite your sympathy more with
           the pursuer or with the pursued? Consider the chiastic arrangement of
           the comparisons in the two similes.
      b.   Both similes have literary antecedents given on the opposite page and
           below. What are the effects of these literary echoes in our present poem?
19.   Comment on the effectiveness of the metaphor contained in the word
      volantem (16), the synecdoche (**rēmīs**, 17), and the juxtaposition of these two
      words.

Passage for Comparison

The simile contained in the words **velut / . . . leporem citus / vēnātor in campīs
nivālis / Haemoniae [adurget]** (17b–20a), is reminiscent of a passage in Horace's
earlier *Satires* 1.2.105b–8, which deals with licit and illicit erotic ambitions of young
men. Some men pursue courtesans whose favors are readily available and easily
purchased, while others prefer to take on the challenges and obstacles of affairs
with married women. To illustrate the latter, Horace inserts in his poem the following lines, which are adapted from an epigram of the Greek poet Callimachus.
Supply **amātor**, *a lover*, as the subject of **cantat** and of **appōnit**:

105b .   .   .   "Leporem vēnātor ut altā
106   in nive sectētur, positum sīc tangere nōlit,"
107   [amātor] cantat, et appōnit, "Meus est amor huic similis; nam
108   trānsvolat in mediō posita et fugientia captat."

      [A lover] sings "how the hunter pursues a hare in the deep snow, [but]
      refuses to touch [a hare] placed thus [i.e., already lying outstretched],"
      and adds, "My love is like this; for it flies past things placed in the mid-
      dle [i.e., that are readily available] and pursues things that flee."

21   **fātālis, -is, -e**, *fateful; deadly.*
      mōnstrum, -ī, n., *an unnatural thing regarded as an omen; a portent; a monster.*
      quae: the connecting relative; translate *but she*, with adversative force.
      generōsus, -a, -um, *noble; noble-spirited; dignified.*
         generōsius: comparative adv., *more nobly.*
22   **muliebriter**, adv., *in a womanly way.*
23   **expavēscō** [**ex-**, intensive + **pavēscō, pavēscere**, *to begin to quake, take fright*],
         expavēscere, expāvī, *to fear greatly, dread.*
      ēnsis, ēnsis, m., *sword.*
      latentīs / . . . ōrās (24): *hidden shores,* i.e., a safe haven.
24   **classis, classis**, f., *group, division; fleet.*
      citus, -a, -um, *swift.*
      reparō [**re-**, *back, again, in place of* + **parō, -āre, -āvī, -ātus**, *to prepare; to arrange;*
         to acquire], **-āre, -āvī, -ātus**, *to obtain/reach X in exchange/in place of.*
            nec (23) **. . . / . . . reparāvit**: she did not reach some safe haven in ex-
               change for giving up her kingdom in Egypt that was now endan-
               gered by the pursuing Octavian, i.e., she did not go into exile.
25   **ausa**: translate as present in reference, *enduring, daring, being bold enough to* +
         infinitive. Alternatively, one may supply **est** and translate **ausa** [**est**] as
         she endured/dared/was bold enough to.
      et, adv., *even.*
      iaceō, iacēre, iacuī, *to lie* (here, in ruins).
      vīsō, vīsere, vīsī, vīsus, *to look upon.*
      rēgia, -ae, f., *palace; royal city.*
26   **vultus, -ūs**, m., *face, expression, countenance.*
         vultū serēnō: i.e., with a stoic quality admired by the Romans.
      fortis . . . / tractāre (27): *brave [enough] to handle.* . . .
      et: adverb again, *even.*
      asper, aspera, asperum, *harsh, rough, scaly.*
27   **tractō** [frequentative of **trahō, trahere, trāxī, tractus**, *to drag*], **-āre, -āvī,**
         -ātus, *to manage; to handle.*
      serpēns, serpentis, m./f., *snake, serpent.*
         asperās (26) **/ . . . serpentīs**: asps are actually smooth, but Horace and his
            readers may not have known this. In any case, Horace is making use of
            word play here, since the Latin word for *asps* is **aspidēs.**
      āter, ātra, ātrum, *black; deadly.*
28   **combibō** [**con-**, intensive + **bibō, bibere, bibī, bibitus**, *to drink*], **combibere,**
         combibī, *to drink in deeply.*
         corpore combiberet: an unusual choice of words.
      venēnum, -ī, n., *poison.*

21 fātāle mōnstrum; quae generōsius
22 perīre quaerēns nec muliebriter
23   expāvit ēnsem nec latentīs
24   classe citā reparāvit ōrās;

25 ausa et iacentem vīsere rēgiam
26 vultū serēnō, fortis et asperās
27   tractāre serpentīs, ut ātrum
28   corpore combiberet venēnum,

continued

Explorations

20. The imperfect subjunctive **daret** (20) introduces a purpose clause in sec-
ondary sequence after **redēgit** (15) and after the intervening similes in lines
17b–20a.
   a. Does the language of the purpose clause (20b–21a) jar with that of the
   similes? Does it clash with the erotic overtones of the passages recalled
   in the simile of the hunter and the hare? After lines 17b–20a do you expect the queen to be referred to as a **fātāle mōnstrum** (21)?
   b. Is the reader to take the phrase **fātāle mōnstrum**, which comes at the
   end of the clause describing Caesar's purpose in pursuing the queen, as
   representing the speaker's view of the queen or Caesar's?
   c. Does the phrase **fatāle mōnstrum** depersonalize, dehumanize, and
   demonize the queen? Has she been depersonalized, dehumanized, or
   demonized earlier in the poem?
21. Why would Caesar want to put the queen in chains (20b–21a)?
22. As the speaker in lines 12b–16 gave only a very condensed account of the
battle of Actium, so in lines 21b–28 he only sketches the queen's actions after
her flight from Actium. What sequence of events can you detect? What does
the speaker present in these lines in place of a detailed narrative account?
23. What is especially striking about the placement of words on either side of the
diaeresis in line 21? Of what importance is the juxtaposition of these words
in the structure of the poem?
24. How has imagery of drinking articulated three stages in the queen's psycho-
logical journey?
25. What sound effects can you find in lines 21b–28?

29   **dēlīberō** [**dē-**, *thoroughly* + **lībra, -ae**, f., *a pair of scales, a balance*], **-āre, -āvī, -ātus**, *to weigh the pros and cons, deliberate;* perfect, *to have resolved upon.*
      dēlīberātā morte: ablative absolute expressing cause and explaining
         ferōcior, *since she had resolved upon death.*
      ferōx, ferōcis, *fierce; fierce-spirited, defiant.*
30   **Liburna, -ae,** f., *Liburnian galley* (a type of small, swift ship that Octavian
         used to great advantage against the fleet of Antony at the battle of Actium).
      saevīs Liburnīs: dative with **invidēns.**
         saevīs: transferred epithet; it is Caesar who, from Cleopatra's point of
            view, is *cruel*, not the ships themselves.
      scīlicet, adv., *certainly, to be sure, clearly.*
         scīlicet: "the word has here none of the ironical force so common to it"
            (Bennett and Rolfe, p. 230). "Her purpose was so clearly shown that we
            may assume that none would dare to question it" (Page, p. 100).
      invideō [**in-**, *on, upon* + **videō, vidēre, vīdī, vīsus**, *to see*], **invidēre, invīdī, invīsus** + dat., *to regard with ill-will; to envy, be jealous of; to refuse to allow; to begrudge.*
31   **prīvātus** [**prīvō, -āre, -āvī, -ātus**, *to deprive* (of), *rob* (of)], **-a, -um**, *private.*
      prīvāta: substantive use of the perfect passive participle, *as a private person*
         (i.e., deprived of her queenship).
      dēdūcō [**dē-**, *down* + **dūcō, dūcere, dūxī, ductus**, *to lead*], *to lead away; to bring
         home* (as one's bride in a wedding ceremony); *to bring* (a person back with
         one to Rome).
      dēdūcī: present passive infinitive, depending on **invidēns**, *to be brought*
         (to Rome).
32   **nōn humilis:** with **mulier.**
      triumphus, -ī, m., *triumph, triumphal procession, victory parade.*
      superbō (31) / . . . **triumphō:** dative of purpose with **dēdūcī,** *for a.* . . .

29   dēlīberātā morte ferōcior,
30   saevīs Liburnīs scīlicet invidēns
31   prīvāta dēdūcī superbō
32   nōn humilis mulier triumphō.

Explorations

26.   What does line 29 add to what has been said in the previous stanza?
27.   What do lines 30–32 tell the reader about the queen's decision to commit sui-
      cide?

"Augustus of Prima Porta"
Vatican Museums and Galleries, Vatican City, Italy

Odes 1.37

1 Nunc est bibendum, nunc pede līberō
2 pulsanda tellūs, nunc Saliāribus
3   ōrnāre pulvīnar deōrum
4   tempus erat dapibus, sodālēs.

5 Antehāc nefās dēprōmere Caecubum
6 cellīs avītīs, dum Capitōliō
7   rēgīna dēmentīs ruīnās
8   fūnus et imperiō parābat

9 contāminātō cum grege turpium
10 morbō virōrum, quidlibet impotēns
11   spērāre fortūnāque dulcī
12   ēbria. Sed minuit furōrem

13 vix ūna sōspes nāvis ab ignibus,
14 mentemque lymphātam Mareōticō
15   redēgit in vērōs timōrēs
16   Caesar ab Ītaliā volantem

17 rēmīs adurgēns, accipiter velut
18 mollīs columbās aut leporem citus
19   vēnātor in campīs nivālis
20   Haemoniae, daret ut catēnīs

21 fātāle mōnstrum; quae generōsius
22 perīre quaerēns nec muliebriter
23   expāvit ēnsem nec latentīs
24   classe citā reparāvit ōrās;

25 ausa et iacentem vīsere rēgiam
26 vultū serēnō, fortis et asperās
27   tractāre serpentīs, ut ātrum
28   corpore combiberet venēnum,

29 dēlīberātā morte ferōcior,
30 saevīs Liburnīs scīlicet invidēns
31   prīvāta dēdūcī superbō
32   nōn humilis mulier triumphō.

Discussion

1. How is this ode structured?

2. Horace's ode does not purport to be a journalistic historical record of Cleopatra's life and of what happened at Actium and afterwards, and in fact at several points what Horace says in the ode is at odds with historical accounts. The following is a brief account of the battle of Actium and its aftermath based on Velleius Paterculus *History of Rome* 2.84–87, Suetonius *Life of Augustus* 17, Plutarch *Life of Antony* 60–87, and Cassius Dio *Roman History* 50.10–51.22. At what points in *Odes* 1.37 does it appear that Horace has taken liberties with historical fact? In each case, what does Horace achieve by distorting the historical record?

> The battle of Actium, which took place on September 2, 31 B.C., marked turning points in the fates of its three main combatants, Octavian, Mark Antony, and Cleopatra. Antony, once a political and personal ally of Octavian (he was a member of the Second Triumvirate with Octavian and Lepidus, created in 43 B.C., and he married Octavian's sister, Octavia, in 40 B.C.), was now at odds with Rome's primary leader.

> After several skirmishes, their two navies met at Actium. Although Antony had more men and more and much larger ships than Octavian had, he was inexperienced as a naval commander. It was at Cleopatra's urging that Antony allowed the battle to be decided at sea, although she was actually planning to flee with the Egyptian contingent. The battle itself developed slowly, owing to the fact that Antony commanded large, well-fortified ships while Octavian's fleet was smaller and swifter. The turning point of the battle took place when Cleopatra suddenly fled with her sixty ships intact, because of either impatience or fear, and Antony followed her. The battle continued, in a state of confusion, with Octavian finally prevailing by desperately assailing Antony's remaining fleet with fire. Suetonius reports that the battle lasted so long that Octavian spent the night on board his ship (*Augustus* 17.2–3). At some time during or after the battle, ships from Octavian's fleet went in pursuit of Antony and Cleopatra but failed to catch them.

> Antony fled into Libya and Cleopatra back to Egypt. Octavian, meanwhile, set off for Greece to administer affairs, to deal with Antony's former troops and allies, and to prevent uprisings among his own men. He then moved on to Asia, keeping tabs on Antony's movements. Plutarch reports that Antony tried to commit suicide while in Libya but was prevented from doing so and was taken to Cleopatra in Alexandria. The winter passed with Octavian dealing with his various military and political concerns apart from Antony and Cleopatra.

> Antony and Cleopatra made preparations for a possible engagement with Octavian's forces in Egypt, but they also made preparations for flight to Spain or to the Red Sea to escape further war, another defeat, and servitude. Meanwhile, they both separately petitioned Octavian for mercy, with Cleopatra asking that her children and country be spared and Antony requesting life as a private citizen in Egypt or Athens.

Octavian, however, was more concerned with adding to his wealth and with his triumph than he was with granting mercy. In a further setback for Antony and Cleopatra, the Arabians burned the ships that Antony and Cleopatra had prepared for the voyage to the Red Sea.

According to Dio, Octavian sent an emissary to Cleopatra to tell her that he was in love with her and that she should do away with Antony; what Octavian really wanted was Cleopatra's vast wealth, but she was tricked by his protestations and was hoping through Octavian to become mistress of the Roman Empire.

In the spring of 30 B.C., Octavian finally made his way to Alexandria via Syria to square off against Antony. After one brief success, Antony was defeated militarily once and for all by Octavian, not without suspicion of Cleopatra's connivance in his defeat.

Cleopatra, fearing for her own fate, sent messengers to Antony letting him know of her "death." Antony rushed off to the tomb she had been preparing. He asked a servant to kill him with his sword, but the servant instead fell upon the sword himself. Antony, in turn, fell upon the same sword, wounding himself seriously, but not fatally. Cleopatra heard the commotion outside the tomb and ordered the wounded Antony to be hoisted up to her tomb at once. Antony succumbed to his wounds in Cleopatra's arms.

Cleopatra now had to turn her mind to saving her own life, while Octavian was intent on adding the queen and her wealth to his triumph, thinking that leading the fallen queen in his triumphal procession would add greatly to its glory. He allowed her to mourn and to give Antony a proper burial in Alexandria. When treacherously trapped by Octavian's henchmen, Cleopatra tried unsuccessfully to kill herself with a dagger that she had concealed under her clothing. Although determined to die, if die she must, as a queen, she made one last, desperate attempt to gain Octavian's favor by turning on all her seductive charms in an interview with her Roman conquerer. Octavian, however, departed without making a clear commitment to her, but gave orders that she be carefully guarded "to adorn his triumph" (Dio 51.13.2).

Cleopatra suspected this to be the case, "and thinking it to be worse than a thousand deaths, she truly desired to die" (Dio 51.13.2). Despite the guards assigned by Octavian to prevent the queen from taking her own life, she did soon commit suicide in August 30 B.C. The only marks on her body were two faint holes on her arm. She is believed either to have had a poisonous asp smuggled into her chamber among fruits or flowers or to have pricked herself with a poison-tipped hairpin. Octavian "both admired and pitied her and was himself greatly distressed, as if deprived of all the glory of his victory" (Dio 51.14.6). Plutarch remarks that Octavian, "although vexed at the woman's death, admired her noble spirit, and ordered that her body be buried with Antony's in magnificent and regal fashion" (*Antony* 86.4).

After the deaths of Antony and Cleopatra, Octavian ordered the deaths of Antony's eldest son, Antyllus, and Cleopatra's son by Julius

Caesar, Caesarion. The Romans granted Octavian a triumph for his defeat of Cleopatra, erecting arches in both Brundisium and Rome. In the third of the triple triumphs that Octavian celebrated in 29 B.C., he included an effigy of Cleopatra with an asp clinging to her. The effigy was accompanied by the two children she bore to Antony, namely, Alexander Helios and Cleopatra Selene.

Dio remarks that Cleopatra, although defeated, attained glory in Rome, "because her adornments are dedicated in our temples and she herself appears in gold in the temple of Venus" (51.22.3).

3. What is Caesar's role in the poem?
4. The last word in the poem is **triumphō**. Who triumphs and who loses in this poem?
5. At the beginning of the poem the reader is told that it is time to drink and dance, and the **sodālēs** are told that it is high time to celebrate with a **lectisternium** and with Salian banquets. Is the reader or are the **sodālēs** ever told why a celebration is appropriate? Now that you have read Horace's ode through to its end, what do you think it is that Horace wants us to celebrate?

Meter: Sapphic

1   **Persicus, -a, -um**, *Persian.*
     Persicōs: note the emphatic placement as the first word of the poem.
     ōdī, ōdisse, ōsus (perfect in form; present in meaning), *to hate.*
     puer: a common form of address to a slave.
     apparātus [ad-, *to, toward,* or intensive + **parō, parāre, parāvī, parātus**, *to*
       prepare], **-ūs**, m., *luxurious preparation; pomp, display; paraphernalia, trappings.*
2   **displiceō [dis-**, *not,* + **placeō, placēre, placuī, placitūrus**, *to be pleasing*],
       displicēre, displicuī, displicitūrus + dat., *to displease.*
       displicent: supply **mihi**; the subject is **corōnae**.
     nectō, nectere, nexī, nexus, *to bind, stitch, weave.*
     philyra [Gr., φιλύρα], -ae, f., *bark* (from the linden tree, especially well-suited
       for binding elaborate wreaths).
         nexae philyrā corōnae: Bennett and Rolfe (p. 231) note that wreaths of
           this sort were "made by sewing flowers on a strip of the inner bark, or
           bast, of the linden-tree (*philyra*); such *coronae* were specially made by
           professional craftsmen and were of great elegance."
3   **mitte**: + infin., *stop* (doing something).
     sector [sequor, sequī, secūtus sum, *to follow* + **-tō**, iterative or intensive suf-
       fix] **-ārī, -ātus sum**, *to follow constantly; to chase; to go about searching for.*
     rosa: the subject of **morētur**.
     quō locōrum: *where of places* (partitive genitive), *in what place, where in the*
       world.
4   **sērus, -a, -um**, *belated; tardy; late-blooming.*
     morētur: from **moror, morārī, morātus sum**; subjunctive in an indirect
       question, with its interrogative phrase **quō locōrum** delayed to second
       place in its clause.

ODES 1.38

Preparations for a Simple Party

The first book of odes ends on a quiet, personal note, in strong contrast to the public spectacle in the previous ode. Despite its seemingly simple expressions, the ode is quite complex.

1 Persicōs ōdī, puer, apparātūs,
2 displicent nexae philyrā corōnae;
3 mitte sectārī, rosa quō locōrum
4   sēra morētur.

continued

Explorations

1. For what two things does the speaker express a dislike in lines 1–2? What is the connection between the two?
2. What poetic device does Horace use in lines 1–2?
3. What does the phrase **mitte sectārī** (3) mean, and what implication does the iterative suffix convey? How is this phrase different from **nōlī petere**? How does the tone of the phrase **mitte sectārī** color the tone of the entire stanza?
4. How does the way the rose is referred to echo the first line to form a ring around the first stanza?

5   **simplex, simplicis,** *plain, simple.*
       allabōrō [ad-, *to, toward; at* + **labōrō, -āre, -āvī, -ātūrus,** *to work*], **-āre,** *to work*
           at; + dat., *to add* (to) *with special effort.*
           Simplicī myrtō nihil allabōrēs: supply **ut** to introduce this indirect
               command dependent on **cūrō** (6a).
6   **sēdulus, -a, -um,** *painstaking, fussy; diligent.*
       sēdulus: translate as an adverb here.
       cūrō: in a context with a negative, this verb can mean *to desire, want;* so here
           with the negative **nihil** (5) in the subordinate clause it means *I desire/want*
           that you not. . . . or better *I do not desire/I do not want you to. . . .*
       minister [minus, minōris, n., *less* + **-ter,** suffix used to form opposing pairs],
           ministrī, m., *one who helps in an inferior capacity, servant.*
           ministrum: in apposition to **tē;** note that the opposite of the word **minis-**
               ter is **magister [magis,** adv., *more* + **-ter,** suffix used to form opposing
               pairs], *commander; ship's captain; manager; master.*
7   **dēdecet [dē-,** negative + **decet, -ēre, -uit,** *it is fitting, suitable*], **-ēre, -uit** + acc.,
           (it) is unsuitable for; (it) is unbecoming to.
           neque (6) . . . **/ dēdecet . . . neque:** litotes; "When combined with a neg-
               ative this verb suggests positive elegance" (Nisbet and Hubbard, p.
               426); one could translate *it graces both . . . and. . . .*
       artus, -a, -um, *thick, dense.*
8   **vītis, vītis,** f., *grape; grape vine.*

5   Simplicī myrtō nihil allabōrēs
6   sēdulus cūrō: neque tē ministrum
7   dēdecet myrtus neque mē sub artā
8   vīte bibentem.

Explorations

5. What does the speaker not want his addressee to do in the second stanza?
6. What words, phrases, and clauses stand in parallel or in contrast to words, phrases, and clauses in the first stanza?
7. The adjective **sēdulus** can modify either the subject of **allabōrēs** or of **cūrō**. Which way do you prefer to take it? Why? Can it be taken with both verbs?
8. What is the main point being made by the speaker in lines 6b–8? How do these lines provide an appropriate conclusion for the poem?

Text

Some editors print **cūrā**, second person singular imperative, *see to it*, instead of the manuscript reading **cūrō** in line 6a.

"Relief of a Banqueter"
ca. 50 B.C.
Museum of Fine Arts, Boston

Odes 1.38

1   Persicōs ōdī, puer, apparātūs,
2   displicent nexae philyrā corōnae;
3   mitte sectārī, rosa quō locōrum
4   sēra morētur.

5   Simplicī myrtō nihil allabōrēs
6   sēdulus cūrō: neque tē ministrum
7   dēdecet myrtus neque mē sub artā
8   vīte bibentem.

Discussion

1. Compare *Odes* 1.38 with the passage from Lucretius *De rerum natura* 2.20–33, quoted below. What contrasting lifestyles is Lucretius describing in this passage? How is the contrast drawn in *Odes* 1.38 similar and how is it different?
2. What relationships can you see between *Odes* 1.38 and the poem that immediately precedes it, *Odes* 1.37?
3. How is *Odes* 1.38 appropriate as the final poem in the first book of odes?

Passage for Comparison

Lucretius *De rerum natura* 2.20–33

20   Ergō corpoream ad nātūram pauca vidēmus
21   esse opus omnīnō, quae dēmant cumque dolōrem,
22   dēliciās quoque utī multās substernere possint;
23   gratius interdum neque nātūra ipsa requīrit,
24   sī nōn aurea sunt iuvenum simulacra per aedēs
25   lampadas igniferās manibus retinentia dextrīs,
26   lūmina nocturnīs epulīs ut suppeditentur,
27   nec domus argentō fulget aurōque renīdet
28   nec citharae reboant laqueāta aurātaque templa,
29   cum tamen inter sē prōstrātī in grāmine mollī
30   propter aquae rīvum sub rāmīs arboris altae
31   nōn magnīs opibus iūcundē corpora cūrant,
32   praesertim cum tempestās adrīdet et annī
33   tempora cōnspergunt viridantīs flōribus herbās.

Therefore we see that all in all our bodily nature needs few things to take away pain, and to be able to spread many delights before us; nor does nature herself meanwhile need anything more pleasant, if there are no golden statues of young men about the house holding fiery torches in their right hands to supply light for nocturnal feasts, and the house does not shine with silver and gleam with gold, and if no paneled and gilded ceilings echo the lyre, when, nevertheless, men, stretched out on soft grass in groups, near a stream of water beneath the limbs of a tall tree pleasantly rest their bodies with no great efforts, especially when the weather smiles on them and the season of the year sprinkles the green grass with flowers.

Meter: Alcaic

1   **aequus, -a, -um,** *even, level; calm.*
     meminī, meminisse, perfect with present sense, *to remember.*
         mementō: imperative.
     arduus, -a, -um, *steep; difficult.*
2   **mēns, mentis,** f., *mind.*
         Aequam . . . (1) / . . . mentem: hyperbaton.
     nōn secus: *not otherwise; likewise.*
     in bonīs: supply **rēbus.**
3   **īnsolēns, īnsolentis [in-,** *not* + **soleō, solēre, solitus sum,** *to be accustomed],*
         unaccustomed; excessive.
     temperō, -āre, -āvī, -ātus, intransitive, *to practice restraint, be moderate;* transi-
         tive, *to moderate, temper;* + **ab** + abl., *to hold* X *back* (from an extreme).
             temperātam: *held back from;* supply **mementō servāre mentem** to com-
                 plete the sense.
4   **laetitia, -ae,** f., *joy; happiness.*
     moritūre: vocative of the future participle of **morior, morī, mortuus sum.**
     Dellius, -ī, m., *Quintus Dellius* (the addressee pursued a varied career in as-
         sociation with some of Rome's most famous and notorious individuals; he
         was aptly called *the circus rider of the civil wars,* **dēsultōrem bellōrum**
         cīvīlium, for changing his allegiance from Caesar to Cassius to Antony
         and finally to Octavian in the course of the civil wars).

ODES 2.3

To Dellius, on Living Well and Dying

Horace asks Dellius to maintain equanimity in the face of the mutability of fortune and in the face of death.

1 Aequam mementō rēbus in arduīs
2 servāre mentem, nōn secus in bonīs
3   ab īnsolentī temperātam
4   laetitiā, moritūre Dellī,

continued

Explorations

1. What does the speaker advise Dellius to do in difficult times (1–2a)?
2. What does the speaker advise Dellius to do in good times (2b–4a)?
3. Which words in lines 1–3 are linked phonetically by the letter combinations *em*, *ent*, and *ment*?
4. In using the striking epithet **moritūre** (4) as he addresses Dellius, what truth about human life does the speaker invoke? What tension is created by placing **laetitiā** and **moritūre** side by side?

5   **seu . . . seu**, conj., *whether. . . or.*
    maestus, -a, -um, *sad, gloomy.*
       maestus: translate as an adverb.
    omnī tempore: ablative expressing duration of time. Alternatively, Quinn
       (p. 201) understands **tempus** more specifically to mean *a critical point in
       time,* and he translates the phrase as *at every (fresh) crisis.*
    vīxeris: future perfect indicative, making it subordinate in time to the tense
       of the participle **moritūre**.
6   **remōtus, -a, -um**, *far off, distant.*
    grāmen, grāminis, n., *grass.*
    diēs / fēstōs (7): days officially designated as free from **negōtium** or busi-
       ness, so *holidays.*
7   **reclīnō, -āre, -āvī, -ātus**, transitive, *to make X lean back;* intransitive, *to lean
       back;* passive in middle sense, *to stretch (oneself) out.*
    beō, -āre, -āvī, -ātus, *to make X happy.*
       beāris: contracted from **beāveris**, future perfect indicative, parallel in con-
          struction to **vīxeris** (5).
          tē (6) **. . . / . . . beāris**: Horace uses this verb with a reflexive pronoun
             to mean *to enjoy oneself.*
8   **interior, interior, interius**, gen., **interiōris**, *inner.*
    nota, -ae, f., *mark; writing; brand.*
       interiōre notā: *with an expensive bottle;* lit., *with an inner brand.* Smith (p.
          112) explains **interiōre** as follows: "The jars farther back in the *apotheca*
          [wine cellar] would be those which had been left undisturbed the
          longest," and of **notā** he says, "properly the stamp or inscription on the
          amphora [large jar], or on a tag attached to it, recording the name and
          date (consuls of the year) of the vintage; hence used in general for qual-
          ity of wine."

5   seu maestus omnī tempore vīxeris,
6   seu tē in remōtō grāmine per diēs
7   fēstōs reclīnātum beāris
8   interiōre notā Falernī.

continued

Explorations

5. Describe the two hypothetical and contrary lifestyles that Horace maps out in lines 5–8.
6. How does the hypothetical lifestyle envisioned in line 5 indicate a failure to adhere to the advice offered in lines 1–2a?
7. Conversely, how does the hypothetical lifestyle envisioned in lines 6–8 indicate a successful adherence to the exhortation in lines 2b–4a?
8. Does the second stanza flow naturally and logically from the first or does it take an unexpected turn?
9. What advice or instruction do you think the speaker will give Dellius in the next section of the poem?

9   **quō**, interrogative adv., *why? for what reason?*

      pīnus, -ī, f., *pine tree.*

      pōpulus, -ī, f., *poplar tree.*

        pīnus . . . pōpulus: note that names of trees are feminine in the second declension. Nisbet and Hubbard (p. 59) identify these two trees as the *pinus pinea*, capable of growing to a height of eighty feet, and the white poplar, also a tall tree, which "loves growing by water. . . and according to Pliny was the only tree whose leaves rustled against each other."

10   **hospitālis, -is, -e**, *inviting, welcome, hospitable.*

      cōnsociō [**con-**, *with, together* + **socius, -ī**, m., *ally*], **-āre, -āvī, -ātus**, *to unite, join.*

        umbram . . . cōnsociāre: Horace has extended the use of the intransitive verb **cōnsociāre** to include an object that expresses the result of the action. In your translation, add a short linking phrase, such as *in making.*

      amant: the personification of the trees becomes clear with **amant**, which, when used with an infinitive, has the meaning *to be accustomed* (to).

11   **quid**, interrogative adv., *why?*

      oblīquus, -a, -um, *slanting, winding.*

        oblīquō: with **rīvō** (12).

      labōrat: this verb too may govern an infinitive, with the meaning *to strive* (to), *to struggle* (to).

12   **lympha, -ae**, f., *water.*

      fugāx, fugācis, *swift, fleeting.*

      trepidō, -āre, -āvī, -ātūrus, *to be alarmed, be in a panic; to scurry, rush.*

13   **nimium**, adv., *exceedingly, very; too.*

14   **amoenus, -a, -um**, *pleasant; charming; lovely.*

      iubē: supply **servum**.

15   **rēs**: *wealth, current situation,* or *circumstances* are possible translations of this word here; compare its meaning in line 1.

      aetās, aetātis, f., *age; time; the passage of time; time of life.*

16   **trium**: genitive of the numeral **trēs**. The appearance of the three sisters, the Fates, augurs a darker second half of the poem. The thread that Clotho spun and Lachesis measured out was ultimately cut by the third sister, Atropos. The blackness traditionally associated with death has been transferred by Horace to the thread of the Fates.

      patior, patī, passus sum, *to suffer; to permit, allow.*

      āter, ātra, ātrum, *black.*

9   Quō pīnus ingēns albaque pōpulus

10   umbram hospitālem cōnsociāre amant

11   rāmīs? Quid oblīquō labōrat

12   lympha fugāx trepidāre rīvō?

13   Hūc vīna et unguenta et nimium brevīs

14   flōrēs amoenae ferre iubē rosae,

15   dum rēs et aetās et sorōrum

16   fīla trium patiuntur ātra.

continued

Explorations

10. Two images in lines 9–12, one static, one dynamic, embedded in rhetorical questions invite us to speculate on nature's purposes. Point out the chiasmus in line 9 and two elisions in line 10. What do the two trees join in doing? What might be the answer to the rhetorical question that Horace poses in lines 9–11a?

11. Describe the flow of the stream (11b–12). Identify an example of hyperbaton. What might be the answer to the rhetorical question that the speaker poses here?

12. To whom is the imperative **iubē** addressed in line 14? What is the speaker inviting that person to do?

13. What items does the speaker insist on in lines 13–14? How does the list create an ascending tricolon? Explain how the items are all essential to a Roman drinking party and symbolic of Horace's philosophy of life as expressed in his poetry.

14. Contained in the list of ingredients for a drinking party in lines 13–14 and then developed more fully in lines 15–16 are some palpable and mythical limitations to their continued enjoyment. What limits the enjoyment of the drinking party? Trace the increasing gravity of the limitations. Where does the second tricolon of the stanza place the most emphasis and why?

15. How does the placement of words in lines 15–16 parallel that in lines 13–14? What effect is produced by making prominent use of elisions in the first tricolon but not in the second?

16. In what direction do you think the urgency of the imperative **iubē** and the multiple restraints on the enjoyment of the drinking party will lead the poem in the next stanza?

17   **cēdō, cēdere, cessī, cessūrus** + dat., *to yield* (to), *give in* (to); + abl., *to go away*
       (from), *depart* (from).
      coemō [con-, *with, together* + **emō, emere, ēmī, ēmptus,** *to buy*], **coemere,**
       coēmī, coēmptus, *to buy up.*
      saltus, -ūs, m., *pastureland.*
         coēmptīs saltibus: the ablative here and in **domō** (17) and **vīllā** (18) round
          out the meaning of **cēdēs,** for Dellius will not only be leaving but he will
          be departing *from* his extensive properties. Shorey and Laing (p. 256)
          translate **coēmptīs** as *bought up on all sides,* which nicely captures
          Dellius's apparent strategy of purchasing adjoining parcels of land in
          order to have large and profitable tracts for herding and grazing.
18   **flāvus, -a, -um,** *yellow, golden-yellow.*
         flāvus . . . Tiberis: for emphasis, the adjective has been pulled out of the
          relative clause. Various explanations have been given for this frequent
          epithet of the Tiber; the presence of light-colored mud or sand in the
          river is the most probable.
      lavō, lavāre or **lavere, lāvī, lavātus** or **lautus,** *to wash.*
19   **exstruō** [ex-, *out;* here, *up* + **struō, struere, struxī, structus,** *to build*],
       exstruere, exstruxī, exstructus, *to build up, pile up.*
      in altum: adverbial, *to great heights, on high.*
20   **potior, potīrī, potītus sum** + abl., *to acquire, take possession of.*

Passage for Comparison

Tibullus 1.1.1–10:

1   Dīvitiās alius fulvō sibi congerat aurō
2   et teneat cultī iugera multa solī,
3   quem labor adsiduus vīcīnō terreat hoste,
4   Martia cui somnōs classica pulsa fugent:
5   mē mea paupertās vītā trādūcat inertī,
6   dum meus adsiduō lūceat igne focus.
7   Iam modo iam possim contentus vīvere parvō
8   nec semper longae dēditus esse viae,
9   sed Canis aestīvōs ortūs vītāre sub umbrā
10   arboris ad rīvōs praetereuntis aquae.

      Let another man pile up wealth for himself with yellow gold and possess
      many acres of well-tilled earth; let constant hassle from a neighboring en-
      emy alarm him and outbursts from a war trumpet drive his sleep away:
      as for me, let my modest belongings guide me in a life of leisure provided
      that my hearth glows with a constant fire. Now at last let me be able to
      live contently on little and not always be enlisted for the long march, but
      let me be able to escape the scorching rise of the Dog Star under the shade
      of a tree next to the waters of a passing stream.

17   Cēdēs coēmptīs saltibus et domō
18   vīllāque flāvus quam Tiberis lavit;
19   cēdēs, et exstructīs in altum
20   dīvitiīs potiētur hērēs.

continued

Explorations

17.   For what event in human life does the speaker use **Cēdēs** (17) as a eu-
      phemism? Why does he repeat the verb in line 19?
18.   What has Dellius acquired over time (17–20)? How is each possession repre-
      sentative of a different sphere of financial activity and social status?
19.   What will happen to Dellius's possessions after his death (19b–20)? How
      does the pointed framing of the fifth stanza by **Cēdēs** at the start and **hērēs** at
      the end contribute to its overall sentiment?
20.   Lines 17–18 offer a list parallel to the list offered in lines 13–14. How do the
      things Horace proposes for enjoyment (13–14) differ from the things Dellius
      has spent his life acquiring (17–18)? How might the realization of the sad
      truth expressed in lines 17–20 affect Dellius?
21.   Horace's younger contemporary, Tibullus, a writer of elegiac love poetry,
      sets forth his poetic persona in the opening lines of the first book of his ele-
      giac poems quoted on the opposite page. How do these lines help you un-
      derstand the philosophy of life of the speaker of *Odes* 2.3?

"A Roman Seaside Villa"
Pompeian fresco, before 79 A.D.

21   **Dīvesne . . . morēris** (23): the poem now shifts to universal statements, ex-
      pressed with a generalizing "you" in this stanza and a generalizing "we"
      in the final stanza. Lines 21–23 are the logical prelude to the devastating
      generalization stated in line 24.
          Dīvesne: when introducing an indirect question, the enclitic **-ne** means
              whether; it is balanced by **an pauper** in the next line.
      nātus: *descended,* from **nāscor, nāscī, nātus sum**, *to be born.*
      Īnachus, -ī, m., *Inachus* (name of the first legendary king of Argos, which
          was a prominent city in ancient Greece).
22   **interest, interesse, interfuit**, impersonal, *it is important; it makes a difference.*
          nīl interest: *it makes no difference at all;* the negating force of **nīl** (short for
              nihil) is stronger than that of **nōn** and comparable to *not at all* or *no . . . at
              all.*
      īnfimus [superlative of **īnferus, -a, -um**, *below*], **-a, -um**, *lowest.*
23   **dīvum, -ī**, n., *the open sky.*
          sub dīvō: *under the open sky,* i.e., on earth and not yet in the underworld.
      moror, -ārī, -ātus sum, *to delay; to stay, linger.*
          morēris: subjunctive in an indirect question; the phrase **sub dīvō morēris**
              in one sense is equivalent to **vīvās**, but the tension between **sub dīvō**
              and its implied opposite (the underworld), joined with the verb **morārī**
              (which suggests a short-term stay), makes the phrase more ominous
              than simply "you live."
24   **victima, -ae**, f., *animal offered in sacrifice, sacrificial victim; victim.*
          victima: in apposition to the subject of **morēris**.
      nīl: see the note on line 22 above.
      miseror, -ārī, -ātus sum, *to have mercy; to show pity.*
      Orcus, -ī, m., *Orcus* (one of the Roman names for the god of the underworld);
          by metonymy, *death.*

21 Dīvesne prīscō nātus ab Īnachō
22 nīl interest an pauper et īnfimā
23   dē gente sub dīvō morēris,
24   victima nīl miserantis Orcī.

continued

Explorations

22. What two features distinguish the two sets of people described in lines 21–23? What difference will such distinctions make as far as Dellius is concerned?
23. How does the placement of the phrase **nīl interest** (22) visually mirror the point that the speaker is making?
24. What do the words **victima** (24) and **nīl** (22 and 24) contribute to the theme of this stanza?

25   **eōdem**, adv., *to the same place.*
     omnium: *everyone's,* possessive genitive with **sors** (27).
26   **versō** [**vertō, vertere, vertī, versus,** *to turn* + **-sō**, intensive or iterative suf-
     fix], **-āre, -āvī, -ātus,** *to keep turning around; to spin;* of an urn, *to shake.*
     urna, -ae, f., *urn.*
       urnā: supply **ab.**
     sērius ōcius: *sooner or later.*
27   **sors, sortis,** f., *fate; lot.*
     exitūra . . . / . . . impositūra (28): future participles reappear and draw out
     the implications of **moritūre** in the opening stanza.
     aeternum: note the hypermetric line with elision over the line-break
       (synapheia).
28   **exsilium, -ī,** n., *exile.*
       exsilium: a charged political word, conjuring up for a Roman the loss of
         privileges and confiscation of property that accompanied expulsion from
         the city.
     cumba, -ae, f., *small boat.*
       cumbae: dative with the compound participle **impositūra.**

25 Omnēs eōdem cōgimur, omnium
26 versātur urnā sērius ōcius
27   sors exitūra et nōs in aeternum
28   exsilium impositūra cumbae.

Explorations

25. How does the first word of the final stanza, **Omnēs** (25), carry forward the theme of the preceding stanza?
26. How does Horace make obvious the all-inclusive reach of death in line 25?
27. Anticipated by the word **victima** in the preceding line, how might the connotation of herding in the verb **cōgimur** (25) link animal and human in the context of the final stanza?
28. How are our final destinies determined (25–28)?
29. To what element of the Greco-Roman mythological picture of the underworld does the action of lines 27–28 allude?
30. What is special and unique about the particular exile that is in store for all of us? How would a Roman aristocrat skilled in political survival like Dellius react to the mention of exile?
31. What is striking about the metrics and the sound of lines 27–28?

"Charon in a Boat, Ferrying Souls across the Styx"
Roman marble relief from a sarcophagus, 3rd century A.D.
Vatican Museums, Vatican State

Odes 2.3

1   Aequam mementō rēbus in arduīs
2   servāre mentem, nōn secus in bonīs
3   ab īnsolentī temperātam
4   laetitiā, moritūre Dellī,

5   seu maestus omnī tempore vīxeris,
6   seu tē in remōtō grāmine per diēs
7   fēstōs reclīnātum beāris
8   interiōre notā Falernī.

9   Quō pīnus ingēns albaque pōpulus
10 umbram hospitālem cōnsociāre amant
11   rāmīs? Quid oblīquō labōrat
12   lympha fugāx trepidāre rīvō?

13 Hūc vīna et unguenta et nimium brevīs
14 flōrēs amoenae ferre iubē rosae,
15   dum rēs et aetās et sorōrum
16   fīla trium patiuntur ātra.

17 Cēdēs coēmptīs saltibus et domō
18 vīllāque flāvus quam Tiberis lavit;
19   cēdēs, et exstructīs in altum
20   dīvitiīs potiētur hērēs.

21 Dīvesne prīscō nātus ab Īnachō
22 nīl interest an pauper et īnfimā
23   dē gente sub dīvō morēris,
24   victima nīl miserantis Orcī.

25 Omnēs eōdem cōgimur, omnium
26 versātur urnā sērius ōcius
27   sors exitūra et nōs in aeternum
28   exsilium impositūra cumbae.

Discussion

1. Why is it advisable to keep a level head (**Aequam . . . mentem**, 1–2a) in both bad times and good? What does the allusion to the inevitability of death (**moritūre**, 4b) add to the advice?

2. With lines 6–12 of *Odes* 2.3, compare lines 19–22 of *Odes* 1.1, quoted in Passages for Comparison I following these questions. What are the similarities between the two passages? How do the rhetorical questions of lines 9–12 of *Odes* 2.3 advance the thought beyond what is contained in lines 19–22 of *Odes* 1.1?

3. The weight of the two clauses in lines 13–16 is on the third image of each list, the short-lived rose and the dark threads. Knowing that wine and perfume can be replenished, what heightened significance do you find in the use of the rose? Although both the rose and the thread are delicate items, what special twist is added by placing this particular thread alongside the rose?

4. A telling chiasmus unfolds in lines 17–20: verb (**Cēdēs**) : ablatives (**coēmptīs saltibus et domō**) :: ablatives (**exstructīs . . . dīvitiīs**) : verb (**potiētur**). Explain how this chiasmus heightens the difference between Dellius and the heir. How will Dellius feel about what is said here?

5. With lines 17–20, compare Lucretius *De rerum natura* 3.894–99, quoted in Passages for Comparison II following these questions. What is missing from the list in *Odes* 2.3? What is Horace suggesting through its absence?

6. There are several ways to discuss the structure of *Odes* 2.3. Consider the strengths of the following approaches:
    a. A tripartite structure: lines 1–8, 9–16, and 17–24
    b. A concentric structure: the fourth stanza surrounded by three stanzas on each side, with the first and seventh, the second and sixth, and the third and fifth stanzas paired off

Passages for Comparison

I.

Odes 1.1.19–22:

    19   Est quī nec veteris pōcula Massicī
    20   nec partem solidō dēmere dē diē
    21   spernit, nunc viridī membra sub arbutō
    22   strātus, nunc ad aquae lēne caput sacrae.

II.

Lucretius *De rerum natura* 3.894–99; hypothetical mourners are addressing a dead man:

894   "Iam iam nōn domus accipiet tē laeta neque uxor
895   optima, nec dulcēs occurrent ōscula nātī
896   praeripere et tacitā pectus dulcēdine tangent.
897   Nōn poteris factīs flōrentibus esse, tuīsque
898   praesidium. Miserō, miserē," āiunt, "omnia adēmit
899   ūna diēs īnfesta tibī tot praemia vītae."

"No longer now (i.e., now that you are dead) will your home nor your excellent wife joyfully receive you, nor will sweet children run up to you to snatch the first kisses and touch your heart with quiet sweetness. You will not be able to provide protection for your flourishing affairs and your family. Sadly," they say, "one adverse day has taken so many of life's rewards from wretched you."

BACKGROUND FOR *ODES* 2.7

Horace's Autobiography

Horace *Epistles* 2.2.41–52a:

41 Rōmae nutrīrī mihi contigit, atque docērī
42 īrātus Grāīs quantum nocuisset Achillēs.
43 Adiēcēre bonae paulō plūs artis Athēnae,
44 scīlicet ut vellem curvō dīnōscere rēctum,
45 atque inter silvās Acadēmī quaerere vērum.
46 Dūra sed ēmōvēre locō mē tempora grātō,
47 cīvīlisque rudem bellī tulit aestus in arma
48 Caesaris Augustī nōn respōnsūra lacertīs.
49 Unde simul prīmum mē dīmīsēre Philippī,
50 dēcīsīs humilem pennīs inopemque paternī
51 et laris et fundī, paupertās impulit audāx
52a ut versūs facerem.

> It was my lot to be fostered at Rome and to be taught how much Achilles in his wrath had harmed the Greeks. Noble Athens added a little more knowledge, so that I would wish to distinguish the straight from the crooked and to seek the truth among the groves of the Academy. But difficult times swept me from my pleasing station, and the tide of civil war bore me, inexperienced though I was, into warfare, unable to match the might of Caesar Augustus. As soon as Philippi had discharged me, humbled with clipped wings and bereft of my father's house and estate, poverty made me bold to write poetry.

Biography of Horace

An extract from Suetonius *Vita Horati:*

> Bellō Philippēnsī excitus ā Marcō Brūtō imperātōre, tribunus mīlitum meruit; victīsque partibus vēniā impetrātā scrīptum quaestōrium comparāvit. Ac prīmō Maecēnātī, mox Augustō īnsinuātus nōn mediocrem in ambōrum amīcitiā locum tenuit.

> In the battle at Philippi Horace served as a tribune of the soldiers, having been raised to that office by Marcus Brutus; and after his party had been defeated, he obtained a pardon and bought a position as a clerk to a quaestor. Then having gotten on good terms, first with Maecenas, and later with Augustus, he held not an ordinary place in the friendship of both.

Meter: Alcaic

1　Ō . . . / **dēducte** (2): modifying **Pompēī** (5a), vocative, the addressee, Pompeius.
　tempus: here, *a critical period of time, a crisis.*
　ultimus, -a, -um, *final; ultimate.*
　　tempus . . . ultimum: *ultimate* (i.e., life-threatening) *crisis, greatest danger;* the reference is to military engagements.

2　**dēdūcō [dē-,** *down, away, from* or expressing thoroughness or completeness
　　+ dūcō, dūcere, dūxī, ductus, *to lead*], **dēdūcere, dēdūxī, dēductus,** *to lead away; to reduce* (to an extreme state); *to lead* (into an extreme course of action).
　Brūtus, -ī, m., *Brutus* (M. Junius Brutus, one of the assassins of Julius Caesar on March 15, 44 B.C.).
　mīlitia, -ae, f., *campaign, military service.*
　　Brūtō mīlitiae duce: ablative absolute. Brutus and Cassius, two of the chief conspirators in the assassination of Julius Caesar, left Rome in August 44 B.C., having failed to gain popular support for the assassination. They went to Greece and the eastern provinces where they gathered a large army with which they could confront Antony and Octavian, who were determined to avenge the murder of Caesar. The philosophically minded Brutus attended lectures of Theomnestus, the Academic, and Cratippus, the Peripatetic, in Athens, where Horace was studying. Brutus attracted Horace and many other young Romans studying there to his cause as the champion of the Republic and of liberty. Horace enlisted in Brutus's army in the summer of 44 or 43 B.C. and probably fought in engagements in the east prior to the great battles against Antony and Octavian at Philippi in Macedonia in October and November 42 B.C. Horace tells us that he served as a tribune in charge of a legion (see background notes a and b on the opposite page).

3　**tē:** i.e., Pompeius (see line 5a), known only from this poem. The name evokes resistance to the Caesarians and allegiance to the defense of the Republic, causes championed by Pompeius Magnus, who was defeated by Julius Caesar at Pharsalus in 48 B.C., and by his son Sextus Pompeius, who was defeated by Octavian's general Agrippa at Naulochus in 36 B.C. The Pompeius addressed in this poem campaigned with Horace in Brutus's army before and at Philippi and continued to campaign after Brutus's defeat. He may have been a fellow student with Horace in Athens.
　redōnō [word probably coined by Horace; **re-,** *back again* + **dōnō, -āre, -āvī, -ātus,** *to make a present of; to forgive, pardon*], **-āre, -āvī, -ātus,** *to give back.*
　　redōnāvit: translate *has given . . . back,* but the verb also implies the granting of a pardon.
　Quirīs, Quirītis, m., *a Roman citizen* (cf. the more usual plural, **Quirītēs, Quirītium,** as used in *Odes* 1.1.7; the term is used of those enjoying the full civil rights of Roman citizens as opposed to soldiers, who would be under military discipline).
　　tē . . . Quirītem: *you [as a] citizen.*

4　**patrius, -a, -um,** *of a father; native; ancestral.*

ODES 2.7

Reunion with a Friend

The speaker welcomes his friend, Pompeius, who has come back to Rome after the civil wars, and prepares a celebration.

1 Ō saepe mēcum tempus in ultimum
2 dēducte Brūtō mīlitiae duce,
3   quis tē redōnāvit Quirītem
4   dīs patriīs Italōque caelō,

continued

Explorations

1. What is the speaker recalling in addressing Pompeius with the words **Ō saepe mēcum tempus in ultimum / dēducte** (1–2)?
2. The words **Brūtō mīlitiae duce** (2) are a self-contained ablative absolute, but the word **duce** at the end of the line resonates with **dēducte** at the beginning. What does the ablative absolute add to the address of Pompeius in the first two lines? What does the echo of **dēducte** in **duce** add to that?
3. What does the rhetorical question beginning with the word **quis** (3) tell us? What is the answer to the question (consider the quotation from Octavian/Augustus in Background Notes III below)? How would the question reassure Pompeius?

Background Notes

I.

Horace (*Satires* 1.6.48) complains that everyone used to carp at him because, although the low-born son of a freedman, a Roman legion obeyed him as its tribune: **quod mihi parēret legiō Rōmāna tribūnō.**

II.

On the other hand, Horace claims to have pleased the foremost men of Rome both in war and in peace (*Epistles* 1.20.23): **mē prīmīs urbis bellī placuisse domīque.**

III

Octavian/Augustus boasted of his clemency to the defeated after the battle of Actium. Writing of himself, he says (*Res gestae* 3) that he spared all citizens who sought pardon: **omnibus veniam petentibus cīvibus pepercī.**

5   **Pompēius, Pompēiī,** m., *Pompeius* (see note to line 3 above).
    Pompēī: pronounced as two syllables by synizesis.
    prīmus, -a, -um, *first; earliest; foremost; most notable, most distinguished; best.*
    prīme: commentators disagree as to whether this means *first* or *best*;
        Shorey and Laing (p. 265) suggest "first and foremost."
    sodālium: see *Odes* 1.37.4; here two meanings are operative, *comrades in arms*
        and *drinking companions.*
6   **moror, -ārī, -ātus sum,** *to delay; to wait; to pass slowly, linger.*
7   **frēgī** and **frācta** (11): note that in addition to *break*, the verb **frangere** can
        mean *to shatter, smash; to exhaust, wear out; to vanquish, destroy; to crush* (in
        spirit or temper).
            morantem . . . diem (6) . . . / **frēgī**: "i.e., shortened the day, which
                otherwise would have gone tediously and heavily" (Lincoln, p. 354) or
                "defeated a wearisome day" (Page, p. 44).
    niteō, nitēre, nituī, *to shine, glisten.*
            nitentīs / . . . capillōs (8): accusative object of **corōnātus**, perfect passive
                participle used in the sense of the Greek middle voice, *having wreathed*
                my hair glistening. . . . ; for the construction, cf. *Odes* 1.1.21b–22a, **membra**
                sub arbūtō / strātus.
8   **mālobathrum** [Gr., μαλάβαθρον, from Sanskrit, *tamālapatram*, "leaf of the
        tamala tree"], **-ī,** n., *malobathrum* (an oil from the fragrant leaves of the
        Indian tamala tree used in perfume).
            mālobathrō: dependent on **nitentīs** (7).
    Syrius, -a, -um, *Syrian* (used in general of goods from the Orient, many of
        which passed through Antioch in Syria).
            mālobathrō Syriō: a touch of local color; an appropriate perfume for the
                speaker to use in drinking parties in the eastern provinces during his
                military service with Brutus before Philippi.

5   Pompēī, meōrum prīme sodālium?
6   Cum quō morantem saepe diem merō
7   frēgī corōnātus nitentīs
8   mālobathrō Syriō capillōs.

continued

Explorations

4. Characterize the style and tone of the opening address to Pompeius (1–5). How are the expression and tone of line 5 appropriate to a welcoming-home poem?
5. The words **Cum quō** and **saepe** in line 6 pick up **saepe** and **mēcum** in line 1, in reverse order. How does what is described in lines 6–8 humorously and ironically complement or present a reverse image of what is said of the speaker and Pompeius's activities in lines 1–2?
6. Compare the scene of drinking here with that in *Odes* 1.1.19–22:

    19   Est quī nec veteris pōcula Massicī
    20   nec partem solidō dēmere dē diē
    21   spernit, nunc viridī membra sub arbutō
    22   strātus, nunc ad aquae lēne caput sacrae.

    How do the words **nec partem solidō dēmere dē diē spernit** in *Odes* 1.1 help explain the clause **morantem . . . diem . . . / frēgī** in *Odes* 2.7.6–7?

9   **Philippī, -ōrum**, m. pl., *Philippi* (a town on the Via Egnatia in eastern
     Macedonia near the Thracian border; the site of battles where Brutus and
     Cassius defended the cause of the Republic against Octavian and Antony
     in October and November of 42 B.C.; in the first battle Cassius's camp was
     overrun by Antony, and Cassius committed suicide; in the second battle
     Brutus was defeated and committed suicide).
     fuga, -ae, f., *flight; retreat.*
       Philippōs et celerem fugam: sometimes (e.g., Quinn, p. 211) understood
         by hendiadys as *the swift retreat at Philippi*, and sometimes taken to mean,
         as Smith (p. 122) insists, "the battle and the flight"—"not a case of hendi-
         adys."
10   **sentiō, sentīre, sēnsī, sēnsus**, *to feel; to experience* X *to one's cost.*
     parmula [word probably coined by Horace; **parma, -ae**, f., *small, round shield
     carried by light infantry and cavalry* + **-ula**, diminutive suffix], **-ae**, f., *little
     shield.*
       parmulā: the diminutive strikes a disparaging tone, *poor little shield;*
         Horace is alluding to the famous gesture of the Greek lyric poets
         Archilochus, Alcaeus, and Anacreon, who abandoned their shields on
         the battlefield and saved their lives (for Archilochus, see the passage
         for comparison below), refusing to adhere to the Spartan saying,
         "Return either with your shield or on it."
11   **frācta**: supply **est**.
     virtūs, virtūtis, f. [= Gr. ἀρετή], *manly spirit; valor; excellence of character; moral
     excellence, virtue.*
       virtūs: both the *valor* of Brutus's soldiers and Brutus's personal *virtue*, for
         which he was famed and respected even by his enemies.
     minācēs: substantive use of the adjective, *threatening [men]*, i.e., the soldiers of
       Brutus; subject of **tetigēre = tetigērunt**.
12   **turpis, -is, -e**, *foul; ugly; disgraceful, shameful, ignominious.*
       turpe: although grammatically modifying **solum**, with which it would
         mean *foul* (with the blood and gore of battle), the word also characterizes
         the entire act of touching the ground with the chin in death and may be
         translated as an adverb, *ignominiously.*
     solum, -ī, n., *earth, ground.*
     mentum, -ī, n., *chin.*

Passage for Comparison

Archilochus, seventh century B.C. Greek poet and warrior from Paros, fragment 5:

1   Ἀσπίδι μὲν Σαΐων τις ἀγάλλεται, ἣν παρὰ θάμνῳ
2   ἔντος ἀμώμητον, κάλλιπον οὐκ ἐθέλων·
3   αὐτὸν δ' ἐξεσάωσα. τί μοι μέλει ἀσπὶς ἐκείνη;
4   ἐρρέτω· ἐξαῦτις κτήσομαι οὐ κακίω.

       Some Saian exults in my shield which I left—a faultless weapon—beside a
       bush against my will. But I saved myself. What do I care about that
       shield? To hell with it! I'll get one that's just as good another time.

9 Tēcum Philippōs et celerem fugam
10 sēnsī relictā nōn bene parmulā,
11   cum frācta virtūs, et mināces
12   turpe solum tetigēre mentō.

continued

Explorations

7. What is reinforced by the repetition of prepositional phrases with **cum** in the first three stanzas?
8. Horace gives only a very truncated account of the battle of Philippi with carefully selected details. What four details does he include?
9. What do the words **celerem fugam / sēnsī** (9–10) tell us about how the speaker views his flight from the battle at Philippi?
10. Consider the passage for comparison from Archilochus on the opposite page. How does the allusion to that passage color the speaker's statement that he left his shield behind in his flight from Philippi (9b–10)?
11. To what do the words **frācta virtūs [est]** (11a) refer? What message do they convey to Pompeius?
12. What contrast is being made by the echo of **frēgī** (7) in **frācta** (11a)?
13. What is the meaning of the clause **mināces / turpe solum tetigēre mentō** (11b–12)? Note the underlined words in the passages for comparison at the bottom of this page as you consider this question.

Passages for Comparison

I.

Agamemnon in *Iliad* 2 prays to Zeus that he may destroy Priam's palace and slay Hector and that "many of his comrades may fall headlong in the dust and <u>seize the earth with their teeth</u>" (2.417b–18).

II.

In Book 11 of the *Iliad*, Nestor reminisces about a battle with the Epeians. When the latter began to flee, Nestor sprang at them and seized fifty chariots. He continues (11.748b–52):

> And about each one two men subdued by my spear <u>seized the earth</u>. And now I would have slain the two Moliones, sons of Actor, if their father, the wide-ruling Earth-Shaker had not saved them from the battle by veiling them in a dense mist.

13 **Mercurius, -ī**, m., *Mercury* (the messenger of the gods, but probably evoked here because as the inventor of the lyre he is a patron of poets. Commonly in epic descriptions of battle, a god will rescue a favored warrior by shrouding him in a dense mist and removing him from the field of battle; see Passages for Comparison I on the opposite page and the second passage from the *Iliad* beneath lines 9–12. Only here in *Odes* 2.7, however, is Mercury said to do this).

14 **dēnsus, -a, -um**, *thick, dense.*
    dēnsō: with **āere**, ablative of place where without a preposition.
  paveō, pavēre, *to be frightened, be terrified.*
    paventem: perhaps from being defeated in battle or from being defenseless with loss of his shield or from being transported aloft by Mercury or for all three reasons.
  āer, āeris, m., *air; fog, mist.*
    dēnsō . . . āere: Horace's translation of the Greek ἠέρι πολλῇ, which we translate "in a dense mist" in the passage from Homer quoted below.

15 **in bellum**: take with both **resorbēns** and **tulit** (16).
  resorbeō [re-, *back, again* + **sorbeō, sorbēre, sorbuī, sorbitus**, *to suck, absorb*], **resorbēre**, *to suck back.*

16 **fretum, -ī**, n., *narrow strait; sea;* pl., *waters, currents.*
  aestuōsus [aestus, -ūs, m., see below + **-ōsus, -a, -um**, adjectival ending], **-a, -um**, *hot, sweltering;* of water, *seething; raging.*

"Mercury"
Bas-relief from the exterior of the Rockefeller Center (1931–1940)
Manhattan, New York City, U.S.A.

13   Sed mē per hostīs Mercurius celer
14   dēnsō paventem sustulit āere;
15   tē rūrsus in bellum resorbēns
16   unda fretīs tulit aestuōsīs.

continued

Explorations

14. How do the words at the beginning of lines 13 (**Sed mē**) and 15 (**tē**) articulate the structure of the fourth stanza ?
15. Consider the first passage for comparison below and the second passage from the *Iliad* beneath lines 9–12. The speaker is obviously not recording a historical fact in lines 13–14. What is he doing here? Why is it Mercury who spirits the speaker away?
16. Why is Mercury described as **celer** (13)? What are some of the implications for the speaker of the swiftness of his rescue?
17. How is the word order of line 14, **dēnsō paventem sustulit āere**, significant?
18. What pictorial image is conveyed by the metaphorical language of lines 15–16? What is its point?

Passages for Comparison

I.

With lines 13–14 of *Odes* 2.7, compare the rescue of the sons of Actor by Poseidon in the second passage from the *Iliad* beneath lines 9–12 on the previous page, and compare the following passage from *Iliad* 3.380b–81 describing Aphrodite's rescue of Paris to prevent his being slain in his duel with Menelaus:

> But Aphrodite snatched him away very easily, as a goddess can, and veiled him in a dense mist.

II.

With the words **fretīs tulit aestuōsīs** in line 16, compare what Horace says of himself (*Epistles* 2.2.47) at the time when he left his studies at the Academy in Athens and joined Brutus's army:

47   Cīvīlis . . . [mē] rudem bellī tulit aestus in arma.

> The tide of civil war bore me, inexperienced though I was, into warfare.

> **aestus, -ūs**, m., *heat; rage, passion, fury;* of the sea, *surge, swell, tide;* metaphorical, *flood, current, tide.*

17   **ergō**, particle, *therefore*.
      obligō [ob-, *in the way of, in payment for* + **ligō, -āre, -āvī, -ātus,** *to tie*], **-āre,**
         -āvī, -ātus, in a religious sense, *to bind, pledge* (with vows or promises made
         to a deity).
      redde: here used as a technical term in the context of fulfilling religious obli-
         gations: *give back* (**re-**) (what is due), *render*.
      daps, dapis, f., *sacrificial feast*.
         dapem: cf. *Odes* 1.37.4, **dapibus**, in a similar context of thanksgiving.
            obligātam . . . dapem: here it is not a matter of a person who has been
               bound or pledged but of a feast that has been pledged or promised.
               The implication is that Pompeius prayed to Jupiter and vowed or
               promised in his prayers that he would offer a sacrificial feast to Jupiter
               if he (Pompeius) would return safely as a **Quirīs**, a citizen with full
               rights, to Italy. Now that Pompeius has returned to Italy and has been
               reinstated as a citizen, the speaker orders him to *render* (**redde**) *the sac-*
               rificial feast (**dapem**) *that had been pledged* (**obligātam**) with vows or
               promises.
18   **fessus, -a, -um**, *tired, weary, exhausted*.
      latus, lateris, n., *side; flank;* by metonymy, *body*.
19   **laurus, -ūs**, f., *laurel tree*.
20   **cadus, -ī**, m., *wine jar*.
      dēstinō, -āre, -āvī, -ātus, *to mark out, set aside*.

Comparison

The archaic Greek poet Hesiod records (*Theogony* 29–32) how the Muses conse-
crated him as a poet by granting that he pluck a branch of laurel (δάφνης . . . ὄζον,
30) to serve as a staff and breathed divine inspiration into him. The staff of laurel
symbolizes Hesiod's calling as a poet.

17 Ergō obligātam redde Iovī dapem
18 longāque fessum mīlitiā latus
19   dēpōne sub laurū meā, nec
20   parce cadīs tibi dēstinātīs.

continued

Explorations

19. How does line 17, **Ergō obligātam redde Iovī dapem**, introduced by **Ergō**, function in relation to the first four stanzas of the poem?
20. Is there any special point to Horace's mentioning the laurel tree (19) as a place for the contemplated drinking party? See the passage from Hesiod in Comparison on the opposite page and the passages below.
21. The verb **parcō, parcere** is often used in military contexts of sparing the defeated and humbled enemy. How is the word used humorously and ironically in line 20?
22. What does the word **dēstinātīs** (20) imply on the part of the speaker?

Passages for Comparison

I.

In *Odes* 3.30.15b–16, Horace asks to be crowned as a poet with Delphic laurel:

15b .   .   .   mihi Delphicā
16   laurō cinge volēns, Melpomenē, comam.

   willingly bind my hair, Melpomene, with Delphic laurel.

II.

In *Res gestae* 34, Augustus reports that the doorposts of his house were decorated with laurel wreaths by decree of the senate:

   In cōnsulātū sextō et septimō, bella ubi cīvīlia exstīnxeram, per cōnsēnsum ūniversōrum potītus rērum omnium, rem pūblicam ex meā potestāte in senātūs populīque Rōmānī arbitrium trānstulī. Quō prō meritō meō senātūs cōnsultō Augustus appellātus sum et laureīs postēs aedium meārum vestītī pūblicē [sunt].

   In my sixth and seventh consulships [i.e., 28–27 B.C.], after I had put an end to the civil wars, having taken charge of all affairs through the consent of all, I transferred the republic from my power to the control of the senate and the Roman people. For this service of mine by a decree of the senate I was given the name Augustus ["the reverend one"], and the doorposts of my house were publicly decorated with laurel wreaths.

21   obliviōsus [cf. oblīvīscor, oblīvīscī, oblītus sum, *to forget*], **-a, -um,**
      causing/bringing forgetfulness.
      Massicum, -ī, n., *Massic wine* (produced in Campania near Mount Massicus;
      cf. *Odes* 1.1.19).
22   **cibōrium** [Gr., κιβώριον, used only here in its Latin transliteration], **-ī,** n.,
      large drinking cup (made from or resembling an Egyptian bean pod; such
      cups would be tall, very large, narrow below, and broad at the top).
      expleō [ex-, *out, completely* + **pleō, plēre,** *to fill*], **explēre, explēvī, explētus,** to
      fill up, fill to the brim.
      fundō, fundere, fūdī, fūsus, *to pour out.*
      capāx, capācis, *capacious.*
23   **unguentum, -ī,** n., *perfume; unguent* (scented oil).
      concha, -ae, f., *sea-shell; sea-shell shaped vessel.*
      Quis: interrogative pronoun, *Who?* or interrogative adjective, **Quis** [supply
      puer], *What [boy/slave]?*
      ūdus, -a, -um, *moist; pliant.*
24   **dēproperō** [word probably used first by Horace with a transitive sense; **dē-,**
      down from, thoroughly + **properō, -āre, -āvī, -ātūrus,** *to hasten*], **-are, -āvī,**
      -ātus, *to make haste to complete; to prepare quickly.*
25   **cūratve:** the enclitic **-ve** should be understood with **myrtō,** to which it would
      be attached in prose.
          cūrat: *is taking care* (to), *is responsible* (for), *has the job* (of) + infin.
      Venus, Veneris, f., *Venus* (the goddess of love, but also a term, as here, for
      the highest throw of four dice, when there is a different number on each
      face; the guest at a drinking party who threw the Venus became **arbiter
      bibendī** and decided on the proportion of wine to water in the mixing
      bowl).
26   **dīcet:** *will name, will appoint.*
      sānē, adv., *sensibly, soberly.*
      Nōn: with **sānius:** *not more sanely,* by litotes = **īnsānius,** *more insanely, more
      wildly.*
27   **bacchor** [Gr., βακχεύω, *to celebrate the mysteries of Bacchus*], **-ārī, -ātus sum,** *to
      celebrate the mysteries of Bacchus; to act like a Bacchante; to rave, rage; to be in a
      Bacchic frenzy* (of intoxication).
      Ēdōnī, -ōrum, m. pl., *Edonians* (a Thracian people notorious for their worship
      of Bacchus; their women were Bacchantes).
      recipiō [re-, *back, again* + **capiō, capere, cēpī, captus,** *to take*], **recipere,
      recēpī, receptus,** *to admit* (a person) *to shelter or entertainment; to make wel-
      come, receive; to admit* (a person to friendship, citizenship, etc.); *to regain pos-
      session of, recover, get back* (usually of material or abstract things).
28   **dulcis, -is, -e,** *sweet; delightful.*
      furō, furere, *to be out of one's mind; to behave wildly.*

21 Oblīviōsō lēvia Massicō
22 cibōria explē; funde capācibus
23   unguenta dē conchīs. Quis ūdō
24   dēproperāre apiō corōnās

25 cūratve myrtō? Quem Venus arbitrum
26 dīcet bibendī? Nōn ego sānius
27   bacchābor Ēdōnīs: receptō
28   dulce mihī furere est amīcō.

Explorations

23. Explain the meaning and overtones of **Oblīviōsō** (21), which is in the emphatic first position of the sixth stanza. Compare the phrase "wine that brings forgetfulness of sorrows" in the passage for comparison from Alcaeus below and compare the advice to Plancus in the lines quoted on the next page from *Odes* 1.7.
24. Comment on the features of the drinking party that the speaker orders to be prepared in the sixth and seventh stanzas (21–28).

Passages for Comparison

I.

Alcaeus 346

Let's drink! Why do we wait for the lamps? There is only a finger's breadth of the day left. Take down, dearest, the big cups intricately designed. For the son of Semele and Zeus has given <u>wine</u> to men <u>that brings forgetfulness of sorrows</u>. Pour in one part water to two of wine and mix, filling it to the brim, and let one cup make way for another.

more on next page

II.

Odes 1.7.15–21a:

15   Albus ut obscūrō dēterget nūbila caelō
16   saepe Notus neque parturit imbrīs
17   perpetuō, sīc tū sapiēns fīnīre mementō
18   trīstitiam vītaeque labōrēs
19   mollī, Plance, merō, seu tē fulgentia signīs
20   castra tenent seu dēnsa tenēbit
21a   Tīburis umbra tuī.

As the South Wind, often bringing clear weather, sweeps away the clouds
from a dark sky and does not produce rain showers continuously, so you
should remember with wisdom to put an end to your sorrow and the
troubles of life with mellow wine, Plancus, whether the military camp
gleaming with standards holds you or the thick shade of your own Tibur.

Discussion

1. How does the speaker bridge the past and the present in welcoming
    Pompeius back?
2. How does the speaker effectively define an autonomous position for himself
    by ignoring or marginalizing Octavian/Augustus?
3. As we have seen, when Horace speaks of leaving his shield behind at
    Philippi, he is alluding to a famous poem of Archilochus. Note that
    Archilochus in that poem consoles himself with the statement that he will get
    a better shield in the future. In another poem (fragment 1) Archilochus
    boasts of being both a warrior and a poet:

    1   εἰμὶ δ᾽ ἐγὼ θεράπων μὲν Ἐνυαλίοιο ἄνακτος
    2   καὶ Μουσέων ἐρατὸν δῶρον ἐπιστάμενος.

    I am the servant of lord Enyalius [God of War] and versed in the
    lovely gift of the Muses.

    Look back at what Horace wrote about himself in *Epistles* 2.2.41–52a quoted at
    the beginning of the material on this ode.

    a. Judging from that passage and the two poems of Archilochus, what simi-
        larities and what differences do you see between the poetic biographies
        of Archilochus and Horace?
    b. When did Horace become a poet, and why was what happened to him at
        the battle of Philippi of importance?
    c. What does *Odes* 2.7 tell us about Horace as a poet?

Odes 2.7

1   Ō saepe mēcum tempus in ultimum
2   dēducte Brūtō mīlitiae duce,
3   quis tē redōnāvit Quirītem
4   dīs patriīs Italōque caelō,

5   Pompēī, meōrum prīme sodālium?
6   Cum quō morantem saepe diem merō
7   frēgī corōnātus nitentīs
8   mālobathrō Syriō capillōs.

9   Tēcum Philippōs et celerem fugam
10 sēnsī relictā nōn bene parmulā,
11   cum frācta virtūs, et minācēs
12   turpe solum tetigēre mentō.

13 Sed mē per hostīs Mercurius celer
14 dēnsō paventem sustulit āere;
15   tē rūrsus in bellum resorbēns
16   unda fretīs tulit aestuōsīs.

17 Ergō obligātam redde Iovī dapem
18 longāque fessum mīlitiā latus
19   dēpōne sub laurū meā, nec
20   parce cadīs tibi dēstinātīs.

21 Oblīviōsō lēvia Massicō
22 cibōria explē; funde capācibus
23   unguenta dē conchīs. Quis ūdō
24   dēproperāre apiō corōnās

25 cūratve myrtō? Quem Venus arbitrum
26 dīcet bibendī? Nōn ego sānius
27   bacchābor Ēdōnīs: receptō
28   dulce mihī furere est amīcō.

Meter: Sapphic

1   **rēctus, -a, -um**, *correct, proper, good.*
    rēctius, comparative adverb, *more correctly/properly; better.*
    Licinius, -ī, m., *Licinius* (sometimes, but with no certainty, identified with
        Aulus Terentius Varro Murena, brother-in-law of C. Maecenas; this man,
        known also as Licinius Murena, defended the ex-governor of Macedonia
        on a charge of treason in 23 or 22 B.C., became involved with Fannius
        Caepio in a conspiracy against the emperor's life, and was executed).
2   **urgendō**: gerund, *by pressing hard upon; by pressing out to*, with **altum** as its
        object.
    procella, -ae, f., *violent wind; storm.*
3   **cautus, -a, -um**, *wary, cautious.*
    cautus: translate as an adverb.
    horrēscō, horrēscere, horruī, *to fear, dread.*
    nimium, adv., *too much.*
        nimium: translate *too closely*, with **premendō**.
    premō, premere, pressī, pressus, *to press; to stay close to; to hug.*
4   **inīquus [in-**, *not* + **aequus, -a, -um**, *equal; fair*], **-a, -um**, *uneven; unfair; harsh;*
        dangerous.

ODES 2.10

The Golden Mean

The speaker admonishes his addressee to steer a middle course between extremes and to prepare himself for the vicissitudes of life.

1 Rēctius vīvēs, Licinī, neque altum
2 semper urgendō neque, dum procellās
3 cautus horrēscis, nimium premendō
4   lītus inīquum.

continued

Explorations

1. What are the speaker's tone and stance as he addresses Licinius in this stanza?
2. What words describe the dangerous alternatives in the voyage of life that the speaker presents?
3. Both alternatives are extremes to be avoided. What words suggest extremes? Why should each extreme be avoided?
4. What words in lines 2–3 are parallel in placement to the words **neque** (1) . . . **urgendō** (2)? Locate a chiastic arrangement of words in lines 1–4.
5. While the two alternatives are carefully described in parallel and chiastic arrangements of words, one of them is developed at greater length. Which one? What reasons can you think of as to why the speaker would devote more than twice the number of words to this alternative?

5   **quisquis, quisquis, quidquid**, indefinite pronoun, *whoever, whatever*.
    mediocritās, mediocritātis, f., *avoidance of extremes, keeping a middle course,*
        the mean.
            Auream . . . mediocritātem: the need to avoid extremes and stay a
                middle course was a commonplace in ancient moral thought.
                "Nothing in excess" (μηδὲν ἄγαν) was inscribed on Apollo's temple at
                Delphi. Horace seems to have coined the phrase, **aurea mediocritās**.
6   **dīligō [dis-/dī-**, *apart* + **legō, legere, lēgī, lēctus**, *to gather; to choose; to read*], *to*
        choose between; to love, hold dear; to have a special regard for, value.
    tūtus, -a, -um, *safe*.
            tūtus: translate as an adverb.
    careō, carēre, caruī, caritūrus + abl., *to need, lack; to be free* (from).
    obsolētus, -a, -um, *worn out with age or use, shabby, dilapidated*.
7   **sordēs, sordis**, f., *dirt, filth, squalor*.
            sordibus: ablative with **caret**.
    tēctum, -ī, n., *covering, roof;* by synecdoche, *house*.
            invidendā: gerundive with **aulā**.
8   **sōbrius, -a, -um**, *reasonable, temperate, sensible*.
            sōbrius: translate as an adverb.
    aula [Gr., αὐλή], -ae, f., of a Greek house, *inner court;* of a Roman house, *at-*
        tached yard or enclosure, entrance hall; generally, *palace*.

5   Auream quisquis mediocritātem
6   dīligit, tūtus caret obsolētī
7   sordibus tēctī, caret invidendā
8   sōbrius aulā.

continued

Explorations

6. Instead of offering Licinius specific advice as he did in the first stanza, what is
    the speaker doing here? What word announces the shift? What is achieved
    by this shift?
7. What alternatives or extremes are set forth in this stanza? How do they cor-
    respond to the alternatives in the first stanza? What is dangerous about the
    alternatives that are set forth in the second stanza?
8. What does the verb **dīligit** (6a) imply about its subject? That is, what stance
    do the people being described here (**quisquis . . . / dīligit**, 5–6a) take toward
    their lives? What is it that such people are seeking and how are they charac-
    terized?
9. Locate examples of the following. What effect does each of these stylistic de-
    vices have?
    a. Line framing
    b. Anaphora
    c. Asyndeton
    d. Parallel word order
    e. Chiastic word order
    f. Other effective word placements and sounds
10. Why might Horace have described the "mean" as "golden"?

9   **agitō [agō, agere, ēgī, āctus,** *to do; to drive* + **-itō,** iterative or intensive suf-
     fix], **-āre, -āvī, -ātus,** *to toss, shake, stir.*
     ingēns, ingentis, *huge.*
10   **pīnus, -ī,** f., *pine tree.*
     celsus, -a, -um, *high, lofty.*
     cāsus, -ūs, m., *fall.*
11   **dēcidō [dē-,** *down* + **cadō, cadere, cecidī, casūrus,** *to fall*], **dēcidere, decidī,**
     dēcāsūrus, *to fall down.*
     turris, turris, f., *tower.*
     summōs: *highest* or *tops of,* with **montīs.**
12   **fulgur, fulguris,** n., *thunderbolt.*

9   Saepius ventīs agitātur ingēns
10 pīnus et celsae graviōre cāsū
11 dēcidunt turrēs feriuntque summōs
12   fulgura montīs.

continued

Explorations

11. The first stanza began with an address to a particular person, and the second stanza generalized the theme on a human level, *Whoever. . . .* How does the third stanza move to a different plane?
12. What three examples are given in lines 9–12? What do they exemplify?
13. The comparatives **Saepius** (9) and **graviōre** (10) invite the reader to imagine alternatives to the examples given in lines 9–12.
    a. What would those alternatives be? Are they things to be avoided or are they something else? If the latter, what?
    b. Are these alternatives exposed to as much danger as the examples that are cited?
14. Examine the three clauses, which form a tricolon: **Saepius ventīs agitātur ingēns / pīnus : celsae graviōre cāsū / dēcidunt turrēs : feriunt . . . summōs / fulgura montīs**.
    a. How many words are there in each clause?
    b. The tricolon is not an ascending tricolon in the sense of having successively longer clauses. How does it, nevertheless, build to a climax?
    c. How are the adjectives **ingēns** (9), **celsae** (10), and **summōs** (11) highlighted by their position?
    d. What is particularly effective about the juxtaposition of **agitātur** with **ingēns**? Of **celsae** with **graviōre**? And of **feriuntque** with **summōs**?
15. What is the lesson of this stanza for mankind? How is it similar to or different from the message conveyed by Artabanus to Xerxes in the passage from Herodotus below?

Passage for Comparison

Herodotus 7.10: the Persian prince Artabanus tries to dissuade Xerxes from his campaign against Greece:

> You see how the god strikes exalted creatures with his thunderbolt and does not allow them to make a show of themselves, but how the small creatures do not provoke him at all. And you see how his shafts always strike the tallest buildings and the tallest trees; for it is the god's habit to cut down all exalted things.

13 **Spērat**: the subject is **bene praeparātum / pectus** (14–15a); supply **alteram sortem** (14) as direct object. The adjectives **alter . . . alter** usually mean *the one . . . the other*; here translate **alteram sortem** as *the opposite lot* after both **spērat** and **metuit**.

īnfestus, -a, -um, *hostile; violent; harmful; dangerous; adverse.*

metuō, metuere, metuī, *to fear.*

secundus [sequor, sequī, secūtus sum, *to follow*], **-a, -um,** *following; second; favorable, prosperous.*

    īnfestīs . . . secundīs: sometimes interpreted as dative neuter plural, *hopes for adversity, fears for prosperity, the opposite lot* (Page, p. 53); alternatively, supply **rēbus** with each adjective, forming ablative absolutes describing attendant circumstances, *when things are adverse = in adversity*, etc.

14 **sors, sortis**, f., *fate, fortune, lot.*

praeparō [prae-, *beforehand* + **parō, -āre, -āvī, -ātus,** *to prepare*], **-āre, -āvī, -ātus,** *to prepare.*

15 **pectus, pectoris**, n., *chest; heart/mind* (including both emotional and mental faculties of a human being).

īnformis, -is, -e, *shapeless; ugly; unsightly.*

16 **īdem**: *the same one, he too, he likewise.*

17 **summoveō [sub-,** *below* + **moveō, movēre, mōvī, mōtus,** *to move*], **summovēre, summōvī, summōtus,** *to take away.*

sī male: ellipsis of **est** in an idiomatic expression, *if things go badly.*

ōlim: with **et,** *hereafter as well,* with the forceful **nōn** at the beginning of the sentence negating it.

18 **quondam**, adv., *formerly; in the future; sometimes.*

19 **suscitō [sub-,** *below* + **citō, -āre, -āvī, -ātus,** *to set in motion, rouse*], **-āre, -āvī, -ātus,** *to awaken.*

    suscitat: Apollō (20) is the subject of this verb, as well as of **tendit** (20).

      tacentem (18b) **/ suscitat Mūsam**: *awakens the silent Muse = brings music to life.*

        Mūsam: by metonymy = *music.*

arcus, -ūs, m., *arch; bow.*

20 **tendo, tendere, tetendī, tēnsus,** *to stretch.*

    tendit: Apollo *stretches* his bow, i.e., he keeps it bent, ready to shoot; for Apollo as a deadly archer, see Homer *Iliad* 1.43–52.

"Apollo with Lyre"
Museo Archeologico Nazionale
Naples, Italy

13   Spērat īnfestīs, metuit secundīs
14   alteram sortem bene praeparātum
15   pectus. Īnfōrmīs hiemēs redūcit
16   Iuppiter, īdem

17   summovet. Nōn, sī male nunc, et ōlim
18   sīc erit: quondam citharā tacentem
19   suscitat Mūsam neque semper arcum
20   tendit Apollō.

continued

Explorations

16. In lines 13–15a, identify: a. parallel word order; b. internal rhyme; c. asyn-
     deton; d. effective word placement; and e. alliteration.
17. What is the message of lines 13–15a?
18. What link can you find between the adjective **īnfestīs** (13a) and the theme of
     the previous stanza?
19. Lines 15b–20 contain three statements of one theme. What is that theme?
     How do the three statements form an ascending tricolon?
20. What word earlier in the stanza is echoed by **Īnformīs** (15b)?
21. How are the verbs **redūcit** (15b), **summovet** (17a), **suscitat** (19), and **tendit**
     (20) highlighted by their placement?
22. How does alliteration of **sī** (17b) and **sīc** (18a) help articulate the meaning
     expressed by the clauses in which they occur?
23. How does the activity of Jupiter (15b–17a) illustrate the aphorism expressed
     in lines 17b–18a (**Nōn, sī male nunc, et ōlim / sīc erit**)? How does the ac-
     tivity of Apollo (18b–20) illustrate that aphorism?
24. How does the placement of the names **Iuppiter** (16a) and **Apollō** (20) high-
     light the importance of these two deities in these stanzas?
25. What is the main characteristic of the world within which humans live as
     Horace describes it here (15b–20)?
26. How does the speaker recommend that humans make the best of their lives
     within that world?
27. Some readers see references to Augustus in the mention of Jupiter and
     Apollo. How would allusions to Augustus affect your understanding of
     these stanzas?
28. Compare the message of these stanzas with that of the first three stanzas.

21 **angustus, -a, -um**, *narrow; impoverished; restricted; tight.*
 animōsus, -a, -um, *bold, spirited.*
22 **fortis, -is, -e**, *courageous, bold, resolute, brave.*
 appareō [ad-, *to, toward,* intensive + **pareō, -ēre, -uī, -itūrus**, *to submit; to obey; to be visible, be seen*], **-ēre, -uī, -itūrus**, *to be seen, to appear;* with predicate adjectives, *to be clearly.*
 sapienter, adv., *wisely.*
 īdem: modifying the subject of **contrahēs** (23), *[you], the same person; [you] too; [you] likewise,* cf. line 16.
23 **contrahō [con-**, *together* + **trahō, trahere, traxī, tractus**, *to drag*], **contrahere, contraxī, contractus**, *to draw in;* of sails, *to furl.*
24 **turgidus, -a, -um**, *swollen.*
 turgida: modified by **ventō ... secundō** (23).
 vēlum, -ī, n., *sail.*

21 Rēbus angustīs animōsus atque
22 fortis appārē; sapienter īdem
23 contrahēs ventō nimium secundō
24   turgida vēla.

Explorations

29. What word in the first line reminds you of a word in the previous pair of stanzas?
30. What two pieces of advice does the speaker give in this stanza?
31. How is this final stanza reminiscent of the first one? Consider the following:
  a. Addressee
  b. Nautical imagery
  c. Repeated diction
32. Two alternatives are presented in the first stanza and two in the last. Show how the alternatives are presented in chiastic order. How are the alternatives similar? How are they different?
33. Compare the alternatives in the final stanza with those presented in lines 13–15a. How are they similar?
34. The word **īdem** (22b) occurred also in line 16b. In what way is the proposed behavior of the person addressed in the last stanza similar to the behavior of Jupiter and Apollo in lines 15b–20?
35. Structure and word placement:
  a. The stanza has a chiastic structure: **Rēbus angustīs : animōsus atque / fortis appārē :: sapienter īdem / contrahēs : ventō nimium secundō / turgida vēla.** Show how the elements correspond in this chiasmus.
  b. What is striking about the sound of the words **angustīs animōsus** and their juxtaposition?
  c. What is significant about the positioning of the word **sapienter** in this stanza?
36. In difficult circumstances (**Rēbus angustīs**, 21), the speaker recommends that one *be clearly* (**appārē**, 22) *spirited and brave* (**animōsus atque / fortis**, 21–22). In excessively favorable circumstances, however, he says *you will wisely draw in your sails [when] swollen with too favorable a wind* (22b–24). Why is it recommended that one *be clearly spirited and brave* in the one instance, while in the other instance action is recommended?

Odes 2.10

1   Rēctius vīvēs, Licinī, neque altum
2   semper urgendō neque, dum procellās
3   cautus horrēscis, nimium premendō
4   lītus inīquum.

5   Auream quisquis mediocritātem
6   dīligit, tūtus caret obsolētī
7   sordibus tēctī, caret invidendā
8   sōbrius aulā.

9   Saepius ventīs agitātur ingēns
10   pīnus·et celsae graviōre cāsū
11   dēcidunt turrēs feriuntque summōs
12   fulgura montīs.

13   Spērat īnfestīs, metuit secundīs
14   alteram sortem bene praeparātum
15   pectus. Īnfōrmīs hiemēs redūcit
16   Iuppiter, īdem

17   summovet. Nōn, sī male nunc, et ōlim
18   sīc erit: quondam citharā tacentem
19   suscitat Mūsam neque semper arcum
20   tendit Apollō.

21   Rēbus angustīs animōsus atque
22   fortis appārē; sapienter īdem
23   contrahēs ventō nimium secundō
24   turgida vēla.

Discussion

1. How is this ode structured? Take the following into account:
   a. Antitheses
   b. Chiastic arrangements within stanzas
   c. Chiastic arrangements within the poem as a whole
   d. Themes in the first, second, and third stanzas
   e. The themes of the fourth and fifth stanzas, which are the only enjambed stanzas in the poem
   f. The relationship between the first and the last stanzas
2. Compare the passages from Ovid quoted below in Passages for Comparison I and II with *Odes* 2.10. How is the advice offered in the passages of Ovid similar to and different from the advice offered in *Odes* 2.10?
3. Compare *Odes* 2.10 with *Odes* 2.3. What do they have in common?
4. Compare the choral ode in Seneca *Agamemnon* 87–107, quoted in Passages for Comparison III following these questions. What has Seneca borrowed from *Odes* 2.10? What major difference has Seneca introduced in lines 103b– 7?

Passages for Comparisons

I.

The story of Phaëthon. Here is part of his father's advice as he is about to drive the chariot of the sun (Ovid *Metamorphoses* 2.134–37):

134   Utque ferant aequōs et caelum et terra calōrēs,
135   nec preme nec summum mōlīre per aethera cursum!
136   Altius ēgressus caelestia tēcta cremābis,
137   īnferius terrās; mediō tūtissimus ībis.

> And so that both sky and earth may bear equal heat, do not go low nor pursue the highest course through the heavens; having gone too high, you will burn up the heavenly homes; too low, the lands. You will go most safely in the middle.

II.

Daedalus's advice to Icarus before they take flight (Ovid *Metamorphoses* 8.203–6):

203   Īnstruit et nātum, "Mediō," que, "ut līmite currās,
204   Īcare," ait, "moneō, nē, sī dēmissior ībis,
205   unda gravet pennās, sī celsior, ignis adūrat:
206   inter utrumque volā."

> He also instructed his son and said, "Icarus, I warn you to fly in a middle course so that if you go too low, the water may not weigh down your wings; if too high, the fire may not burn them. Fly between the two.

III.

Choral ode in Seneca *Agamemnon*, 87–107:

87	Licet arma vacent cessentque dolī,
88	sīdunt ipsō pondere magna
89	cēditque onerī Fortūna suō.
90	Vēla secundīs īnflāta Notīs
91	ventōs nimium timuēre suōs;
92	nūbibus ipsīs īnserta caput
93	turris pluviō vāpulat Austrō,
94	dēnsāsque nemus spargēns umbrās
95	annōsa videt rōbora frangī;
96	feriunt celsōs fulmina collēs,
97	corpora morbīs maiōra patent,
98	et cum in pastūs
99	armenta vagōs vīlia currant,
100	placet in vulnus maxima cervīx.
101	Quidquid in altum Fortūna tulit,
102	ruitūra levat.
103	Modicīs rēbus longius aevum est.
104	Fēlīx mediae quisquis turbae sorte quiētus
105	aurā stringit lītora tūtā
106	timidusque marī crēdere cumbam
107	rēmō terrās propiōre legit.

Although arms may lie dormant and treachery may cease, greatness
sinks by its own weight, and Fortune retreats because of its own burden.
Sails swollen with favorable Notus fear winds too strongly their own; the
tower with its head inserted among the clouds themselves takes a beating
from the rainy Auster, and the grove, spreading dense shade, sees its ancient oak trees broken; thunderbolts strike the high hills, larger bodies lie
open to diseases, and when common herds roam into vagrant pastures,
the greatest head is the first to be slaughtered. Whatever Fortune raises
on high she lifts up only to hurl it down. Modest things have a longer
lifespan. Happy is the one who, content with the lot of the middling
crowd, keeps close to the shore with a safe breeze, and fearing to trust his
skiff to the open sea hugs the land with a closer oar.

Meter: Alcaic

1   **fugāx, fugācis** [**fugiō, fugere, fūgī**, *to run away, flee*], *prone to run away;* of
       time, *swiftly passing, fleeting.*
       Postumus, -ī, m., *Postumus* (the person to whom this poem is addressed; he
       cannot be identified with certainty; the name, from the root **post**, means
       born after the father's death).
2   **lābor, lābī, lāpsus sum**, *to slip, glide along/by.*
       pietās, pietātis, f., *dutifulness, devotion; piety* (respect in relationships with
       human beings and with gods.).
       mora, -ae, f., *delay.*
3   **rūga, -ae**, f., *wrinkle.*
       īnstō [**in-**, *in, upon, against* + **stō, stāre, stetī, stātūrus**, *to stand*], **īnstāre, īn-**
       stitī, *to press* (in a hostile manner); *to loom; to threaten.*
       senecta, -ae, f., *old age.*
4   **adferō** [**ad-**, *to, toward* + **ferō, ferre, tulī, lātus**, *to bring*], **adferre, attulī, al-**
       lātus, *to bring to.*
       indomitus [**in-**, *not* + **domitus, -a, -um** (perfect passive participle of **domō**,
       -āre, -āvī, -ātus, *to tame*), *tamed*], **-a, -um**, *untamed;* of animals, *unbroken;*
       wild, fierce; unconquered; unconquerable.
           indomitae . . . mortī: Horace may be alluding to Homer *Iliad* 9.158b–59,
            where Agamemnon describes Hades, the god of death and of the
            underworld, as ἀδάμαστος, *untamed/unconquered.*

ODES 2.14

A Wake-up Call to Life

Postumus is warned of the inevitability of death and advised not to keep his precious wine locked up for his heir to enjoy.

1 Ēheu fugācēs, Postume, Postume,
2 lābuntur annī nec pietās moram
3   rūgīs et īnstantī senectae
4   adferet indomitaeque mortī:

continued

Explorations

1. How does the vocabulary of the first line and a half and the positioning of the words establish a melancholy tone?
2. How are the juxtaposition of **pietās** and **moram** and the placement of **moram** at the end of line 2 especially meaningful? With what other words in the stanza are these words linked by alliteration?
3. What rhetorical devices and what other effective patterns of sounds can you find in this stanza?
4. What differences or contrasts can you find between the imagery and themes of the first line and a half (**fugācēs . . . / lābuntur annī**, 1–2a) and the imagery and themes in the ascending tricolon (2b–4), especially in the phrases **īnstantī senectae** (3) and **indomitae . . . mortī** (4)?

5   **trecēnī** [**trēs**, *three* + **centum**, *hundred*], **-ae, -a**, *three hundred at a time*.
      trecēnīs: modifying **taurīs** (7a); the sacrifice of a hundred bulls, what the
        Greeks called a hecatomb (Greek ἑκατόν, *hundred* + βοῦς, *ox*), represents
        a traditional ceremony of appeasement of the gods that recalls both the
        heroic standards of the Homeric epics (see, for example, *Iliad* 1.65, 2.306,
        6.115, 7.450, 9.535, etc.) and the grand scale of public offerings made by
        the Roman people, such as the rites that included sacrifice of three hun-
        dred oxen after the defeat of the Roman army at Lake Trasimene in 217
        B.C. (Livy 22.10.7).
    quotquot, indeclinable adjective, *however many*.
      quotquot eunt diēs: *however many days go by*, i.e., *every day of your life*.
6   **plācō** [**placeō, placēre, placuī, placitus**, *to please*], **-āre, -āvī, -ātus**, *to concili-*
    ate; to appease; to placate.
      plācēs: present subjunctive. The present tense represents progressive
        action that has not been completed, which in this context can be inter-
        preted as a repeated attempt to do something. The subjunctive func-
        tions in a future-less-vivid protasis of a mixed condition, the apodosis
        of which is expressed by the ellipsis implied by **nōn** (5): *[piety will] not*
        [bring delay], [even] if you were repeatedly to try to placate. . . .
    illacrimābilis [**in-**, *not* + **lacrimō, -āre**, *to shed tears* + **-bilis**, *able to*], **-is, -e**, *tear-*
    less; merciless, pitiless.
7   **Plūtō, Plūtōnis**, m., *Pluto* (the god of the underworld).
      Plūtōna: Greek accusative.
    taurus, -ī, m., *bull*.
    amplus, -a, -um, *having ample bulk, large, huge*.
      ter amplum: *thrice-huge*, but with a reference to the triple-body of the giant
        Geryon.
8   **Gēryōn, Gēryonis**, m., *Geryon* (a triple-bodied giant, king of Erytheia or
        Erythrea, the modern Cadiz in Spain; he owned a vast herd of cattle that
        were stolen by Hercules, who slew the giant when he attempted to get
        them back).
      Gēryonēn: Greek accusative.
    Tityos, Tityī, m., *Tityus* (a giant slain while trying to rape Leto, the mother
        of Apollo and Artemis, and punished in Hades by being stretched out over
        nine acres of ground and having his heart or liver eaten out by vultures or
        snakes).
      Tityon: Greek accusative.

5   nōn sī trecēnīs quotquot eunt diēs,
6   amīce, plācēs illacrimābilem
7   Plūtōna taurīs, quī ter amplum
8   Gēryonēn Tityonque trīstī

continued

Explorations

5. Why is Pluto described as **illacrimābilem** (6b)?
6. What rhetorical figure is Horace using in the words **trecēnīs, quotquot eunt diēs** (5)? How is it reinforced by the tense and mood of **plācēs** (6b)? What does the future-less-vivid conditional sentence here imply about Postumus's actual actions?
7. What uses of alliteration stand out in this stanza?
8. How do the figures of Geryon and Tityus suggest the immense power of Pluto?

"Pluto with Cerberus"
4th century Graeco-Roman period
Sanctuary of Isis, Gortyna, Crete, Greece

9 **compēscō, compēscere, compēscuī,** *to restrain; to confine, imprison.*
   undā: modified by **ēnāvigandā** (11a); the reference is to the river Styx, which
      wound nine times around the underworld to form its boundary.
   scīlicet, adv., *certainly, to be sure, clearly, surely.*
   omnibus: dative of agent with the gerundive **ēnāvigandā** (11a).
10 **quīcumque, quaecumque, quodcumque,** indefinite relative pronoun, *who-*
      ever, everyone who; whatever, everything that.
11 **ēnāvigō [ex-/ē-,** *thoroughly* + **nāvigō, -āre, -āvī, -ātūrus,** *to sail*], **-āre, -āvī,**
      -ātus, intransitive, *to sail forth;* transitive, *to sail across.*
   sīve . . . sīve, conj., *whether . . . or.*
   rēgēs: *kings,* or, as often in Horace, *rich men.*
12 **inops [in-,** *not* + **ops, opis,** f., *power; wealth*], **inopis,** *resourceless; poor.*
   erimus: i.e., at the time of our death.
   colōnus, -ī, m., *farmer* (often not owning the land he farms, and thus poor).

9   compēscit undā, scīlicet omnibus,
10   quīcumque terrae mūnere vēscimur,
11   ēnāvigandā, sīve rēgēs
12   sīve inopēs erimus colōnī.

continued

Explorations

9. What is the significance of the placement and the meaning of **omnibus** (9b)?
10. What is the point of Horace's allusion in the words **quīcumque terrae mūnere vēscimur** (10) to Homeric phrases such as those cited below?
11. What is achieved by the prepositional prefix in the word **ēnāvigandā** (11a) and by its gerundive form?
12. What is achieved by the dichotomy signaled by **sīve . . . / sīve** (11b–12)?

Passages for Comparison

With the words **quīcumque terrae mūnere vēscimur** (10), Horace is echoing phrases that Homer uses in the *Iliad* to emphasize the mortality of warriors about to engage in single combat:

Iliad 6.142–43, Diomedes confronts Glaucus on the battlefield and says:

> "If you are of mortal men, who eat the fruit of the field, come closer that you may sooner enter the snares of destruction."

Iliad 21.462–67, Apollo addresses Poseidon:

> "Earth-Shaker, you would not say that I am of sound mind, if I make war on you for the sake of mortal men, pitiful creatures, who at one time like leaves are full of flaming life, eating the fruit of the field, but at another time waste away and are dead. But let us right away stop our fighting; and let them fight their battles on their own."

13   **cruentus, -a, -um,** *bloody.*
      Mārs, Mārtis, m., *Mars* (the god of war); by metonymy, *war.*
      careō, carēre, caruī, caritūrus + abl., *to lack, need; to be free from; to avoid.*
14   **raucus, -a, -um,** *hoarse; noisy; howling.*
      flūctus, -ūs, m., *wave, billow* (of the sea).
          frāctīs . . . flūctibus: *billows broken* (on the shore); *breakers.*
      Hadria, -ae, m., *the Adriatic Sea.*
15   **autumnus, -ī,** m., *autumn.*
          per autumnōs: *through each succeeding autumn.*
16   **metuō, metuere, metuī,** *to fear.*
      Auster, Austrī, m., *Auster, the South Wind* (today called "Sirocco," a hot, op-
          pressive wind blowing from North Africa across parts of southern Europe;
          it is especially unhealthy during autumn, and wealthy Romans retired to
          their country villas or to the seaside during this season).

13 Frūstrā cruentō Mārte carēbimus

14 frāctīsque raucī flūctibus Hadriae,

15   frūstrā per autumnōs nocentem

16   corporibus metuēmus Austrum:

continued

Explorations

13. This stanza begins a new sentence, the second of the ode. What is the theme of the stanza? How does it reinforce what has been said in the first three stanzas?

14. Identify examples of the following and discuss their rhetorical effects:
     a. Anaphora
     b. Interlocked word order or synchysis
     c. Alliteration
     d. Parallelism
     e. Tricolon

17   vīsō, vīsere, vīsī, *to look upon; to go and see; to visit.*
         vīsendus: supply **est**, making a passive periphrastic construction, and, as
              the dative of agent, supply **nōbīs omnibus** (cf. **omnibus**, 9b, **carēbimus**,
              13, and **metuēmus**, 16), *by us all, by all of us.*
      āter, ātra, ātrum, *black.*
      flūmen, flūminis, n., *river, stream.*
      languidus, -a, -um, *drooping; sluggish, languid.*
18   Cōcȳtos [Gr., κωκυτός, *wailing*], -ī, m., *Cocytus* (the river of lamentation in
              the underworld).
      Danaus, -ī, m., *Danaus* (the father of fifty daughters called the Danaïdes; all
              but one of them killed their husbands on their wedding night and were
              punished in the underworld by having to fill leaky jars with water for-
              ever).
      genus, generis, n., *race, stock, nation; descendants, offspring.*
19   īnfāmis [in-, *not* + fāma, -ae, f., *reputation*], -is, -e, *having a bad name, notorious;*
              disgraced, infamous.
      damnō, -āre, -āvī, -ātus + gen., *to punish with, to condemn to.*
      longī / . . . labōris (20): understatement; Sisyphus's labor was eternal.
20   Sīsyphus, -ī, m., *Sisyphus* (see below).
      Aeolidēs [Aeolus, -ī, m., *Aeolus* (guardian of the winds) + -idēs, a
         patronymic suffix], -ae, m., *son of Aeolus.*
         Sīsyphus Aeolidēs: *Sisyphus, son of Aeolus;* for some unknown act of
              impiety, Sisyphus was sentenced in the underworld to a frustrating
              eternity of pushing a huge rock up a hill only to have it roll back down
              (*Odyssey* 11.593–600).

17   vīsendus āter flūmine languidō
18   Cōcȳtos errāns et Danaī genus
19   īnfāme damnātusque longī
20   Sīsyphus Aeolidēs labōris:

continued

Explorations

15.   Identify the members of a tricolon in this stanza.
16.   What impression of the underworld does the speaker create through the use of adjectives in this stanza?
17.   Does the description of the underworld and its inhabitants in this stanza convey any ethical message or moral warning to Postumus?
18.   Identify meaningful alliteration in this stanza and explain its purpose.

21   **tellūs, tellūris**, f., *earth* (as consisting of soil for cultivation); *the earth* (as op-
        posed to the sky or the underworld).
            tellūs: both meanings of the word as given above are intended.
        domus: compare **domō / vīllāque**, *Odes* 2.3.17–18.
22   **hārum . . . arborum**: genitive with **ūlla** (24); the speaker seems to be point-
        ing to Postumus's trees on his country estate. This may imply that the
        speaker has been invited to Postumus's country estate and is addressing
        this poem to him there.
        colō, colere, coluī, cultus, *to worship; to cherish; to cultivate*.
            colis: note the range of meanings of this verb; both *cherish* and *cultivate*
            may be operative here.
23   **invīsus** [perfect passive participle of **invideō, invidēre, invīdī, invīsus**, *to
        regard with ill will or envy*], **-a, -um**, *hated*.
        cupressus, -ī, f., *cypress* (a tree sacred to Pluto, branches of which were placed
            around funeral pyres and which was planted around graves).
24   **dominum**: *master, proprietor* (of an estate).

21 linquenda tellūs et domus et placēns
22 uxor, neque hārum quās colis arborum
23   tē praeter invīsās cupressōs
24   ūlla brevem dominum sequētur:

continued

Explorations

19. Identify the elements of a tricolon in lines 21–22a.
20. What has Horace taken in lines 21–22a from the passage of Lucretius below? What has he left out?
21. What is the significance of the use of the second person in **colis** (22b)?
22. How does Horace play upon the emotions in this stanza?
23. What theme is brought to the fore by Horace's description of Postumus as a *short-lived proprietor* (**brevem dominum**, 24)?

Passage for Comparison

With lines 21–22a, **linquenda tellūs et domus et placēns / uxor**, compare the following passage from Lucretius, who is quoting the grieving words of mourners addressing a dead man (*De rerum natura* 3.894–96a):

894 "Iam iam nōn domus accipiet tē laeta neque uxor
895 optima, nec dulcēs occurrent ōscula nātī
896a praeripere."

> "No longer now [i.e. now that you are dead] will your home joyfully receive you nor your excellent wife, nor sweet children run up to you to snatch the first kisses."

Later in this passage, Lucretius counters the sorrow usually felt for the dead with the following observation of his own (900–903):

900 Illud in hīs rēbus nōn addunt: "Nec tibi eārum
901 iam dēsiderium rērum super īnsidet ūnā."
902 Quod bene sī videant animō dictīsque sequantur,
903 dissoluant animī magnō sē angōre metūque.

> In these circumstances they do not add the following: "No longer now does any yearning for these things weigh upon you with life's passing." If they were to see this clearly in mind and follow it in their speech, they would free themselves from great torment and fear of mind.

25 **absūmō** [ab-, *completely, thoroughly* + **sūmō, sūmere, sūmpsī, sūmptus,** *to take up; to take* (food or drink)], **absūmere, absūmpsī, absūmptus,** *to use up entirely; to consume.*

hērēs: cf. **hērēs,** *Odes* 2.3.20.

Caecubus, -a, -um, *Caecuban.*

    Caecuba: supply **vīna** (the plural indicates quantity), *Caecuban wine;* Caecuban was a particularly prized vintage (cf. *Odes* 1.37.5).

dignus, -a, -um, *worthy.*

26 **centum**: hyperbole; cf. **trecēnīs** (5).

clāvis [cf. **claudō, claudere, clausī, clausus,** *to close, shut up*], **clāvis,** f., *key.*

    centum clāvibus: we would say "with/by a hundred locks."

27 **tingō, tingere, tīnxī, tīnctus,** *to wet, soak; to dye, stain.*

    absūmet (25) and **tinget pavīmentum** (27): presumably the wine will be consumed at dinner parties, and some of it will be poured on the floor as libations (see Background on the next page); the wine used in libations was always unmixed (**merō**, 26).

superbus, -a, -um, *haughty, disdainful, proud.*

28 **pontifex, pontificis,** m., *priest.*

potior [comparative of **potis, -is, -e,** *having power*], **potiōris,** *stronger; better; preferable.*

cēnīs: ablative of comparison with **potiōre,** which modifies **merō** (26), literally, *with wine preferable to the banquets of priests,* but usually taken more expansively as *with wine preferable to [the wine served at] the banquets of priests.*

25 absūmet hērēs Caecuba dignior
26 servāta centum clāvibus et merō
27   tinget pavīmentum superbō,
28   pontificum potiōre cēnīs.

Explorations

24. In the previous stanza (21–24), the speaker says that Postumus will have to leave four things behind when he dies: his land, his home, his wife, and his trees, except for the cypresses. What fifth thing will he have to leave behind as well (25–28)? What attachment does Postumus appear to have had to it?
25. How does this final stanza develop the **carpe diem** theme brought to the fore in the word **brevem** (24)?
26. Why is the heir described as **dignior** (25)?
27. The word **superbō** (27) grammatically describes the wine (**merō**, 26), but it may also work as a transferred epithet. Explain. Various editors, however, suggest that Horace actually wrote **superbus** or **superbum** or **superbīs**. Which reading do you prefer?
28. Identify striking examples of alliteration in the final stanza.
29. How does the comparison of the wine with that served at the banquets of priests make what will happen to it all the more painful to Postumus?

Background

The feasting at a Roman dinner party was often followed by a **cōmissātiō** or drinking bout. After the guests chose a **magister bibendī**, the drinking would begin with libations poured in honor of the gods:

> When the guests reclined around a communal table, they passed the wine bowl to each other. One would hold the beaker in his left hand by one handle, while the next took it with his right hand.
> Once a guest had the cup, he would perform a libation (*libatio*): he took one of the handles of the drinking bowl between two fingers, and made the wine swirl inside the bowl, as wine-tasters still do today, and allowed some to splash over the edge as a sacrifice. Sometimes sawdust was scattered over the floor to protect it against frequent libations. It was customary to dedicate at least one libation to Jupiter or Apollo, but Neptune, Bacchus and many others were likewise honoured.
> According to etiquette, the libation was paired with a hymn of praise to the gods.

> —Patrick Faas. *Around the Roman Table*. Translated from the Dutch by Shaun Whiteside. New York: Palgrave Macmillan, 2003, page 94.

Odes 2.14

1   Ēheu fugācēs, Postume, Postume,
2   lābuntur annī nec pietās moram
3   rūgīs et īnstantī senectae
4   adferet indomitaeque mortī:

5   nōn sī trecēnīs quotquot eunt diēs,
6   amīce, plācēs illacrimābilem
7   Plūtōna taurīs, quī ter amplum
8   Gēryonēn Tityonque trīstī

9   compēscit undā, scīlicet omnibus,
10   quīcumque terrae mūnere vēscimur,
11   ēnāvigandā, sīve rēgēs
12   sīve inopēs erimus colōnī.

13   Frūstrā cruentō Mārte carēbimus
14   frāctīsque raucī flūctibus Hadriae,
15   frūstrā per autumnōs nocentem
16   corporibus metuēmus Austrum:

17   vīsendus āter flūmine languidō
18   Cōcȳtos errāns et Danaī genus
19   īnfāme damnātusque longī
20   Sīsyphus Aeolidēs labōris:

21   linquenda tellūs et domus et placēns
22   uxor, neque hārum quās colis arborum
23   tē praeter invīsās cupressōs
24   ūlla brevem dominum sequētur:

25   absūmet hērēs Caecuba dignior
26   servāta centum clāvibus et merō
27   tinget pavīmentum superbō,
28   pontificum potiōre cēnīs.

Discussion

1. How do the first line and a half of the poem (**Ēheu fugācēs . . . /lābuntur annī**) anticipate the themes of the final two stanzas (21–28)?

2. The second and third stanzas are the only ones in the poem that are connected to one another by a flow of thought and grammar from one stanza to the next. What structural parallels can you find between these two stanzas?

3. The poem contains three gerundives (**ēnāvigandā**, 11a, **vīsendus**, 17, and **linquenda**, 21). Only one of them (**ēnāvigandā**, 11a) is accompanied by a dative of agent (**omnibus**, 9b). The dative phrase **nōbīs omnibus** may be supplied with **vīsendus** (17). What two different datives of agent could be supplied with **linquenda** (21)? How does this series of gerundives help to structure the poem?

4. The poem contains a number of words and phrases that are opposite or antithetical to one another, such as the following:

    undā (9a) :: **terrae** (10)

    frāctīs raucī flūctibus Hadriae (14) :: **āter flūmine languidō / Cōcӯtos errāns** (17–18)

    vīsendus (17) :: **linquenda** (21)

    flūmine (17) :: **tellūs** (21)

    longī (19) :: **brevem** (24)

    linquenda (21) :: **sequētur** (24)

    placēns (21) :: **invīsās** (23)

    absūmet (25) :: **servāta** (26)

    How do these opposed or antithetical words and phrases help to structure the thought of the poem?

5. The speaker states that in the underworld we will have to see Cocytus, the Danaïdes, and Sisyphus (17–20). Then in the last stanza he conjures up a vivid picture not of what Postumus will see in the underworld but of what will happen in this world after Postumus's death, namely his heir's consuming Postumus's precious wine. Which will be more painful for Postumus to contemplate: the mythological figures of the underworld or his heir consuming his wine?

6. What similarities and what differences can you find between this poem and *Odes* 2.3?

Meter: Alcaic

1   **ōdī, ōdisse, ōsus** [perfect with present force], *to have an aversion to; to hate.*
    profānus [pro-, *in front of, before, outside* + **fānum, -ī,** n., *a consecrated area, tem-*
    ple], **-a, -um,** *not consecrated; profane; uninitiated; unhallowed.*
    vulgus, -ī, n., *the common people; a crowd of ordinary people; the mob.*
    arceō, -ēre, -uī, *to prevent X from coming near; to keep X at a distance, keep X*
    away.
        profānum vulgus . . . arceō: uninitiated, sacrilegious people are to be
        kept away from the sacred rites, as in Callimachus *Hymn to Apollo* 2b,
        Away, away, whoever is sinful!
            Ōdī . . . arceō: line framing.
2   **faveō, favēre, fāvī, fautūrus** + dat., *to favor, be favorable* (to); + abl. **linguīs,**
    religious idiom, *to be favorable in speech, to speak favorably* = *to keep holy silence*
    (**sacrum silentium,** since only by being silent can one be sure not to mar a
    ritual or say something ill-omened).
        favēte linguīs: a formulaic expression (the Greeks said εὐφημεῖτε, *speak*
        well!, i.e., *be silent!*) uttered by priests before beginning a sacrifice, reli-
        gious ritual, or initiation into mysteries. Note the short opening sylla-
        ble here in line 2 and in line 26.
    carmen, carminis, n., *song* (originally referring to solemn, rhythmic, and al-
    literative song associated with sacred chants); *oracle; prophecy;* (any)
    song/poem.
    nōn prius / audīta (3): these words state Horace's claim to originality in the
    first six odes of Book 3, all in the Alcaic meter and all dealing with issues of
    public concern.
3   **sacerdōs, sacerdōtis,** m., *priest.*

ODES 3.1

The Poet as Priest of the Muses

Against the backdrop of raw power relationships within the cosmic hierarchy, the poet, as priest of the Muses, sings to boys and girls about how to avoid fear, threats, and anxiety, and he states his own preference for a simple life in his Sabine valley.

1   Ōdī profānum vulgus et arceō;
2   favēte linguīs: carmina nōn prius
3   audīta Mūsārum sacerdōs
4   virginibus puerīsque cantō.

continued

Explorations

1. How does the singer portray himself and his songs in these lines?
2. How does the singer define his audience?

"Chorus of Diana"
This 3rd century A.D. mosaic from the Temple of Diana at Capua gives some idea of what Horace's audience of girls and boys might have looked like.
Museo Campano, Capua, Italy

217

5   **Rēgum timendōrum**: supply **imperium est** from line 6.
     in, prep. + acc., *into; over*.
     proprius, -a, -um, *one's own*; with plural antecedent, *their own*.
     grex, gregis, m., *flock* (of animals, usually sheep); *a population, people*.
6   **rēgēs in ipsōs**: adversative asyndeton.
     imperium, -ī, n., *authority; dominion; power*.
7   **clārus, -a, -um**, *bright*; + abl., *famous* (for).
     Gigantēus, -a, -um, *of/belonging to/over the Giants* (the Giants were the off-
       spring of Ge, goddess of the earth, and Uranus, god of the sky; they made
       war on the Olympian gods).
     triumphus, -ī, m., *triumph, victory*.
8   **supercilium, -ī**, n., *eyebrow*.
     moventis: *shaking*.

Passage for Comparison

Odes 3.4.42b–48; Jupiter is the subject of the verb **sustulerit** (44):

42b   .   .   .   Scīmus ut impiōs
43   Tītānas immānemque turbam
44   fulmine sustulerit cadūcō,

45   quī terram inertem, quī mare temperat
46   ventōsum, et urbēs rēgnaque trīstia
47   dīvōsque mortālīsque turmās
48   imperiō regit ūnus aequō.

We know how [Jupiter] destroyed the impious Titans and their monstrous
horde with his descending thunderbolt, he who regulates the motionless
land and the windy sea and who by himself alone rules cities, the gloomy
underworld, gods, and troops of mortal men with power that is right and
fair.

5   Rēgum timendōrum in propriōs gregēs,
6   rēgēs in ipsōs imperium est Iovis,
7   clārī Gigantēō triumphō,
8   cūncta superciliō moventis.

continued

Explorations

3. Homer described Agamemnon as "shepherd of the people" (*Iliad* 2.243b). How is this description recalled in line 5? Are the kings described here shepherds of their people? If not, what kind of rulers are they?
4. In lines 5–6, locate examples of:
    a. Anaphora
    b. Polyptoton
    c. Chiasmus
    d. Line framing
    e. Effective juxtaposition
5. Lines 7–8:
    a. Locate a chiasmus.
    b. What do these lines add to the statement that is made in line 6?
    c. Compare the passage from *Odes* 3.4 on the opposite page, describing Jupiter's triumph over the Titans. The Titans, offspring of Ge and Uranus prior to the birth of the Giants, included Cronus, who overthrew Uranus and in turn was overthrown with the other Titans by his son Zeus. What descriptions of the Titans and of Jupiter are present in the passage from *Odes* 3.4 that are not present in *Odes* 3.1.7–8 above? On what is the singer's focus in *Odes* 3.1.7–8?
6. What is the main message of lines 5–8? What is the tone?

9   **Est ut**: introducing a substantive clause of result with the subjunctive, *It is*
      [true] that, It is [the case] that.
      lātus, -a, -um, *broad, wide.*
          lātius: comparative adv., *over a wider area.*
      ōrdinō, -āre, -āvī, -ātus, *to set in ranks* (as of soldiers) or *rows* (as of trees).
10   **arbustum, -ī,** n., *woods;* pl., *trees;* here of trees on which grape vines are
      trained to grow, producing a *vineyard.*
      sulcus, -ī, m., *furrow; trench.*
      generōsus, -a, -um, *of noble birth, nobly born.*
11   **dēscendat**: the word describes the nobles coming down from the hills where
      they lived to the Forum or the Campus Martius, but it is also used of entry
      into combat or competition.
      Campum: the Campus Martius, where assemblies were held for the election
      of Roman magistrates.
      petītor, petītōris, m., *one who seeks; a candidate* (for political office).
13   **contendō** [**con-**, intensive + **tendō, tendere, tetendī, tentus,** *to stretch out; to*
      exert oneself, strive], **contendere, contendī, contentus,** *to strive; to compete,*
      contend (often, as here, for political office).
14   **aequus, -a, -um,** *level; equal; just, impartial.*
      lēx, lēgis, f., *law; condition, term* (for the fulfillment of a contract).
          aequā lēge: *on equal terms, impartially.*
      Necessitās [personification of **necessitās, necessitātis,** f., *necessity*], **Neces-**
      sitātis, f., *Necessity* (here representing the inevitability of death).
15   **sortior, -īrī, -ītus sum,** *to assign, determine* (by lot); *to determine the fate of X by*
      lot, to allot the fate of.
      īnsignis [**in-**, intensive + **signum, -ī,** n., *mark; sign* (by which someone or
      something is recognized)], **-is, -e,** *easily recognizable; remarkable; outstand-*
      ing, distinguished.
      īmus, -a, -um, *lowest* (in the social order).
16   **capāx, capācis,** *able to hold much; capacious.*
      movet: i.e., *shakes* (in casting lots).
      urna, -ae, f., *urn* (here used in casting lots).

Passage for Comparison

Odes 2.3.21–28:

      21   Dīvesne prīscō nātus ab Īnachō
      22   nīl interest an pauper et īnfimā
      23   dē gente sub dīvō morēris,
      24   victima nīl miserantis Orcī.

      25   Omnēs eōdem cōgimur omnium
      26   versātur urna sērius ōcius
      27   sors exitūra et nōs in aeternum
      28   exsilium impositūra cumbae.

9   Est ut virō vir lātius ōrdinet

10   arbusta sulcīs, hic generōsior

11   dēscendat in Campum petītor,

12   mōribus hic meliorque fāmā

13   contendat, illī turba clientium

14   sit maior: aequā lēge Necessitās

15   sortītur īnsignīs et īmōs;

16   omne capāx movet urna nōmen.

continued

Explorations

7. Look closely at lines 9–14a.
    a. Locate the four comparative words. How do they serve to characterize the men being described? What do the men have in common?
    b. Locate examples of:
        i.   Effective juxtaposition
        ii. Polyptoton
        iii. Line framing
        iv. Enjambment
    c. What prominent positions do the verbs occupy in these lines?
8. On what occasions would a noble Roman be in the presence of a large group of his clients (**turba clientium**, 13b)?
9. Does the singer invite the reader to take any particular attitude toward the four people or types of people described in lines 9–14a?
10. Note the adversative asyndeton in line 14 and the effective juxtaposition of **maior** with **aequā**. What is the effect of these two rhetorical devices?
11. What ideas and words from *Odes* 2.3.21–28, quoted on the opposite page, are echoed here in *Odes* 3.1.14b–16?
12. Look closely at line 16, **omne capāx movet urna nōmen**.
    a. How are the adjectives, nouns, and verb arranged? What is the technical label for a line of poetry with this arrangement of words?
    b. How many syllables does each word have?
    c. What words are highlighted by their placement?
13. How do lines 14b–16 comment on the activities of the men described in lines 9–14a?

17   dēstringō [dē-, *away* + stringō, stringere, strīnxī, strīctus, *to bind; to tighten;
     to draw, unsheathe* (a sword)], dēstringere, dēstrīnxī, dēstrīctus, *to strip off;
     to draw, unsheathe* (a sword).
     ēnsis, ēnsis, m., *sword.*
        dēstrīctus ēnsis: the words are placed outside the relative clause of which
        they serve as subject. For the proverbial sword of Damocles, see the pas-
        sage from Cicero's *Tusculan Disputations* in Passages for Comparison I at
        the end of the material for this ode.
        cui: *whose,* dative of possession with impiā / cervīce (18a); as an antecedent,
        supply eī, *for/to him,* or alicui, *for/to anyone,* dative of reference with
        ēlabōrābunt (19) and indirect object with redūcent (21a).
     impius, -a, -um, *impious* (neglecting obligations toward gods and men).
18   cervīx, cervīcis, f., *neck.*
        impiā (17) / cervīce: transferred epithet; impiā logically modifies the im-
        plied eī or alicui, *for him/for any impious person over whose neck.* . . .
     Siculus, -a, -um, *Sicilian.*
     daps, dapis, f., *feast, banquet.*
        Siculae dapēs: the Sicilian cities were proverbial for wealth, luxury, and
        cultivation of the culinary arts.
19   dulcis, -is, -e, *sweet; pleasant.*
     ēlabōrō [ex-/ē-, *thoroughly* + labōrō, -āre, -āvī, -ātus, *to work; to work at*
        (something)], -āre, -āvī, -ātus, *to work up to perfection, perfect; to produce.*
     sapor, sapōris, m., *taste, flavor.*
20   avium: here, apparently, caged birds valued for their soothing songs.
     cantus, -ūs, m., *singing; music.*
        avium citharaeque cantūs: zeugma through cantūs, i.e., *the singing of
        birds and the music of a lyre.*
21   redūcent: note the force of the prefix: *will not bring back* the sleep that the im-
        pious person no longer enjoys because of his anxieties.
     somnus: adversative asyndeton; sleep in Horace is often a "symbol of free-
        dom from care" (Quinn, p. 243).
     agrestis, -is, -e, *of/dwelling in the country.*
        agrestium / . . . virōrum (22): related by position to somnus . . . / lēnis
        (22), but dependent on humilīs domōs (22).
22   lēnis, -is, -e, *gentle.*
     nōn: modifying fastīdit (23).
23   fastīdiō [fastīdium, -ī, n., *aversion, distaste*], -īre, -īvī, -ītus, *to disdain, spurn.*
     somnus (21b) . . . / . . . / fastīdit: mild personification.
     umbrōsus, -a, -um, *shady.*
24   nōn: repeat fastīdit from line 23. Note the repetition and the positions of the
        word nōn in lines 18, 20, 22, and 24.
     zephyrus [Gr., ζέφυρος] -ī, m., *zephyr* (the gentle west wind).
     agitō [agō, agere, ēgī, āctus, *to do; to drive* + iterative/intensive suffix -itō],
        -āre, -āvī, -ātus, *to set in motion, move, stir.*
     Tempē [Gr., Τέμπη], n. pl. indecl., *Tempe* (the Peneus river valley in Thessaly,
        between Mts. Ossa and Olympus, famous for its beauty and for worship of
        Apollo); sometimes by metonymy, *valley.*

17 Dēstrīctus ēnsis cui super impiā
18 cervīce pendet, nōn Siculae dapēs
19   dulcem ēlabōrābunt sapōrem,
20   nōn avium citharaeque cantūs

21 somnum redūcent: somnus agrestium
22 lēnis virōrum nōn humilīs domōs
23   fastīdit umbrōsamque rīpam,
24   nōn zephyrīs agitāta Tempē.

continued

Explorations

14. Compare lines 17–21a with the story of Dionysius I (ca. 430–367 B.C.), tyrant of Syracuse, and Damocles as told by Cicero in *Tusculan Disputations* 5.21, quoted in Passages for Comparison I at the end of the material for this ode. Who is the person referred to in lines 17–18a?
15. Comment on the effects produced by the following in lines 17–21a:
    a. Prominent placement of words
    b. Line framing
    c. Alliteration
16. What is unusual about the way the verb **ēlabōrābunt** is used in line 19?
17. What effect is produced by the repetition **somnum . . . somnus** (21) and the adversative asyndeton?
18. Note that the three adjective-noun phrases, **humilīs domōs** (22), **um-brōsamque rīpam** (23), and **zephyrīs agitāta Tempē** (24) come at the end of their respective lines.
    a. How do the three phrases complement one another in meaning?
    b. Do they build to a climax?
    c. Are the three locations mentioned to be thought of as inhabited or enjoyed only by **virī agrestēs**? Might others enjoy a shady river bank? Why does Horace use the word **Tempē**, which evokes the landscape of Greek poetry, instead of a Latin word for valley? It should be observed that while the word **Tempē** (often lowercase) may be used by metonymy for any beautiful valley, Horace uses it elsewhere only of the fabled valley in Thessaly (*Odes* 1.7.4 and 1.21.9).
19. What contrasts are being drawn between the type of person alluded to in lines 17–21a and the people referred to in lines 21b–24? Why can the latter sleep while the former cannot?

25 **Dēsīderantem:** substantive use of the participle, *The/A person who desires.*

26 **tumultuōsus, -a, -um,** *filled with uproar/commotion, tumultuous, violent.*

sollicitō, -āre, -āvī, -ātus, *to trouble, disturb.*

sollicitat: the subjects of this singular verb are **mare** (26), **impetus** (28), **vīneae** (29), and **fundus** (30a); the direct object is **Dēsīderantem** (25).

27 **Arctūrus** [Gr., Ἀρκτοῦρος], **-ī,** m., *Arcturus* (the name of the brightest star in the constellation Boötes or the name of the whole constellation).

cadentis: *falling = setting.*

28 **impetus, -ūs,** m., *attack; onset.*

saevus (27) . . . **/ impetus:** the reference is to the *savage onset* of stormy autumnal weather associated with the rising of Haedus (early October) and the setting of Arcturus (end of October).

Haedus, -ī, m., *Haedus, Kid* (the name of one or two stars; usually plural, **Haedī,** two stars in the arm of the constellation Auriga; Vergil, *Aeneid* 9.668, associates them with rain).

29 **grandō, grandinis,** f., *hail.*

30 **mendāx, mendācis,** *untruthful; deceiving.*

fundus . . . mendāx: personification, continued in the ablative absolute, **arbore . . . / culpante** (31a).

mendāx: the farm deceives its owner because the crops that it promised turn out badly.

arbore: i.e., a fruit tree, making excuses for not producing as much fruit as expected.

aquās: i.e., *rain, rainfall;* pl., *rain storms.*

31 **culpō, -āre, -āvī, -ātus,** *to blame.*

culpante: governing three direct objects, **aquās** (30b), **sīdera** (32a), and **hiemēs** (32b) in a tricolon; note also the anaphora, **nunc** (30b), **nunc** (31b), and **nunc** (32b).

torreō, torrēre, torruī, tostus, *to scorch, parch.*

32 **sīdus, sīderis,** n., *planet; star.*

sīdera: probably referring to the Dog Star, Sirius, the rising of which in late July was regarded as a harbinger of the hottest weather of the year.

inīquus [**in-,** *not* + **aequus, -a, -um,** *equal; fair*], **-a, -um,** *uneven; unfair; harsh;* of seasons, *stormy, inclement.*

25 Dēsīderantem quod satis est neque
26 tumultuōsum sollicitat mare
27   nec saevus Arctūrī cadentis
28   impetus aut orientis Haedī,

29 nōn verberātae grandine vīneae
30 fundusque mendāx, arbore nunc aquās
31   culpante, nunc torrentia agrōs
32   sīdera, nunc hiemēs inīquās.

continued

Explorations

20. How does the type of person referred to in the phrase **Dēsīderantem quod satis est** (25) compare with
   a. the kings described in line 5;
   b. the four types of Romans described in lines 9–14a;
   c. the people over whose heads hang swords of Damocles (17–21a);
   d. the types of people who can sleep easily (21b–24)?
21. The type of person described in the words **Dēsīderantem quod satis est** is characterized as not being troubled by four things (26–30a). What are these four things? What would be the occupations of people who *are* troubled by these four things?
22. Locate a chiasmus in lines 27–28.
23. Locate examples of personification and humor in lines 30–32.
24. The person who desires only what is enough is free from what (25–32)?

33   **contrahō** [**con-**, *together* + **trahō, trahere, traxī, tractus**, *to draw*], **contrahere, contraxī, contractus**, *to draw together, contract.*
      Contracta: supply **esse**.
    piscis, piscis, m., *fish.*
    sentiō, sentīre, sēnsī, sēnsus, *to feel; to experience to one's cost.*
      sentiunt: cf. **sēnsī**, *Odes* 2.7.10.

34   **mōlibus**: i.e., blocks of masonry or boulders let down into the sea to serve as foundations for a villa projecting beyond the shoreline.
    frequēns, frequentis, *crowded, thronged.*

35   **caementum** [**caedō, caedere, cecīdī, caesus**, *to cut*], **-ī**, n., *small stones, rubble* (used in making a kind of concrete); *concrete* (incorporating small stones).
    dēmittit: *lets down.*
    redēmptor, redēmptōris, m., *contractor.*
      frequēns (34b) **/ . . . redēmptor**: commentators differ on the meaning of the phrase; some take it with **cum famulīs** (36), *the contractor with his throng of laborers*; some translate **frequēns** as *busy*; others translate *many a contractor*; yet others translate **frequēns** in an adverbial sense, *often, repeatedly*, going with **dēmittit**.

36   **famulus, -ī**, m., *slave.*

37   **fastīdiōsus, -a, -um**, *having a distaste for food; hard to satisfy;* + objective gen., *not satisfied/content* (with).
      fastīdiōsus: cf. **fastīdit** (23).
    Minae [personification], **-ārum**, f. pl., *Threats.*

38   **scandō, scandere**, *to climb up, ascend.*
    eōdem, adv., *to the same place.*

39   **dēcēdō** [**dē-**, *down from, away* + **cēdō, cēdere, cessī, cessūrus**, *to go; to go away*], **dēcessī, dēcessūrus**, *to go away;* + abl., *to go away from, leave.*
    aerātus [**aes, aeris**, n., *bronze*], **-a, -um**, of ships, *with bronze fittings/weapons; bronze-fitted.*
    trirēmis, trirēmis, f., *trireme* (a ship having three banks of oars).
      aerātā trirēmī: if the reference is still to the **dominus** of line 38a, this would be a private yacht ornamented with bronze (cf. *Epistle* 1.1.93, **prīva trirēmis**), on which the **dominus** sails for pleasure; the reference may, however, be to bronze-fitted warships (cf. *Odes* 2.16.21, **aerātās . . . nāvīs**).

40   **eques, equitis**, m., *horseman; cavalryman.*
      equitem: either the **dominus** of line 38a, out riding for pleasure, or the reference may be to cavalrymen on the battlefield or mustered for review.
    āter, ātra, ātrum, *black; gloomy.*
    Cūra [personification], **-ae**, f., *Care, Anxiety.*

33   Contracta piscēs aequora sentiunt
34   iactīs in altum mōlibus; hūc frequēns
35   caementa dēmittit redēmptor
36   cum famulīs dominusque terrae

37   fastīdiōsus: sed Timor et Minae
38   scandunt eōdem quō dominus, neque
39   dēcēdit aerātā trirēmī et
40   post equitem sedet ātra Cūra.

continued

Explorations

25.   How might the statement **Contracta piscēs aequora sentiunt** (33) be hyperbolic? How might it be humorous? How might it evoke pathos?

26.   Describe in as precise detail as possible the scene in lines 33–38a and the people involved. What is happening? What are the motives of the **dominus**? Why is the emphasis on the solidity of the foundations?

27.   To what might the words **Timor et Minae** (37b) refer? What does the **dominus** have to fear?

28.   With lines 38b–40, compare *Odes* 2.16.21–22:

21   Scandit aerātās vitiōsa nāvīs
22   Cūra nec turmās equitum relinquit.

Vicious Anxiety climbs aboard bronze-fitted warships and does not leave troops of cavalrymen alone.

Cūra, *Anxiety*, operates similarly in both passages. In *Odes* 2.16.21–22, however, **Cūra** plagues warships and squadrons of cavalrymen.

Most commentators interpret *Odes* 3.1.38b–40 as referring to the **dominus** of line 38a, sailing in his pleasure yacht and riding on horseback for pleasure on his country estate, presumably the estate on which he is building his villa out over the sea. The reference, however, could shift to a warship (any warship) and a cavalryman (as in *Odes* 2.16.21–22). Which interpretation makes better sense or a more vivid picture or series of pictures? Can the lines be read now one way and now the other?

29.   Locate two examples of chiasmus in lines 37b–40.

41   **quodsī**, conj., *but if.*
      doleō, -ēre, -uī, -itūrus, *to suffer bodily pain; to suffer mental pain/distress/ anxiety.*
          dolentem: substantive use of the participle, *the/a person who suffers mental anxiety;* cf. the use of **dēsīderantem** (25).
      Phrygius, -a, -um, *Phrygian, of Phrygia* (a country in Asia Minor).
          Phrygius lapis: marble with purple and violet markings from Synnada in Phrygia, used for columns, as, for example, in the Pantheon.
42   **purpura, -ae,** f., *purple-dyed cloth* (used for clothing, wall hangings, and bed spreads; associated with the rich and the powerful, especially kings and emperors); *the purple-striped tunic* (worn by senators and knights); *the purple-bordered toga* (worn by consuls).
      sīdere: see note to line 32.
43   **dēlēniō [dē-,** *down; completely* + **lēniō, -īre, -īvī** or **-iī, -ītus,** *to soften; to alleviate*], **-īre, -iī, -ītus,** *to soften; to soothe, comfort.*
      ūsus, -ūs, m., *use; wearing.*
      Falernus, -a, -um, *Falernian, of/belonging to Falernus* (an area in northern Campania, famous for its choice wine).
44   **vītis, vītis,** f., *grape-vine.*
          Falerna (43) / **vītis:** metonymy = Falernian wine.
      Achaemenius, -a, -um, *Achaemenian* (Achaemenes was the legendary ancestor of the Persian kings); *Persian; royal.*
      costum [Gr., κόστον**], -ī,** n., *costum* (a fragrant plant used in making perfumes, imported, actually, from India, not Persia); *scent.*
45   **invidendīs postibus:** perhaps marble columns flanking the doorway or supporting the ceiling of the atrium; ablative of description with **ātrium** or ablative of means with **moliar** or ablative of respect with **sublīme.**
      novō / . . . rītū (46): *in a new/unusual manner.*
46   **sublīmis, -is, -e,** *lofty, high.*
          sublīme: proleptic; translate after **ātrium.**
      mōlior, -īrī, -ītus sum, *to construct, build* (with great effort).
      ātrium: the part of the Roman house in which clients and guests were received.
47   **vallēs, vallis,** f., *valley.*
      permūtō [per-, *thoroughly* + **mūtō, -āre, -āvī, -ātus,** *to exchange*], *to exchange;* + acc. and abl., *to take* X (acc.) *in exchange for* Y (abl.).
      Sabīnus, -a, -um, *Sabine* (belonging to the Sabines or their country).
          valle . . . Sabīnā: Horace's villa was located in a Sabine valley; he refers to it frequently in his poetry and comments on his contentment with it, e.g., **satis beātus ūnicīs Sabīnīs,** *sufficiently happy with my unparalleled Sabine property* (*Odes* 2.18.14).
48   **operōsus [opera, -ae,** f., *effort*], **-a, -um,** *involving much effort, laborious; hard-won;* here, apparently, *burdensome, troublesome.*

41 Quodsī dolentem nec Phrygius lapis
42 nec purpurārum sīdere clārior
43   dēlēnit ūsus nec Falerna
44   vītis Achaemeniumque costum,

45 cūr invidendīs postibus et novō
46 sublīme rītū mōliar ātrium?
47   Cūr valle permūtem Sabīnā
48   dīvitiās operōsiōrēs?

Explorations

30. What people or types of people referred to earlier in the poem suffer anxiety, as does the type of person referred to with the word **dolentem** (41)?
31. The substantive participle **dolentem** (41) is the object of the verb **dēlēnit** (43), which has four nouns as its subject. Locate these four nouns and comment on the significance of their placement in the stanza.
32. Point out the transferred epithet in lines 42–43. What rhetorical figure is present in **sīdere clārior** (42)?
33. What do the four things referred to in lines 41–44 have in common?
34. What words in lines 45–46 suggest the singer's negative attitude toward what he is describing?
35. What would be the motive of a person constructing an atrium such as the one envisioned here (45–46)?
36. What is the effect of the anaphora: **cūr** (45) and **Cūr** (47)?
37. Note that the last line consists of two words only. Is this the case with the last line of any other stanza in the poem? What is achieved by having the line consist of only two words, one of which contains six syllables?

Odes 3.1

1   Ōdī profānum vulgus et arceō;
2   favēte linguīs: carmina nōn prius
3   audīta Mūsārum sacerdōs
4   virginibus puerīsque cantō.

5   Rēgum timendōrum in propriōs gregēs,
6   rēgēs in ipsōs imperium est Iovis,
7   clārī Gigantēō triumphō,
8   cūncta superciliō moventis.

9   Est ut virō vir lātius ōrdinet
10   arbusta sulcīs, hic generōsior
11   dēscendat in Campum petītor,
12   mōribus hic meliorque fāmā

13   contendat, illī turba clientium
14   sit maior: aequā lēge Necessitās
15   sortītur īnsignīs et īmōs;
16   omne capāx movet urna nōmen.

17   Dēstrīctus ēnsis cui super impiā
18   cervīce pendet, nōn Siculae dapēs
19   dulcem ēlabōrābunt sapōrem,
20   nōn avium citharaeque cantūs

21   somnum redūcent: somnus agrestium
22   lēnis virōrum nōn humilīs domōs
23   fastīdit umbrōsamque rīpam,
24   nōn zephyrīs agitāta Tempē.

25   Dēsīderantem quod satis est neque
26   tumultuōsum sollicitat mare
27   nec saevus Arctūrī cadentis
28   impetus aut orientis Haedī,

29   nōn verberātae grandine vīneae
30   fundusque mendāx, arbore nunc aquās
31   culpante, nunc torrentia agrōs
32   sīdera, nunc hiemēs inīquās.

33   Contracta piscēs aequora sentiunt
34   iactīs in altum mōlibus; hūc frequēns
35   caementa dēmittit redēmptor
36   cum famulīs dominusque terrae

37   fastīdiōsus: sed Timor et Minae
38   scandunt eōdem quō dominus, neque
39   dēcēdit aerātā trirēmī et
40   post equitem sedet ātra Cūra.

41   Quodsī dolentem nec Phrygius lapis
42   nec purpurārum sīdere clārior
43   dēlēnit ūsus nec Falerna
44   vītis Achaemeniumque costum,

45   cūr invidendīs postibus et novō
46   sublīme rītū mōliar ātrium?
47   Cūr valle permūtem Sabīnā
48   dīvitiās operōsiōrēs?

Discussion

1. This is the first of a series of poems that Horace addresses to maidens and boys (**virginibus puerīsque**, 4). In what way is the teaching embodied in the second stanza the most important thing for these maidens and boys to learn? How is the teaching embodied in the third and fourth stanzas the next most important thing for them to learn?
2. Trace the progression of themes in the stanzas comprising lines 17–48.
3. The words **Dēsīderantem quod satis est** (25) come in the middle of the poem; there are 24 verses before the line in which they occur and 23 after it. What is the special significance of these words in the poem as a whole?
4. Lines 17–40 contain three pairs of stanzas. What structural and thematic similarities are there between the first of the three pairs (stanzas 5 and 6) and the last of the three pairs (stanzas 9 and 10)?
5. Compare *Odes* 3.1 with lines 5–8 of *Odes* 2.10, quoted in Passages for Comparison II following these questions. What similarities and what differences do you find?
6. Compare *Odes* 3.1 with the passage from the prologue to Book 2 of Lucretius *De rerum natura*, given in translation in Passages for Comparison III following these questions. Note that the words Lucretius uses for pain, fear, and anxiety, concepts prominent in *Odes* 3.1, are given in boldfaced Latin. Locate statements or clauses in the passage from Lucretius that correspond to the following topics in *Odes* 3.1:
    a. The vain strivings of men (9–14a)
    b. The uselessness of wealth, nobility, and glory (9–16)
    c. Anxiety and fear existing among kings and powerful men (17–21a and 37b–38a)
    d. The shady river bank (23)
    e. Desiring only what is enough (25)
    f. Anxiety and fear not dispelled by military might (38b–40)
    g. Anxiety and fear not shunning men with splendid trappings (41–43a)
    h. The uselessness of luxurious trappings (41–44)
    i. No need for luxurious surroundings (41–46)

Passages for Comparison

I.

The following is an English translation of Cicero's story of Dionysius I (ca. 430–367 B.C.), tyrant of Syracuse, and Damocles (*Tusculan Disputations* 5.21):

> This tyrant himself gave judgment as to just how happy he was. For when one of his flatterers, Damocles, was recalling in a conversation Dionysius's resources, wealth, the extent of his domination, the abundance of his possessions, and the magnificence of his royal dwelling, and when he was denying that anyone was happier, Dionysius said, "Do you then wish, Damocles, since this life pleases you, to taste it and to experience my fortune?" When he said that he did desire this, Dionysius ordered the man to be placed on a golden couch

spread with a very beautiful woven coverlet adorned with magnificent pictures, and he furnished several sideboards with silver and embossed golden
vessels. Then he ordered chosen boys of exceptional beauty to station themselves at his table and to serve him, diligently attentive to his every wish. Per-
fumes and wreaths were there; incense was burning; the tables were set with
most exquisite feasts. Damocles thought he was lucky indeed. In the middle of
this magnificence, Dionysius ordered a gleaming sword to be let down from
the paneled ceiling by a horse hair, so that it hung threateningly above the
neck of that happy man. Then he ceased looking at those beautiful servants
and the artfully decorated silver, and he was not reaching his hand out to the
table. Now the wreaths slipped down from his head of their own accord. Finally he pleaded with the tyrant that he be permitted to leave, since now he
did not wish to be "happy." Does Dionysius seem to have made it sufficiently
clear that there is no happiness for the man over whom some terror always
hangs? . . . As a youth, at an age when he had no thought for the future, he had
entangled himself in such misdeeds and had committed such crimes that he
was not able to be safe.

II.

Odes 2.10.5–8:

    5   Auream quisquis mediocritātem
    6   dīligit, tūtus caret obsolētī
    7   sordibus tēctī, caret invidendā
    8   sōbrius aulā.

III.

Lucretius *De rerum natura* 2.7–54:

But nothing is sweeter than to have peaceful, lofty temples, well defended by
the teachings of the wise, from which you can look down upon others and see
them wander here and there and, straying about, seek the path of life, as they
compete with their wits, strive for precedence with their good birth, and night
and day contend with outstanding effort to come out on top in wealth and to
gain power. Oh, the pitiable minds of men! Oh, their blind hearts! In what
darkness of life, in what great dangers is this poor span of life spent! Do you
not see that nature cries out for nothing more than this, that pain (**dolor**) should
be absent, unyoked from the body, and that the mind should enjoy pleasant
feelings remote from care (**cūrā**) and fear (**metū**)? Therefore we see that all in
all our bodily nature needs few things to take away pain (**dolōrem**), and to be
able to spread many delights before us; nor does nature herself meanwhile
need anything more pleasant, if there are no golden statues of young men
about the house holding fiery torches in their right hands to supply light for
nocturnal feasts, and the house does not shine with silver and gleam with gold,
and if no paneled and gilded ceilings echo the lyre, when, nevertheless, men,
stretched out on soft grass in groups, near a stream of water beneath the limbs
of a tall tree pleasantly rest their bodies with no great efforts, especially when

the weather smiles on them and the season of the year sprinkles the green grass with flowers. And no more quickly do hot fevers depart from the body, if you lie on decorated bed spreads and blushing purple, than if you must lie on a commoner's blanket. Therefore, since riches do no good for your body nor noble birth nor the glory of regal power, the conclusion is that we must think that these things are of no advantage for the mind either; unless by chance, when you see your legions swarming across the plain stirring up mock battles, strengthened with great forces in reserve and masses of cavalry, equipped equally with arms and spirit, then frightened by these things your superstitious fears flee panic stricken from your mind, and fear of death (**mortis . . . timōrēs**) then leaves your heart unburdened and free from care (**cūrā**). But if we see that these things are ridiculous and a mockery, and truly men's fears (**metūs**) and haunting cares (**cūrae . . . sequācēs**) do not fear the clang of weapons nor cruel spears and boldly roam about with kings and potentates and do not reverence either the gleam of gold or the bright sheen of purple garments,] why do you doubt that this is wholly in the power of reason, especially since all life struggles in darkness.

Meter: Second Asclepiadean

1   **dōnec**, conj., *while, as long as.*
     tibi: i.e., Lydia, the female speaker in this dialogue.
       grātus . . . tibi: *pleasing to you, in favor with you.*

2   **quisquam, quisquam, quicquam**, adjective here, *any.*
     potior [comparative of **potis, -is, -e**, *having power*], **potiōris**, *stronger; better; preferable; preferred, more favored.*
       quisquam potior . . . / . . . iuvenis (3): translate together.
     bracchium, -ī, n., *arm.*
     candidus, -a, -um, *white; beautiful.*

3   **cervīx, cervīcis**, f., *neck.*
     dabat: = **circumdabat** + dat., *was putting* [his arms] *around.*

4   **Persae, -ārum**, m. pl., *the Persians.*
     Persārum . . . rēge: the Persian king was understood to be powerful and wealthy beyond compare and was thus proverbial for a man at the pinnacle of human happiness.
     vigeō, vigēre, viguī, *to be active, lively; to thrive, flourish.*
     beātus, -a, -um, *fortunate; wealthy; supremely happy, blissful, blessed.*

6   **ārdeō, ārdēre, ārsī, ārsūrus**, *to burn, blaze*; + abl., *to burn with love/passion* (for).
     Lȳdia [Gr., Λυδία], **-ae**, f., *Lydia* (the speaker of the second, fourth, and sixth stanzas; see the vocabulary note on the name at *Odes* 1.13.1).
     Chloē [Gr., χλόη, *the first green shoot of plants in spring*], **Chloēs**, f., *Chloe* (see the vocablary note on the name at *Odes* 1.23.1).
       Chloēn: Greek accusative.

7   **multī**: = **magnī.**
     nōmen, nōminis, n., *name; fame, repute.*
       multī . . . nōminis: genitive of description or quality; the phrase is patterned on the Greek adjective πολυώνυμος [πολύ, *much* + ὄνομα, *name*], *having many names; of great name, famous.*

8   **Īlia, -ae**, f., *Ilia* (another name for Rhea Silvia, daughter of Numitor and mother, by Mars, of Romulus and Remus).

ODES 3.9

A Dialogue of Lovers

A lovers' spat over infidelities leads to a reconciliation.

1   Dōnec grātus eram tibi
2 nec quisquam potior bracchia candidae
3   cervīcī iuvenis dabat,
4 Persārum viguī rēge beātior.

5   "Dōnec nōn aliā magis
6 ārsistī neque erat Lȳdia post Chloēn,
7   multī Lȳdia nōminis
8 Rōmānā viguī clārior Īliā."

continued

Explorations

1. What was the male speaker's relationship to his addressee in the past (1)?
2. What do lines 2 and 3 suggest that the male speaker valued in his past relationship with his addressee?
3. How did the male speaker's privileged position with his partner make him feel (4)? What are the implications of the language used in this line?
4. The verbs in the first stanza are all in past tenses. What does this imply about the present? What do you suppose has happened and why?
5. What words in the first stanza are echoed by words in the second? What do these echoes suggest that the speaker of the second stanza is doing?
6. How does the speaker of the second stanza reveal her name?
7. What was the past relationship between the two speakers? What changed it?
8. What appeared to be the intention or purpose of the male speaker as he began the dialogue? How does Lydia respond?
9. What use of alliteration do you find in Lydia's response (5–8)?
10. How does Lydia assert herself in lines 7–8 over against the male speaker in his line 4?

9   **Thraessus, -a, -um,** *Thracian, of Thrace* (an area of northern Greece that was not renowned for sophistication and was a source of slaves).
10   **dulcis, -is, -e,** *sweet.*
     doctus, -a, -um, *learned;* + acc., *versed* (in).
     modus, -ī, m., *manner; limit; rhythmic pattern;* pl., *measures (of verse), poems, songs.*
     sciēns, scientis + gen., *knowledgeable* (in), *skilled* (in).
11   **metuō, metuere, metuī,** *to fear.*
     metuam: future indicative in the protasis of a future more vivid condition.
12   **anima, -ae,** f., *air, breath; soul; life;* as a term of endearment, *beloved.*
     superstes, superstitis, adjective, *remaining alive after the death of another, surviving.*
         superstitī: proleptic, *and grant that she may live.*
13   **torreō, torrēre, torruī, tostus,** *to burn, scorch.*
14   **Thūrīnus, -a, -um,** *belonging to Thurii* (a Greek colony on the gulf of Tarentum in southern Italy, founded in 444 B.C. on or near the site of the Greek colony Sybaris, a town famed for refinement and luxury, which was destroyed in 510 B.C.).
     Calais [Gr., Κάλαϊς, a Greek proper name taken from the word ἡ κάλαϊς, *turquoise* (the precious stone), or from καλός, *beautiful*], **Calais,** m., *Calais* (the name of Lydia's lover recalls the mythical Calais, the winged son of Boreas, the Thracian god of the north wind, and the Athenian Oreithyia, the daughter of Erechtheus; the mythical Calais and his brother Zetes sailed with the Argonauts to fetch the golden fleece; Apollonius Rhodius devoted thirteen lines to these brothers in his catalogue of the Argonauts in *Argonautica* 1.211–23).
     Ornytus [Gr., ᾿Ορνυτος], **-ī,** m., *Ornytus* (the name of the father of Lydia's lover recalls the mythical Ornytus, king of Phocis in Greece and the grandfather of the Argonaut Iphitus; the latter and his grandson Ornytus are mentioned in Apollonius's catalogue of the Argonauts just four lines before Calais is mentioned; this fact suggests that with the names Calais and Ornytus Horace is deliberately alluding to the catalogue of Argonauts in Apollonius's poem; on Lydia's lips these allusions grace the names of her lover and his father with an aura of mythical grandeur; the fact that Lydia cites the name of the father of Calais indicates that the latter is a freeborn citizen, in pointed contrast to the Thracian slave or freedwoman Chloe).
15   **patiar:** future indicative in a future more vivid condition.

9   Mē nunc Thraessa Chloē regit,
10   dulcīs docta modōs et citharae sciēns,
11   prō quā nōn metuam morī,
12   sī parcent animae fāta superstitī.

13   "Mē torret face mūtuā
14   Thūrīnī Calais fīlius Ornytī,
15   prō quō bis patiar morī,
16   sī parcent puerō fāta superstitī."

continued

Explorations

11. What words in the third stanza (9–12) are echoed by words in the fourth (13–16)?

12. How does Lydia trump the male speaker here?

"Greek Woman Playing a Lyre"
Attic Greek white-ground lekythos
Ashmolean Museum, Oxford, United Kingdom

17   **prīscus, -a, -um**, *ancient; former.*
18   **dīdūcō** [dis-/dī-, *asunder, apart, in different directions* + **dūcō, dūcere, dūxī, ductus**, *to lead*], **dīdūcere, dīdūxī, dīductus**, *to draw apart, divide, separate.*

   dīductōs: supply **eōs**, *those who have been* . . . , keeping the thought general here.

   iugum, -ī, n., *yoke.*

   cōgit: note that this verb, meaning *to compel, force*, comes from **con-**, *together* + **agō, agere**, *to drive;* it thus expresses the opposite of the verbal idea contained in **dīductōs**.

   aēneus, -a, -um, *of bronze.*
19   **flāvus, -a, -um**, *golden-yellow; blonde.*

   excutiō [ex-, *out of, off* + **quatiō, quatere, quassus**, *to shake*], **excutere, excussī, excussus**, *to shake off.*
20   **rēiciō** [re-, *back* + **iaciō, iacere, iēcī, iactus**, *to throw*], **rēicere, rēiēcī, rē-iectus**, *to throw back, repel; to reject.*

   rēiectae . . . Lȳdiae: dative, with the participle best taken as concessive, *to Lydia even though she had been rejected.*

   pateō, patēre, patuī, *to be open.*
21   **sīdus, sīderis**, n., *star.*
22   **ille**: i.e., Calais.

   ille est, tū: adversative asyndeton.

   levis, -is, -e, *light; fickle.*

   cortex, corticis, m./f., *cork.*

   improbus, -a, -um, *not good; shameless, without decent limits, wanton.*

   improbō: "a word which might be used of a lover" here "transferred to the sea" (Quinn, p. 262).
23   **īrācundus, -a, -um**, *prone to anger; bad tempered; temperamental.*

   Hadria, -ae, m., *the Adriatic Sea* (an arm of the Mediterranean Sea to the east of Italy, proverbial for its violent storms).
24   **obeō** [ob-, *against* + **eō, īre, iī** or **īvī, itūrus**, *to go*], **obīre, obiī** or **obīvī, obitūrus**, *to meet with;* with or without **mortem** or **diem**, *to meet one's death, die.*

   libēns, libentis: = **libenter**, *gladly.*

Passage for Comparison

With lines 17–18, compare *Odes* 1.33, in which a beautiful woman named Lycoris burns with passionate love for Cyrus. Cyrus, however, will have nothing to do with her but instead loves a heartless woman named Pholoe. Pholoe, however, will have nothing to do with the disgraceful Cyrus. In lines 10–12, the speaker comments :

10 Sīc vīsum Venerī, cui placet imparīs   Such is the will of Venus, who en-
11 fōrmās atque animōs sub iuga aēnea   joys sending ill-matched bodies
12   saevō mittere cum iocō.   and minds under bronze yokes as
                                                    part of a cruel game.

17   Quid sī prīsca redit Venus
18   dīductōsque iugō cōgit aēneō,
19   sī flāva excutitur Chloē
20   rēiectaeque patet iānua Lȳdiae?

21   "Quamquam sīdere pulchrior
22   ille est, tū levior cortice et improbō
23   īrācundior Hadriā,
24   tēcum vīvere amem, tēcum obeam libēns."

Explorations

13.   In the first two exchanges, Lydia echoed words and phrases in the male speaker's stanzas. In Lydia's final stanza (21–24), does she echo any words or phrases in the male speaker's previous stanza (17–20)?

14.   In lines 17–20 the speaker is implicitly proposing that Lydia might again become his number one. What purposes are served by his using only third person indicative verbs and by avoiding overt reference to himself or Lydia until the very last word?

15.   How is the power of Venus in *Odes* 1.33 (see the passage for comparison on the opposite page) similar to her power in lines 17–18 of *Odes* 3.9 above?

16.   What does Lydia do in her final stanza instead of echoing and trumping the language of the male speaker?

17.   How do the words on either side of **ille est, tū** (22) form a chiasmus? What contrast does this chiasmus reinforce?

18.   The second half of Lydia's last line (24b) echoes the first half of that line in much the same way as echoes have functioned earlier in the poem.
      a.   How does the second half of line 24 echo or respond to the first half?
      b.   How do the two halves of this line respond to themes earlier in the poem?
      c.   How does the final line bring the poem to a conclusion?

Odes 3.9

1   Dōnec grātus eram tibi
2 nec quisquam potior bracchia candidae
3   cervīcī iuvenis dabat,
4 Persārum viguī rēge beātior.

5   "Dōnec nōn aliā magis
6 ārsistī neque erat Lȳdia post Chloēn,
7   multī Lȳdia nōminis
8 Rōmānā viguī clārior Īliā."

9   Mē nunc Thraessa Chloē regit,
10 dulcīs docta modōs et citharae sciēns,
11   prō quā nōn metuam morī,
12 sī parcent animae fāta superstitī.

13   "Mē torret face mūtuā
14 Thūrīnī Calais fīlius Ornytī,
15   prō quō bis patiar morī,
16 sī parcent puerō fāta superstitī."

17   Quid sī prīsca redit Venus
18 dīductōsque iugō cōgit aēneō,
19   sī flāva excutitur Chloē
20 rēiectaeque patet iānua Lȳdiae?

21   "Quamquam sīdere pulchrior
22 ille est, tū levior cortice et improbō
23   īrācundior Hadriā,
24 tēcum vīvere amem, tēcum obeam libēns."

Discussion

1. What is the structure of this ode?
2. How does the poem create contrasting portraits of the two lovers?
3. Compare *Odes* 3.9 with Catullus's poem 45 on the love relationship of Acme and Septimius, which may have inspired Horace's ode. Catullus 45 is given in Passages for Comparison I following these questions.
4. What relationships can you see among *Odes* 1.8, 1.13, 1.25, and 3.9, which involve Lydia, and *Odes* 1.23, 3.9, and 3.26, which involve Chloe? *Odes* 1.8 is given in Passages for Comparison II at the end of the material for *Odes* 1.13, and *Odes* 3.26 is given in Passages for Comparison II following these questions.

Passages for Comparison

I.

Catullus 45:

```
 1   Acmēn Septimius suōs amōrēs
 2   tenēns in gremiō, "Mea," inquit, "Acmē,
 3   nī tē perditē amō atque amāre porrō
 4   omnēs sum assiduē parātus annōs,
 5   quantum quī pote plūrimum perīre,
 6   sōlus in Libyā Indiāque tostā
 7   caesiō veniam obvius leōnī."
 8   Hoc ut dīxit, Amor sinistrā ut ante
 9   dextrā sternuit approbātiōnem.
10       At Acmē leviter caput reflectēns
11   et dulcis puerī ēbriōs ocellōs
12   illō purpureō ōre suāviāta,
13   "Sīc," inquit, "mea vīta Septimille,
14   huic ūnī dominō ūsque serviāmus,
15   ut multō mihi maior ācriorque
16   ignis mollibus ārdet in medullīs."
17   Hoc ut dīxit, Amor sinistrā ut ante
18   dextrā sternuit approbātiōnem.
19       Nunc ab auspiciō bonō profectī
20   mūtuīs animīs amant amantur.
21   Ūnam Septimius misellus Acmēn
22   māvult quam Syriās Britanniāsque:
23   ūnō in Septimiō fidēlis Acmē
24   facit dēliciās libīdinēsque.
25   Quis ūllōs hominēs beātiōrēs
26   vīdit, quis Venerem auspicātiōrem?
```

Septimius, holding his beloved Acme on his lap, said, "My Acme, if I don't love you desperately and am not prepared to love you on and on unceasingly for all my years, as desperately as the most desperate lover can, may I alone in Libya or scorched India meet face-to-face a green-eyed lion." When he said this, Amor sneezed his approval as before on the left [so] on the right. But Acme, gently bending back her head and kissing with those rosy lips of hers the drunken eyes of her sweet boy, said, "Dear Septimius, my life, so may we continuously serve this one master, as surely as a much greater and fiercer fire burns in my tender marrow." When she said this, Amor sneezed his approval as before on the left [so] on the right. Now having set out after this good omen, they love and are loved with mutual hearts. Wretched little Septimius prefers Acme alone to all Syrias and Britains: faithful Acme finds her pleasure and lovemaking/pleasurable lovemaking with Septimius alone Who has seen any persons more blessed, who has seen a more auspicious Venus/more auspicious lovemaking?

II.

Odes 3.26:

```
1   Vīxī puellīs nūper idōneus
2   et mīlitāvī nōn sine glōriā;
3       nunc arma dēfunctumque bellō
4           barbiton hic pariēs habēbit,

5   laevum marīne quī Veneris latus
6   custōdit. Hīc, hīc pōnite lūcida
7       fūnālia et vectīs et arcūs
8           oppositīs foribus minācēs.

9   Ō quae beātam dīva tenēs Cyprum et
10  Memphin carentem Sīthoniā nive,
11      rēgīna, sublīmī flagellō
12          tange Chloēn semel arrogantem.
```

I lived until recently a suitable match for girls and performed military service not without glory; but now this wall will hold my weapons and my lyre which is finished with war, [this wall] which guards the left side of seaborn Venus. Here, here put the shining torches and the crowbars and bows that threaten the blocking doors. O you who hold sway over blessed Cyprus and Memphis that is free of Sithonian snow, queen, with upraised whip touch arrogant Chloe just once.

Meter: Fourth Asclepiadean

1   **Ō**: this interjection with the vocative case is common in Greek and Roman hymns.

      fōns, fontis, m., *fountain, spring.*

      Bandusia, -ae, f., *Bandusia* (the name the speaker gives to a spring addressed in this poem and perhaps the name also of a water nymph thought to inhabit the spring. Horace mentions a spring on his Sabine farm near the modern town of Licenza in other poems, e.g., *Satires* 2.6.2 and *Epistles* 1.16.12–13, but he uses the name Bandusia only here).

      splendidus, -a, -um, *bright, shining; splendid, brilliant; glittering.*

      vitrum, -ī, n., *glass.*

2   **dulcis, -is, -e**, *sweet.*

      dignus, -a, -um + abl., *worthy* (of).

3   **dōnō, -āre, -āvī, -ātus** + abl., *to present* (with).

      haedus, -ī, m., *young goat, kid.*

4   **cui**: *whose*, dative of reference indicating possession.

      turgidus, -a, -um, *swollen.*

      cornū, -ūs, n., *horn.*

Fōns Bandusiae

ODES 3.13

The Fōns Bandusiae

Horace pays tribute to and immortalizes his Bandusian spring.

1   Ō fōns Bandusiae splendidior vitrō,
2   dulcī digne merō nōn sine flōribus,
3   crās dōnāberis haedō,
4   cui frōns turgida cornibus

continued

Explorations

1. Identify the following poetic devices in this stanza and comment on their effects:
    a. Formal interjection
    b. Alliteration
    c. Litotes
2. How does the speaker praise and compliment the spring? How does he surpass what would appear to be normal from the passage below?

Passage for Comparison

Varro, *On the Latin Language* 6.22:

Fontīnālia ā Fonte, quod is diēs fēriae eius; ab eō tum et in fontēs corōnās iaciunt et puteōs corōnant.

Fontinalia [Festival of the Springs], from Fons [god of springs]; because that day [October 13] is his holiday; on his account they then throw garlands into springs and they wreathe wells [with garlands].

5   **cornibus** (4) / **prīmīs**: *with the tips of its horns* or *with its first horns.*
     venus, veneris, f., *sexual appetite; sexual activity; mating.*
     proelium, -ī, n., *battle.*
        et venerem et proelia: i.e., butting contests with rivals for access to females.
     dēstinō, -āre, -āvī, -ātus + acc., *to mark out, destine, preordain.*
6   **gelidus, -a, -um**, *cold, chilly.*
     īnficiō [**in-**, *in* + **faciō, facere, fēcī, factus,** *to make*], **īnficere, īnfēcī, īnfec-**
        tus, *to stain, dye, discolor.*
        īnficiet: the subject is **subolēs** (8).
     tibi: dative of reference; translate as a possessive with **rīvōs** (7).
7   **ruber, rubra, rubrum,** *red.*
8   **lascīvus, -a, -um,** *playful, frisky; lustful.*
     subolēs [**sub-**, *under* + **alō, alere, aluī, altus,** *to nurture, sustain*], **subolis**, f.,
        offspring (used here with the implication that the offspring in question is
        vital to maintenance of the flock).
     grex, gregis, m., *flock.*
        lascīvī . . . gregis: goats were proverbially known for their lustiness.

5   prīmīs et venerem et proelia dēstinat;
6   frūstrā: nam gelidōs īnficiet tibi
7   rubrō sanguine rīvōs
8   lascīvī subolēs gregis.

continued

Explorations

3. How is the kid described (4–5)? At what stage of its life is it? What response does it elicit from the reader?
4. What do the embedded word order of **gelidōs** . . . / **rubrō sanguine rīvōs** (6b–7) and the adjectives contribute to the description of what will happen?
5. What word earlier in the poem does line 8, **lascīvī subolēs gregis,** recall? How does this phrase round out the description of the kid and the first half of the poem? Of what importance to the flock could the kid have been?

9   **flagrō, -āre, -āvī**, *to burn, blaze.*
     atrōx, atrōcis, *fierce, savage, cruel.*
     hōra, -ae, f., *hour;* by metonymy, *season.*
     Canīcula [canis, canis, m./f., *dog* + **-cula**, diminutive suffix] **-ae**, f., *Canicula,*
         Little Dog (the Dog Star, Sirius, the rising of which in late July was
         regarded as a harbinger of the hottest weather of the year).
10   **nesciō, nescīre, nescīvī** or **nesciī, nescītus**, *not to know;* + infin., *not to know*
         how to, not to be able to.
     frīgus, frīgoris, n., *cold, chill, coolness.*
     amābilis, -is, -e, *lovable; cherished.*
11   **fessus, -a, -um**, *wearied, tired.*
     vōmer, vōmeris, n., *plowshare;* by synecdoche, *plow;* by metonymy, *plowing.*
         vōmere: ablative of cause.
     taurus, -ī, m., *bull; ox.*
12   **pecus, pecoris**, n., a collective noun, *farm animals, livestock, herd, flock*
         (particularly of sheep or cattle, but here perhaps of goats, cf. **gregis**, 8).
     vagus, -a, -um, *roaming, wandering.*

9   Tē flagrantis atrōx hōra Canīculae
10 nescit tangere, tū frīgus amābile
11   fessīs vōmere taurīs
12   praebēs et pecorī vagō.

continued

Explorations

6. Locate examples of anaphora and asyndeton. What words correspond to one
    another in lines 9–10? Locate a chiasmus in lines 11–12.
7. Paraphrase the statement that is being made in lines 9–10a. What is the ef-
    fect of the embedded word order in line 9? How is the star portrayed as ani-
    mate?
8. What does the **fōns** offer (10b–12)? What similar benefits does the spring of-
    fer in the epigram of Anyte of Tegea translated below?
9. The two phrases **gelidōs . . . / . . . rīvōs** (6b–7) and **frīgus amābile** (10b)
    both refer to the chill water of the spring. What very different relationships
    does the water of the spring in these two phrases have to the animals on the
    farm?

Passage for Comparison

Anyte of Tegea (4th–3rd centuries B.C.) *A.P.* 16.228:

> Stranger, rest your wearied limbs beneath the elm. The breeze speaks sweetly
> in the green leaves. Drink the cool water from the spring, for indeed this is a
> resting place dear those traveling in the burning heat of the sun.

13 **fīēs**: *you will become* (one) + partitive genitive, **nōbilium . . . fontium**.
nōbilis, -is, -e, *renowned, famed*.
fontium: cf. **fōns** (1); the echo creates a ring composition. Horace assures his
fōns Bandusiae that it will join the ranks of famous Greek springs such as
Castalia, Hippocrene, Pirene, and Dirce, which were regarded as haunts of
the Muses and sources of poetic inspiration.

14 **mē dīcente**: causal ablative absolute.
dīcente: participle of **dīcō, dīcere, dīxī, dictus**, here meaning *to tell of, celebrate* (in song); cf. Vergil *Georgics* 2.95b, **quō tē carmine dīcam?** *with
what song shall I celebrate you?*
cavus, -a, -um, *hollow*.
impōnō [in-, *in, on* + **pōnō, pōnere, posuī, positus**, *to put, place*], **impōnere,
imposuī, impositus** + dat., *to place on/over; to position on/over*.
īlex, īlicis, f., *ilex, holm oak* (an evergreen tree with dark holly-like leaves).
īlicem: direct object of **dīcente**.

15 **saxum, -ī**, n., *rock*.
saxīs: dative with the compound participle **impositam**.
loquāx, loquācis, *talkative, babbling*.
loquācēs: best translated as predicate after **dēsiliunt**.

16 **lympha** [related to Greek νύμφη, *nymph*], **-ae**, f., *water-nymph;* poetic, *water*.
lymphae: poetic plural for singular.
dēsiliō [dē-, *down* + **saliō, salīre, saluī** or **saliī, saltūrus**, *to jump, leap*],
dēsilīre, dēsiluī, *to jump/leap down*.

13 Fīēs nōbilium tū quoque fontium,
14 mē dīcente cavīs impositam īlicem
15   saxīs, unde loquācēs
16   lymphae dēsiliunt tuae.

Explorations

10. Identify the following poetic devices in this stanza and comment on their effect:
    a. Apostrophe
    b. Personification
    c. Alliteration
11. What similarities are there between *Odes* 3.13 and the epigram of Leonidas of Tarentum translated below?
12. How does the final stanza of *Odes* 3.13 echo the first stanza to create a ring composition?

Passage for Comparison

Leonidas of Tarentum (3rd century B.C.) *A.P.* 6.334.1–2 and 5–6:

> Caves and holy hill of the Nymphs, springs from beneath the rock, and pine tree near the waters, . . . graciously receive these sacrificial barley cakes and this cup full of wine, gifts of Neoptolemus who is descended from Aeacus.

Odes 3.13

1   Ō fōns Bandusiae splendidior vitrō,

2   dulcī digne merō nōn sine flōribus,

3   crās dōnāberis haedō,

4   cui frōns turgida cornibus

5   prīmīs et venerem et proelia dēstinat;

6   frūstrā: nam gelidōs īnficiet tibi

7   rubrō sanguine rīvōs

8   lascīvī subolēs gregis.

9   Tē flagrantis atrōx hōra Canīculae

10 nescit tangere, tū frīgus amābile

11   fessīs vōmere taurīs

12   praebēs et pecorī vagō.

13 Fīēs nōbilium tū quoque fontium,

14 mē dīcente cavīs impositam īlicem

15   saxīs, unde loquācēs

16   lymphae dēsiliunt tuae.

Discussion

1. *Odes* 3.13 contains some elements of a hymn. Compare the hymn in Catullus 34, which is quoted in Passages for Comparison I following these questions.
    a. What similarities do you find?
    b. What differences do you find?
    c. Is there anything in *Odes* 3.13 to correspond to the prayers in the last two stanzas of Catullus's hymn? If not, what does the speaker of *Odes* 3.13 offer in his last stanza?
2. What benefit does the spring provide that could motivate the speaker as master of his Sabine farm to sacrifice the kid to it? What parallel can you find in the epigram of Leonidas of Tarentum translated in Passages for Comparison II following these questions?
3. What does the speaker as poet do for the spring in the final stanza of the poem? What does the spring do for the poet? How is the relationship between the spring and the poet reciprocal?
4. It has been remarked that in this poem "the hymn to Bandusia is a hymn to [Horace's] own poetry" (Nussbaum, p. 156). With this in mind, look back through the poem and consider how each of the following can be associated with Horace's poetry:
    a. The spring and the comparison with glass (**splendidior vitrō**, 1)
    b. The wine and flowers (2)
    c. The sacrifice of the kid that is preordained in vain for **venerem et proelia** (5)
    d. The benefactions of the spring (9–12)
    e. The description of the spring and its ambience (13–16)

Passages for Comparison

I.

Catullus 34:

1	Diānae sumus in fidē	We are under Diana's protection, girls and
2	puellae et puerī integrī:	boys who are chaste: <of Diana let us sing,
3	<Diānam puerī integrī>	boys and girls> who are chaste.
4	puellaeque canāmus.	
5	Ō Lātōnia, maximī	O daughter of Latona, great child of greatest
6	magna prōgeniēs Iovis,	Jove, to whom your mother gave birth be-
7	quam māter prope Dēliam	side the olive tree on Delos,
8	dēposīvit olīvam,	
9	montium domina ut forēs	that you might be the mistress of mountains
10	silvārumque virentium	and of green forests and of secluded wooded
11	saltuumque reconditōrum	pastures and of resounding rivers:
12	amniumque sonantum:	
13	tū Lūcīna dolentibus	you have been called Juno Lucina by women
14	Iūnō dicta puerperīs,	suffering in childbirth, you have been called
15	tū potēns Trivia et nothō es	powerful Trivia and the Moon with bor-
16	dicta lūmine Lūna.	rowed light.
17	Tū cursū, dea, mēnstruō	You, goddess, who measure out the year's
18	mētiēns iter annuum,	path with your monthly course, fill up the
19	rūstica agricolae bonīs	farmer's country sheds with good produce.
20	tēcta frūgibus explēs.	
21	Sīs quōcumque tibi placet	Be sanctified by whatever name you please,
22	sāncta nōmine, Rōmulīque,	and as you were accustomed of old, with
23	antīquē ut solita es, bonā	good aid preserve Romulus's race.
24	sōspitēs ope gentem.	

II.

Leonidas of Tarentum (3rd century B.C.) *A.P.* 9.326.1–2 and 5b–6:

Greetings, cool water leaping down from a rock split in two, and greetings, wooden images of Nymphs made by shepherds! . . . I, Aristocles the traveler, give you this as a gift, this cup that I dipped in your water to dispel my thirst.

Meter: First Asclepiadean

1   **exigō** [**ex-**, *thoroughly* + **agō, agere, ēgī, āctus**, *to do; to drive*], **exigere, exēgī, exāctus**, *to complete*.
     monumentum [**moneō, monēre, monuī, monitus**, *to remind* + **-mentum**, suffix added to stems of verbs to form nouns denoting concrete objects], **-ī**, n., *statue/building constructed as a memorial; tomb; monument*.
     aes, aeris, n., *bronze* (the metal itself or something made of bronze such as a coin, a statue, an inscribed tablet, or letters sunk in stone on monuments or public buildings).
     perennis [**per-**, *through* + **annus, -ī**, m., *year*], **-is, -e**, *lasting through the years, enduring*.
2   **rēgālis, -is, -e**, *royal*.
     rēgālī: modifying **situ**, but may be taken with **pȳramidum** as a transferred epithet.
     situs [**sinō, sinere, sīvī, situs**, *to leave, let*], **-ūs**, m., *site; structure*.
     situ: in addition to the word **situs** given above and meaning *site* or *structure*, there is another word with the same spelling but of uncertain derivation meaning *neglect, disuse; rottenness; decay*. The meaning *decay* may be relevant at some level of interpretation of lines 1–5.
     pȳramis [Gr., πυραμίς], **pȳramidis**, f., *pyramid* (the tomb of an ancient Egyptian king or Pharaoh).
     altus, -a, -um, *high; lofty*.
3   **edāx** [**edō, ēsse, ēdī, ēsus**, *to eat*], **edācis**, *devouring, voracious; destructive*.
     Aquilō, Aquilōnis, m., *the North Wind*; by metonymy, *wind*.
     impotēns, impotentis, *powerless, impotent; lacking in self-control; violent, raging*.
4   **dīruō** [**dis-/dī-**, *thoroughly* + **ruō, ruere, ruī**, *to make* X *collapse*], **dīruere, dīruī, dīrutus**, *to make* X *collapse*.
     innumerābilis, -is, -e, *innumerable*.
5   **seriēs, -ēī**, f., *series*.
     fuga, -ae, f., *flight*.

The Pyramids of Giza

ODES 3.30

The poet reflects on his achievement.

*The speaker has completed an enduring monument, invites the Muse to take
deserved pride in his accomplishment, and requests that she encircle his hair with a
laurel wreath.*

1 Exēgī monumentum aere perennius
2 rēgālīque sitū pȳramidum altius,
3 quod nōn imber edāx, nōn Aquilō impotēns
4 possit dīruere aut innumerābilis
5 annōrum seriēs et fuga temporum.

continued

Explorations

1. Why would the speaker place the verb first in line 1?
2. What three things are special about the **monumentum** that the speaker has completed?
3. Identify an ascending tricolon in lines 3–5. Identify a chiasmus in the third member of the tricolon.
4. How could rain, wind, and the passage of time cause a **monumentum** to collapse?
5. What is the function of a **monumentum**? What is the speaker's **monumentum**?

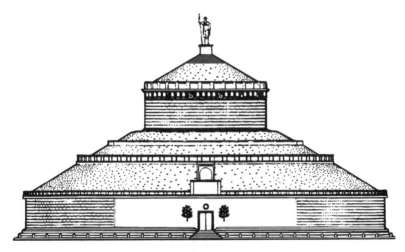

The Mausoleum of Augustus

259

6 **omnis**: translate as an adverb, *entirely*.
 multa: = **magna**.
 meī: genitive of **egō**.
7 **Libitīna, -ae**, f., *Libitina* (the Roman goddess of funerals; the records of Roman burials were kept in her grove in an unsavory quarter of Rome possibly on the Esquiline Hill, and the headquarters of the undertakers and funerary masons were there as well); by metonymy, *the rites of death*.
 ūsque, adv., *all the way; continuously*.
  ūsque: with **crēscam**.
 posterā / . . . laude (8): *later praise* = **posterōrum laude**, *praise of/offered by those who come after*; ablative of cause with **crēscam** and **recēns**.
8 **crēscō, crēscere, crēvī, crētūrus**, *to grow*.
 laus, laudis, f., *praise*.
 recēns, recentis, *newly done; new, recent, fresh*.
 Capitōlium, -ī, n., *the Capitol* (see the vocabulary note on *Odes* 1.37.6).
9 **scandō, scandere**, *to climb*.
  scandet: i.e., up the **clīvus Capitōlīnus**, the winding road from the Forum up the Capitoline Hill to the **Capitōlium**; this was the same road taken by victorious generals in their triumphal processions.
 tacitus, -a, -um, *silent*.
  tacitā: referring to the necessity of silence in religious ritual; see the vocabulary note on **favēte linguīs** (*Odes* 3.1.2).
 virgine: i.e., *Vestal Virgin*; the Vestal Virgins were a group of six unmarried priestesses of the goddess Vesta; they kept the sacred flame of Vesta burning in her temple, which was situated near the **Rēgia**, the official residence of the **Pontifex Maximus**.
 pontifex, pontificis, m., *priest*.
  pontifex: perhaps the **Pontifex Maximus**, the High Priest of the Roman state religion.

6 Nōn omnis moriar, multaque pars meī
7 vītābit Libitīnam: ūsque ego posterā
8 crēscam laude recēns, dum Capitōlium
9 scandet cum tacitā virgine pontifex.

continued

Explorations

6. How does alliteration work with the meter to enhance the meaning of line 6?
7. How does the statement **Nōn omnis moriar, multaque pars meī /vītābit Libitīnam** (6–7a) follow logically from what is said in lines 1–5?
8. What effects are achieved by use of the name of the goddess, **Libitīna**, in line 7a instead of a word for death or for the rites of death?
9. How do lines 7b–8a, **ūsque ego posterā / crēscam laude recēns**, go beyond what has been said so far?
10. What do lines 8b–9, **dum Capitōlium / scandet cum tacitā virgine pontifex**, add to what is said in lines 7b–8a, **ūsque ego posterā / crēscam laude recēns**?

10   **Dīcar**: take with **prīnceps** . . . (13) / **dēdūxisse** (14a), *I will be said [to have
      been] the first to have brought.* . . . ; for an alternative translation, see the note
      on **prīnceps** below.

      quā, adv., *where, [in the region] where.*

      obstrepō [**ob-**, *against* + **strepō, strepere, strepuī, strepitus**, *to make a loud
      noise; to shout in protest*], **obstrepere, obstrepuī, obstrepitūrus**, *to make a
      loud noise in opposition/competition;* here of a river, *to roar in opposition.*

      Aufidus, -ī, m., *the Aufidus* (a river in southern Italy, ten miles from Venusia,
      where Horace was born).

11   **pauper, pauperis**, *poor;* + gen., *lacking in.*

      Daunus, -ī, m., *Daunus* (the legendary founder and first king of Daunia, the
      part of Apulia where Horace was born; before founding Daunia, Daunus
      was famed in his native Illyrium; this Daunus is not the same as Turnus's
      father of the same name in Vergil's *Aeneid*).

      agrestis, -is, -e, *rustic; of/belonging to the country.*

12   **rēgnāvit**: the use of this intransitive verb with an object in the genitive case
      (**populōrum**) is an imitation of Greek grammatical usage.

      humilī: masculine, *a humble [man]*, or generally, *a humble [status].*

      potēns, potentis, *powerful.*

13   **prīnceps** [**prīmus, -a, -um**, *first* + **-ceps**, *one who takes something*], **prīncipis**,
      adj., *first.*

           prīnceps . . . / **dēdūxisse** (14a): translate with **Dīcar**; see note on line 10
           above. The word **prīnceps** may also be a noun meaning *initiator, orig-
           inator, innovator; master* (in a particular activity); *leading citizen; leader;
           princeps* (the title adopted by Augustus). If **prīnceps** is taken as a
           noun, one would translate **Dīcar** . . . / . . . / . . . **potēns / prīnceps** . . .
           / **dēdūxisse** (10a–14a) as *I, a powerful master [of song], will be said to have
           brought.* . . .

      Aeolius, -a, -um, *from Aeolia, Aeolian.*

      carmen, carminis, n., *song.*

           Aeolium carmen: referring to Greek lyric poetry written in the Aeolic di-
           alect by Sappho and Alcaeus.

14   **dēdūcō** [**dē-**, *down* + **dūcō, dūcere, dūxī, ductus**, *to lead*], **dēdūcere, dēdūxī,
      dēductus**, *to lead away; to bring.*

           dēdūxisse: literally, *to have brought*, but the word may also be used of set-
           tling immigrants in a colony, of spinning thread, of composing fine
           poetry, and of bringing a captive to Rome for a triumph (for this mean-
           ing, see *Odes* 1.37.31).

      modus, -ī, m., *measure; rhythm, meter;* pl., *meters; poems; poetry.*

10   Dīcar, quā violēns obstrepit Aufidus
11   et quā pauper aquae Daunus agrestium
12   rēgnāvit populōrum, ex humilī potēns
13   prīnceps Aeolium carmen ad Ītalōs
14a   dēdūxisse modōs.

continued

Explorations

11.   What is the speaker claiming when he says **Dīcar . . . / . . . / . . . ex humilī
      potēns / prīnceps Aeolium carmen ad Ītalōs / dēdūxisse modōs** (10a–
      14a)?
12.   What significance can you see in the way the Aufidus River is described
      (10b)?
13.   What significance can you see in the way Daunus is described (11–12a)?
14.   How does the phrase **ex humilī** (12b) relate the speaker to Daunia as it is de-
      scribed in lines 11–12a?
15.   How, if at all, do the speaker's achievement and reputation derive from his
      native Daunia?

14 **sūmō, sūmere, sūmpsī, sūmptus**, *to take up, accept.*
superbia, -ae, f., *pride.*
    superbiam: with overtones of the pride felt by a general at his triumph; cf.
    Odes 1.37.31–32, **superbō / . . . triumphō**.
15 **quaerō, quaerere, quaesīvī, quaesītus**, *to seek, look for; to obtain; to earn.*
meritum, -ī, n., *meritorious achievement* (i.e., one that deserves recognition).
mihi: take as possessive with **comam** (16).
Delphicus, -a, -um, *Delphic, from Delphi* (Delphi was the site of the oracle of
    Apollo, the god of music and poetry).
16 **laurus, -ī**, f., *laurel tree, laurel branch, laurel crown* (the laurel is the symbol of
    Apollo; a wreath of laurel was the prize for victory at Apollo's Pythian
    Games, held at Delphi, which may have included competitions in poetry;
    at Rome a slave carried a laurel crown over the head of a victorious gen-
    eral, a **triumphātor**, during his triumphal procession).
cingō, cingere, cīnxī, cīnctus, *to surround, encircle.*
volēns, volentis, *willing, gracious.*
    volēns: translate as an adverb.
Melpomenē [Gr., Μελπομένη, participle of μέλπομαι, *to sing, dance*],
    Melpomenēs, f., *Melpomene* (one of the nine Muses; she is at times associ-
    ated particularly with tragedy, but here she is invoked in a general way as
    the muse of Horace's lyrics; cf. *Odes* 1.24.3).
coma, -ae, f., *hair.*

14b   Sūme superbiam
15   quaesītam meritīs et mihi Delphicā
16   laurō cinge volēns, Melpomenē, comam.

Explorations

16.   What is meant by **superbiam** (14b)? What are the *meritorious achievements*
       (**meritīs**, 15)? Whose *meritorious achievements* are they?
17.   What negotiation takes place between the speaker and Melpomene in lines
       14b–16?

Odes 3.30

1   Exēgī monumentum aere perennius
2   rēgālīque sitū pȳramidum altius,
3   quod nōn imber edāx, nōn Aquilō impotēns
4   possit dīruere aut innumerābilis
5   annōrum seriēs et fuga temporum.
6   Nōn omnis moriar, multaque pars meī
7   vītābit Libitīnam: ūsque ego posterā
8   crēscam laude recēns, dum Capitōlium
9   scandet cum tacitā virgine pontifex.
10   Dīcar, quā violēns obstrepit Aufidus
11   et quā pauper aquae Daunus agrestium
12   rēgnāvit populōrum, ex humilī potēns
13   prīnceps Aeolium carmen ad Ītalōs
14   dēdūxisse modōs. Sūme superbiam
15   quaesītam meritīs et mihi Delphicā
16   laurō cinge volēns, Melpomenē, comam.

Discussion

1.   How is the poem structured?
2.   What significance might the following political and military associations of
      the words **prīnceps** (13), **dēdūxisse** (14a), and **laurō** (16a) have for the mean-
      ing of *Odes* 3.30?
      a.   The word **prīnceps**, in addition to being an adjective meaning *first* or a
            noun meaning *initiator, originator; master,* may also as a noun mean *lead-*

ing citizen. It was also the title adopted by Augustus as a political leader in Rome.

    b.   The verb **dēdūcere**, seen in the form **dēdūxisse** in line 14a, is sometimes used in the very specific sense of bringing a captive king or queen to Rome to be paraded in a triumphal procession, as it is in *Odes* 1.37.31–32.

    c.   The laurel with which the speaker asks to be wreathed is specifically described as Delphic (**Delphicā / laurō**, 15–16a), thus relating it to the cult of Apollo at Delphi and to the wreaths of laurel with which victors in the Pythian games and choral competitions held at Delphi were crowned. Wreaths of laurel were, however, also associated with victorious generals, **triumphātōrēs**, as they made their way up the **Capitōlium** in Rome to celebrate their triumphs.

3.   *Odes* 1.1 and 3.30 begin and end the collection of *Odes* that Horace published in 23 B.C. They are both in the same meter, and that meter is not used in any other poem in the collection. What echoes of *Odes* 1.1 can you find in *Odes* 3.30, and what other connections can you find between the two poems?

4.   *Odes* 2.20 comes at the end of the second book in the collection of odes published in 23 B.C. It is given with English translation in Passages for Comparison I following these questions. What are some of the main similarities and differences between *Odes* 2.20 and *Odes* 3.30?

5.   What similarities can you find between *Odes* 3.30 and the passages from earlier poetry quoted in Passages for Comparison II?

6.   What similarities can you find between *Odes* 3.30 and the passages from later poetry quoted in Passages for Comparison III?

Passages for Comparison

I.

Horace, *Odes* 2.20:

  1   Nōn ūsitātā nec tenuī ferar
  2   pennā biformis per liquidum aethera
  3   vātēs, neque in terrīs morābor
  4   longius, invidiāque maior

  5   urbīs relinquam. Nōn ego pauperum
  6   sanguis parentum, nōn ego quem vocās,
  7   dīlēcte Maecēnās, obībō
  8   nec Stygiā cohibēbor undā.

  9   Iam iam resīdunt crūribus asperae
10   pellēs, et album mūtor in ālitem
11   superne, nāscunturque lēvēs
12   per digitōs umerōsque plūmae.

13   Iam Daedaleō nōtior Īcarō
14   vīsam gementis lītora Bosphorī
15   Syrtīsque Gaetūlās canōrus
16   āles Hyperboreōsque campōs.

` 17 Mē Colchus et quī dissimulat metum
18 Mārsae cohortis Dācus et ultimī
19   nōscent Gelōnī, mē perītus
20   discet Hiber Rhodanīque pōtor.

21 Absint inānī fūnere nēniae
22 lūctūsque turpēs et querimōniae;
23   compēsce clāmōrem ac sepulcrī
24   mitte supervacuōs honōrēs.

I, a poet with two shapes, will be carried through the clear sky with a wing that is neither ordinary nor slender. I will not stay longer on earth, and, superior to envy, I will leave cities behind. I, the offspring of poor parents, will not die; I, whom you invite, dear Maecenas, will not be held in by the wave of the Styx. Now, even now, rough skin is settling on my legs, and above I am changing into a white bird. Light feathers are sprouting from my fingers and shoulders. As a singing bird more famous than Daedalus's son Icarus, I will soon see the shores of the mournful Bosphorus, the Gaetulian Syrtes, and the plains of the Hyperboreans. Colchis will come to know me and the Dacian who hides his fear of our Marsian cohorts, and the most remote Gelonians will come to know me as well. Learned Spaniards and men who drink the water of the Rhone will get to know me. Let dirges be absent and my funeral be empty, and let there be no unbecoming laments and complaints. Hold back your loud expressions of grief and forbear purposeless honoring of my tomb.

II.

Pindar's *Pythian* 6 was written on the occasion of the chariot victory of Xenocrates of Akragas, father of Thrasyboulos, in 490 B.C. The poet proclaims that a metaphorical treasure house of hymns has been built, the facade of which commemorates Xenocrates' victory (7–18):

A readily available treasure house of songs has been built in the richly-golden valley of Apollo. Neither the wintry thunder-storm coming from afar, the relentless army of the roaring cloud, nor the wind shall strike it with rubbish of all sorts and drive it into the depths of the sea. In the clear light of day, its facade announces your chariot's victory in the folding hills of Crisa, Thrasybulus, a victory shared by your father and all your family and honored by words of men.

Simonides 531 is a poem honoring Leonidas and the Spartans who fell at Thermopylae (480 B.C.) defending Greece against the Persians:

The fortune of those who perished at Thermopylae is glorious and beautiful is their doom. Their grave is an altar, and instead of weeping there is memory and lamentation over them takes the form of praise. Such a burial shroud neither dank decay nor all-consuming time shall cause to fade. This tomb of brave and noble men has taken the honor of Greece as its inhabitant. And Leonidas, king of Sparta, is the witness, who has left behind a great ornament of courage and everlasting fame.

The following epitaph was composed for himself by the early Roman poet Ennius (239–169 B.C.). In collections of the fragments of Ennius, this poem is given as lines 9–10 of his *Epigrams:*

9   Nēmō mē lacrimīs decoret nec fūnera flētū
10   faxit. Cūr? Volitō vīvus per ōra virum.

Let no one honor me with tears nor make a funeral for me with lamentation. Why? I fly, living, through the mouths of men.

Catullus 1.8–10; the speaker is giving his little papyrus roll of poems to his friend Cornelius Nepos:

8   Quārē habē tibi quidquid hoc libellī
9   quālecumque; quod, <ō> patrōna virgō,
10   plūs ūnō maneat perenne saeclō.

And so, take for yourself whatever kind of booklet this is and of whatever worth; and, o patroness maiden, may it last for more than one century.

Lucretius *De rerum natura* 5.306–11:

306   Dēnique nōn lapidēs quoque vincī cernis ab aevō,
307   nōn altās turrīs ruere et putrēscere saxa,
308   nōn dēlūbra deum simulācraque fessa fatīscī,
309   nec sānctum nūmen fātī protollere fīnīs
310   posse neque adversus nātūrae foedera nītī?
311   Dēnique nōn monimenta virum dīlāpsa vidēmus?

Finally, do you not see that stones too are conquered by the passage of time, that tall towers fall into ruin and that rocks disintegrate, that shrines of the gods and their statues wear out and crack open, and that the sacred power of the gods is able neither to prolong the ends of fate nor to struggle against the settled arrangements of nature? Finally do we not see that memorials of men have collapsed?

Vergil *Georgics* 3.8b–15:

8b   .   .   .   Temptanda via est, quā mē quoque possim
9   tollere humō victorque virum volitāre per ōra.
10   prīmus ego in patriam mēcum, modo vīta supersit,
11   Āoniō rediēns dēdūcam vertice Mūsās;
12   prīmus Idūmaeās referam tibi, Mantua, palmās
13   et viridī in campō templum dē marmore pōnam
14   propter aquam, tardīs ingēns ubi flexibus errat
15   Mincius et tenerā praetexit harundine rīpās.

I must attempt a path by which I, too, may raise myself from the earth and fly victorious on the lips of men. I, if life will only last, will be the first to return and bring the Muses with me in triumph to my country from their Aonian (= Greek) peak. I will be the first to bring back to you, O Mantua, palms of Idumaea,* and I will establish a temple of marble in the green meadow near the waterside, where the huge Mincius River wanders with its lazy bends and decorates the banks with tender reeds.

*palms of Idumaea: Idumaea = Judaea; branches of palm from the Orient were given as rewards for victory the Greek games.

III.

Propertius 3.1.1–12:

1   Callimachī Mānēs et Cōī sacra Philītae,
2   in vestrum, quaesō, mē sinite īre nemus.
3   Prīmus ego ingredior pūrō dē fonte sacerdōs
4   Ītala per Graiōs orgia ferre chorōs.
5   Dīcite, quō pariter carmen tenuāstis in antrō
6   quōve pede ingressī? Quamve bibistis aquam?
7   Āh valeat, Phoebum quīcumque morātur in armīs!
8   Exāctus tenuī pūmice versus eat,
9   quō mē Fāma levat terrā sublīmis, et ā mē
10   nāta corōnātīs Mūsa triumphat equīs,
11   et mēcum in currū parvī vectantur Amōrēs,
12   scrīptōrumque meās turba secūta rotās.

Spirit of Callimachus and sacred rites of Philitas of Cos, allow me, I pray you, to enter into your grove. I enter as the first priest, from the pure fountain, to bring Italian rites in Greek rhythms. Tell me, in what cave did you together make your song fine, or with what foot did you enter? And what water did you drink? Oh, get lost, whoever keeps Apollo delaying in arms! Let my verse go forth, polished with fine pumice stone; for by means of it lofty Fame raises me from the earth, and the Muse born from me triumphs with horses crowned [with laurel]; and little Cupids ride with me in the chariot, and a crowd of writers follows my wheels.

Vergil *Aeneid* 9.446–49; the poet apostrophizes Nisus and Euryalus, killed in a bold nighttime mission:

446   Fortūnātī ambō! Sī quid mea carmina possunt,
447   nūlla diēs umquam memorī vōs eximet aevō,
448   dum domus Aenēae Capitōlī immōbile saxum
449   accolet imperiumque pater Rōmānus habēbit.

Oh, how fortunate both are! If my poems can do anything at all, no day will ever forget your memory, as long as Aeneas' descendants dwell on the unshakeable rock of the Capitoline Hill and a Roman father holds power.

Ovid *Amores* 1.15.7b–8, 25–26, 31–33, and 41–42:

7b .   .   .   Mihi fāma perennis
8   quaeritur, in tōtō semper ut orbe canar.

25   Tītyrus et segetēs Aenēiaque arma legentur,
26   Rōma triumphātī dum caput orbis erit.

31   Ergō, cum silicēs, cum dēns patientis arātrī
32   dēpereant aevō, carmina morte carent.
33   Cēdant carminibus rēgēs rēgumque triumphī.

41   Ergō etiam cum mē suprēmus adēderit ignis,
42   vīvam, parsque meī multa superstes erit.

Fame for all time is what I seek, so that I might be sung always over all the earth.

Tityrus and the crops of the farm and Aeneas's arms will be read as long as Rome is the head of the world she has conquered.

Therefore, even though rocks and the tooth of the enduring plow may perish in time, poetry has no death. May kings and the triumphs of kings yield to poetry.

Therefore, even when the final fire has eaten me up, I shall live, and a great part of me will survive.

Ovid *Metamorphoses* 15.871–79:

871   Iamque opus exēgī, quod nec Iovis īra nec ignis
872   nec poterit ferrum nec edāx abolēre vetustās.
873   Cum volet, illa diēs, quae nīl nisi corporis huius
874   iūs habet, incertī spatium mihi fīniat aevī:
875   parte tamen meliōre meī super alta perennis
876   astra ferar, nōmenque erit indēlēbile nostrum,
877   quāque patet domitīs Rōmāna potentia terrīs,
878   ōre legar populī, perque omnia saecula fāmā,
879   sīquid habent vērī vātum praesāgia, vīvam.

I have now completed my work, which neither Jove's anger nor fire nor corrosive old age will be able to destroy. Whenever it wishes, let that day, which has claim over nothing but this body of mine, bring an end to the length of my uncertain lifespan; the better part of me will nevertheless last through the years and be borne above the stars on high, and my name will never be effaced. Wherever Roman power stretches over the lands of its dominions, I will be read with men's lips, and through all ages, if the predictions of bards have any truth, I will live in fame.

Ovid *Epistulae ex Ponto* 4.8.47–51a:

47   Carmine fit vīvāx virtūs, expersque sepulchrī
48   nōtitiam sērae posteritātis habet.

49 Tabida cōnsumit ferrum lapidemque vetustās,
50   nūllaque rēs maius tempore rōbur habet.
51 Scrīpta ferunt annōs.

Through poetry virtue comes to have a long life; having no part of the
tomb, it gains the notice of distant posterity. Decaying old age consumes
iron and stone, and nothing has greater strength than time. Writing lasts
through the years.

Shakespeare, Sonnet 55.1–2:

1 Not marble nor the gilded monuments
2 Of princes shall outlive this pow'rful rhyme.

Meter: Archilochian

1 **diffugiō** [**dis-**, *apart* + **fugiō, fugere, fūgī**, *to flee*], **diffugere, diffūgī**, *to scatter, flee apart.*
    diffūgēre: = **diffūgērunt**.
  nix, nivis, f., *snow.*
  grāmen, grāminis, n., *grass.*
  campīs: *to the fields*, poetic dative of the goal of motion (equivalent to **ad** + accusative), so also **arboribus** (2).
2 **coma, -ae**, f., *hair; leaf, foliage.*
  comae: nominative plural.
3 **mūtō, -āre, -āvī, -ātus**, *to change*; intransitive, *to undergo a change.*
  vicis (gen.), f., *turn; exchange*; pl., *successive forms/conditions.*
    mūtat terra vicēs: *the earth goes through her changes*; here **mūtat** is intransitive and **vicēs** is an example of an inner or cognate accusative.
  dēcrēscō [**dē-**, *down* + **crēscō, crēscere, crēvī, crētus**, *to grow, increase*], **dēcrēscere, dēcrēvī, dēcrētus**, *to subside, wane.*
4 **flūmen, flūminis**, n., *river.*

ODES 4.7

The Return of Spring

The coming of spring evokes in the poet thoughts of human mortality.

1 Diffūgēre nivēs, redeunt iam grāmina campīs
2   arboribusque comae;
3 mūtat terra vicēs, et dēcrēscentia rīpās
4   flūmina praetereunt;

continued

Explorations

1. Is an early or an advanced stage of spring described in this stanza?
2. In this first stanza there are four finite verbs and one participle. What is common about what they describe?
3. The first word of the poem, **Diffūgēre**, is a striking metaphor when paired with its subject, **nivēs**. What might be some of Horace's reasons for choosing this particular verb? What figure of speech is present here?
4. Identify an example of chiasmus and an example of rhyme. Note also where each of the four finite verbs comes in its clause. What is the effect of the placement of words in this stanza?

5 **Grātia, -ae**, f., *a Grace* (personification of beauty).
   cum ... geminīsque sorōribus: *with her two sisters*; there were traditionally three Graces.
   Nympha, -ae, f., *Nymph* (minor female deity of the natural world).
6 **nūdus, -a, -um**, *nude*.
   chorus [Gr., χορός], **-ī**, m., *group of dancers; dancing; a dance*.
7 **Immortālia**: Latin often uses the neuter plural substantive of an adjective where English would use an abstract noun; *immortal things = immortality*.
   nē, conj., *that ... not*.
   Immortālia nē spērēs: *that you should not hope for immortality*, indirect command after **monet** with the conjunction **nē** delayed.
   annus, -ī, m., *year*; here, *the changing seasons*.
   almus, -a, -um, *nourishing, nurturing*.
8 **quae**: the antecedent is **hōra**.
   hōra: the antecedent of **quae** is embedded in the relative clause; **hōra** is a second subject of **monet** (7b) along with **annus**.

5 Grātia cum Nymphīs geminīsque sorōribus audet
6   dūcere nūda chorōs.
7 Immortālia nē spērēs, monet annus et almum
8   quae rapit hōra diem:

continued

Explorations

5. What do the figures of the Graces and the Nymphs add to the description of
    spring? What is implied by the words **audet** (5) and **nūda** (6)?
6. What does Horace abruptly introduce in lines 7–8?
7. Consider the word order of **Immortālia nē spērēs, monet annus** and of **al-
    mum / quae rapit hōra diem**. How does the placement of words add em-
    phasis? How does it reinforce the point Horace is making?
8. With the phrase **almum / <u>quae rapit hōra diem</u>** Horace is alluding to one of
    his own most famous poetic statements: **Dum loquimur, fūgerit invida /
    aetās: <u>carpe diem</u>, quam minimum crēdula posterō** (*Odes* 1.11.7b–8).
    What is the main difference between these two expressions? What might be
    some possible reasons for the change? Where else in the first two stanzas of
    this poem is there an echo of the same lines from *Odes* 1.11?

"Mercury and the Three Graces"
Detail of "La Primavera"
Sandro Botticelli (1444–1510)
Uffizi, Florence, Italy

9   **frīgus, frīgoris**, n., *cold, chill.*
    mītēscō [**mītis, -is, -e**, *mild, soft, ripe*], **mītēscere**, *to soften; to ripen; to grow mild.*
    Zephyrus, -ī, m., *Zephyr* (the west wind).
        Zephyrīs: *by the west winds, on account of the west winds,* ablative of means or cause (as if the verb were passive).
    vēr, vēris, n., *spring.*
    prōterō [**prō-**, *forward* + **terō, terere, trīvī, trītus**, *to rub; to tread; to wear away*], **prōterere, prōtrīvī, prōtrītus**, *to trample down; to tread on the heels of.*
        prōterit: in addition to the idea of treading on the heels of X, the verb may suggest the threashing of grain or a military rout.
10 **intereō** [**inter-**, *between* + **eō, īre, iī** or **īvī, itūrus**, *to go*], **interīre, interiī, interitūrus**, *to die.*
        interitūra: *destined to die, which will die,* future active participle.
    simul: = **simul ac**, *as soon as.*
11 **pōmifer** [possibly a Horatian coinage; **pōmum, -ī**, n., *apple, fruit* + **ferō, ferre, tulī, lātus**, *to bring, bear*], **pōmifera, pōmiferum** *fruit-bringing, fruitful.*
    Autumnus, -ī, m., *Autumn.*
    frūx, frūgis, f., *fruit, produce, crop.*
    effūderit: *will have poured out,* suggesting the image of the cornucopia; the word may also mean *expend, use up.*
    mox: in dactylic hexameter an accented monosyllable at the end of a line is very emphatic.
12 **brūma** [contraction of **brevissima** or **brevūma**, superlative of **brevis, -is, -e**, *short*], **-ae**, f., *the shortest day of the year, the winter solstice;* by metonymy, *winter.*
    recurrō [**re-**, *back* + **currō, currere, cucurrī, cursūrus**, *to run*] **recurrere, recurrī, recursūrus**, *to run back.*
    iners [**in-**, *without* + **ars, artis**, f., *skill, competence*], **inertis**, *lazy; sluggish.*
        recurrit iners: *comes running back motionless,* paradox or oxymoron, an example of what Horace in his *Ars poetica* calls **callida iūnctūra**, *a clever juxtaposition.*

9 frīgora mītēscunt Zephyrīs, vēr prōterit aestās
10   interitūra simul
11 pōmifer Autumnus frūgēs effūderit, et mox
12   brūma recurrit iners.

continued

Explorations

9. What is described in this third stanza (9–12)? How does what is described here relate to the first two stanzas?
10. Identify examples of personification in these lines. Are there others in the preceding lines?
11. What are the overriding characteristics of the depiction of nature in the first twelve lines of this poem?
12. What is significant about the placement of words in line 9?
13. Note examples of enjambment and effective placement of words, particularly at the beginnings and ends of lines, in this stanza. How is the placement of **iners** in line 12 next to **recurrit** both paradoxical and appropriate?
14. Consider the etymological meaning of the word **brūma** (12). Why is this an appropriate word for "winter" here?

13 **damnum, -ī,** n., *damage; loss.*

reparō [**re-,** *back, again, in place of* + **parō, -āre, -āvī, -ātus,** *to prepare; to arrange; to acquire*], **-āre, -āvī, -ātus,** *to obtain in exchange (for); to get again, recover.*

> **Damna . . . reparant:** *recover their losses;* the metaphor is drawn from business and accounting, while there are also overtones of the technical language of astronomy, e.g., of the waning of the moon.

caelestis [**caelum, -ī,** n., *sky, heaven*], **-is, -e,** *heavenly.*

lūnae: *moons* or *months.*

14 **nōs:** adversative asyndeton. Note that this line is at the center of the twenty-eight-line poem.

dēcidō [**dē-,** *down* + **cadō, cadere, cecidī, cāsūrus,** *to fall*], **dēcidere, dēcidī,** *to fall down.*

> **dēcidimus:** a euphemism for dying; the word may also suggest processes of the natural world, such as leaves falling from trees and the setting of the sun.

15 **quō,** adv., *to where.*

pater Aenēās: *father Aeneas* (the Trojan son of Anchises and Venus, who was the ancestor of the Romans). In place of **pater** many manuscripts have **pius,** *pious.* The words **pater Aenēās** allude to Vergil's *Aeneid* (e.g., 1.699), published approximately four years before this poem. The word **pius** is the distinctive epithet for Aeneas in Vergil's poem, and some editors prefer to print it here because it makes the connection to the *Aeneid* even stronger.

Tullus, -ī, m., *Tullus Hostilius* (legendary third king of Rome; Livy 1.31.1, comments on the great glory and prosperity of Rome under his rule).

Ancus, -ī, m., *Ancus Marcius* (legendary fourth king of Rome noted for his goodness; Ennius calls him **bonus Ancus,** *Annales* 154, as does Lucretius *De rerum natura* 3.1025).

16 **pulvis et umbra:** i.e., what becomes of the physical body after death and the insubstantial ghost that goes to the underworld.

13   Damna tamen celerēs reparant caelestia lūnae:
14   nōs ubi dēcidimus
15   quō pater Aenēās, quō Tullus dīves et Ancus,
16   pulvis et umbra sumus.

continued

Explorations

15.   How does the epithet **celerēs** (13) relate to the theme of the preceding
      stanza?
16.   What new theme is introduced in this stanza? What role does the adversa-
      tive asyndeton in line 14 (**nōs**) play in reinforcing the new theme? How do
      the personification of nature earlier in the poem and the word **interitūra** (10)
      ironically anticipate the new theme?
17.   Why are legendary figures chosen as examples in line 15? What individual
      characteristics of Aeneas and Tullus are introduced? What do all these fig-
      ures have in common? What is the tone of the line?

17   **an**, conj., introducing an indirect question, *whether.*
      adiciō [**ad-**, *to, toward* + **iaciō, iacere, iēcī, iactus**, *to throw*], **adicere, adiēcī,**
         adiectus, *to throw to, put to; to put in addition, add.*
         adiciant: pronounced **adjiciant**, making the first syllable long.
      hodiernus [**hodiē**, adv., *today*], **-a, -um**, *of today, today's.*
      crāstinus [**crās**, adv., *tomorrow*], **-a, -um**, *of tomorrow, tomorrow's.*
      summa, -ae, f., *amount; total, sum.*
18   **superus, -a, -um**, *above.*
19   **avidus, -a, -um**, *greedy.*
         manūs avidās . . . hērēdis: *the greedy hands of your heir*, metonymy with a
            slight transferred epithet. With the theme of the heir here, compare
            Odes 2.3.19b–20 and 2.14.25.
      fugiō, fugere, fūgī, *to flee;* here transitive, *to flee from, escape.*
      amīcus, -a, -um, *friendly, dear;* here, *one's own.*
         amīcō: the adjective is used here in imitation of the Greek adjective φίλος,
            literally, *dear*, but by extension, *one's own.* Cf. numerous Homeric
            phrases such as φίλον ἦτορ, *his own heart* (*Iliad* 9.705).
20   **dederīs**: future perfect indicative second person singular. In the second per-
            son singular the quantity of the last syllable was originally long in the per-
            fect subjunctive and short in the future perfect indicative, but the two ter-
            minations were used interchangeably by the poets.
      animus, -ī, m., *mind; heart, spirit; self.*
         amīcō (19b) **/ . . . animō** (20), probably dative, *to your dear/your own self.*

17   Quis scit an adiciant hodiernae crāstina summae
18   tempora dī superī?
19   Cūncta manūs avidās fugient hērēdis, amīcō
20   quae dederīs animō.

continued

Explorations

18.   What common Horatian theme is implied in lines 17–20?
19.   Why is mention of an *heir* (**hērēdis**, 19a) appropriate in a poem dealing with
      mortality? How is what is said here similar to the advice implicitly given to
      Postumus in *Odes* 2.14.21–28 quoted below?

Passage for Comparison

Odes 2.14.21–28:

21   linquenda tellūs et domus et placēns
22   uxor, neque hārum quās colis arborum
23   tē praeter invīsās cupressōs
24   ūlla brevem dominum sequētur:

25   absūmet hērēs Caecuba dignior
26   servāta centum clāvibus et merō
27   tinget pavīmentum superbō,
28   pontificum potiōre cēnīs.

21 **Cum semel**: *When once.*
   occidō [**ob-**, *in front of* + **cadō, cadere, cecidī, cāsūrus,** *to fall*], **occidere, oc-
   cidī, occāsūrus,** *to fall; to perish, die.*
      occiderīs: see above on **dederīs** (20).
   et dē tē: note the three heavy monosyllables following the caesura.
   splendidus, -a, -um, *splendid; distinguished; brilliant.*
   Mīnōs [Gr., Μίνως], **Mīnōis,** m., *Minos* (legendary king of Crete who was a
      favorite of Zeus and after death became, along with Aeacus and
      Rhadamanthus, a judge in the underworld).
22 **arbitrium, -ī,** n., *judgment.*
   arbitria: plural for singular.
23 **Torquātus, -ī,** m., *Torquatus* (perhaps a Manlius Torquatus, but not surely
      identifiable; a Torquatus is also addressed by Horace at *Epistles* 1.5.3; in that
      poem as in this one, it is indicated that he practices law; perhaps this is rea-
      son to believe that the two are the same person).
   genus, generis, n., *race; high birth.*
      genus: if the individual here is Manlius Torquatus, it may be relevant that
         the Manlii Torquati were among the most grand of Roman aristocratic
         families; Livy (7.9–10) tells the story of how their ancestor earned his
         cognomen by defeating a massive Gaul in battle and taking his golden
         neck-collar, called a **torquis**.
   fācundia, -ae, f., *eloquence.*
   tē: for the final monosyllable, see above on **mox** (11).
24 **restituō** [**re-**, *back* + **statuō, statuere, statuī, statūtus,** *to cause to stand, set up,
      fix*], **restituere, restituī, restitūtus,** *to set up again, replace, restore.*
   pietās, pietātis, f., *dutifulness, devotion; piety* (respect in relationships with
      human beings and with gods.).

21   Cum semel occiderīs et dē tē splendida Mīnōs
22   fēcerit arbitria,
23   nōn, Torquāte, genus, nōn tē fācundia, nōn tē
24   restituet pietās;

continued

Explorations

20.   What earlier verb does **occiderīs** (21) recall in sense?
21.   What contrast is implied by the epithet **splendida** (21)?
22.   What poetic devices are present in lines 23–24 and why are they effective? What does the sentence emphasize?
23.   From lines 23–24 what can you deduce about Torquatus's career? In the light of the rest of the poem, why might Horace have singled out the qualities he mentions here?
24.   Consider **restituet** in line 24. Identify three other verbs compounded with **re-** in the preceding stanzas. What do the other three verbs have in common? How is the use of **restituet** different? Why might Horace have arranged this sequence in this way?

Passage for Comparison

With the theme of **pietās** in lines 23–24 above, compare *Odes* 2.14.1–4:

1   Ēheu fugācēs, Postume, Postume,
2   lābuntur annī nec pietās moram
3   rūgīs et īnstantī senectae
4   adferet indomitaeque mortī.

25 **īnfernus, -a, -um**, *of the underworld.*
neque enim: *for neither.*
tenebrae, -ārum, f., *shadows, twilight, darkness.*
 tenebrīs: ablative of separation, *from the darkness of the underworld*, with
 līberat.
Diāna, -ae, f., *Diana* (the Greek Artemis; daughter of Jupiter, virgin goddess
 of hunting and the wild countryside).
pudīcus, -a, -um, *chaste.*
 pudīcum: cf. the position in the line of the parallel **cārō** (27).
26 **līberat**: present tense, cf. **valet** (27); the present tense implies that the attempts of Diana and Theseus to rescue their beloveds from the underworld
 are ongoing.
Hippolytus, -ī, m., *Hippolytus* (the son of Theseus and a devotee of Diana/
 Artemis who preferred hunting in the woods to relationships with women.
 Horace follows the Greek version of the myth represented by Euripides'
 tragedy *Hippolytus*. Hippolytus's death was caused by the bitterness of his
 stepmother Phaedra, whose advances, under the influence of Venus/
 Aphrodite, toward him he scorned. Vergil and Ovid, however, follow a
 different version of Hippolytus's story in which he is brought back to life
 by Diana, to live in her sacred grove at Aricia in Italy under the name
 Virbius: *Aeneid* 7.761–77; *Metamorphoses* 15.533–46.
27 **Lēthaeus [Lēthē** (Gr., λήθη, *forgetting; forgetfulness*), **Lēthēs**, f., *Lethe* (the river
 of forgetfulness in the underworld)], **-a, -um** *Lethean* (i.e., having to do with
 the underworld, death, and oblivion).
 Lēthaea: Quinn (1980, p. 313) comments: "The chains are called 'Lethaea'
 to conjure up a picture of Pirithoos chained by the River of Forgetfulness: he has forgotten his friend; Theseus still remembers."
valet: + infin., *is strong enough* (to).
Thēseus, -ī, m., *Theseus* (legendary king of Athens).
 Thēseus: the letters *eu* are pronounced as one syllable by synizesis.
abrumpō [ab-, *away* + **rumpō, rumpere, rūpī, ruptus**, *to break, burst*],
 abrumpere, abrūpī, abruptus, *to break away, break off.*
28 **vinculum [vinciō, vincīre, vīnxī, vīnctus**, *to bind*], **-ī**, n., *a means of binding,*
 fetter.
Pīrithous [also spelled Pērithous], -ī, m., *Pirithous* (legendary king of the
 Lapiths; a drunken disturbance at his wedding led to the fight of the
 Lapiths and Centaurs, a favorite subject of Greek art).
 cārō (27) / ... **Pīrithoō**: dative of separation or dative of advantage.
 Thēseus (27) ... / ... **Pīrithoō**: the two friends Theseus and Pirithous
 journeyed to the underworld to kidnap Persephone and were both
 condemned to eternal imprisonment there. Theseus, but not Pirithous, was later freed by Hercules. In some versions Pirithous too
 was rescued.

25 īnfernīs neque enim tenebrīs Dīāna pudīcum
26   līberat Hippolytum,
27 nec Lēthaea valet Thēseus abrumpere cārō
28   vincula Pīrithoō.

Explorations

25. What is the general point made by the mythological examples in lines 25–28? What do Hippolytus and Pirithous have in common? How do these examples relate to those in line 15?

Odes 4.7

1 Diffūgēre nivēs, redeunt iam grāmina campīs
2   arboribusque comae;
3 mūtat terra vicēs, et dēcrēscentia rīpās
4   flūmina praetereunt;

5 Grātia cum Nymphīs geminīsque sorōribus audet
6   dūcere nūda chorōs.
7 Immortālia nē spērēs, monet annus et almum
8   quae rapit hōra diem:

9 frīgora mītēscunt Zephyrīs, vēr prōterit aestās
10   interitūra simul
11 pōmifer Autumnus frūgēs effūderit, et mox
12   brūma recurrit iners.

13 Damna tamen celerēs reparant caelestia lūnae:
14   nōs ubi dēcidimus
15 quō pater Aenēās, quō Tullus dīves et Ancus,
16   pulvis et umbra sumus.

17 Quis scit an adiciant hodiernae crāstina summae
18   tempora dī superī?
19 Cūncta manūs avidās fugient hērēdis, amīcō
20   quae dederīs animō.

21 Cum semel occiderīs et dē tē splendida Mīnōs
22   fēcerit arbitria,
23 nōn, Torquāte, genus, nōn tē fācundia, nōn tē
24   restituet pietās;

25 īnfernīs neque enim tenebrīs Dīāna pudīcum
26   līberat Hippolytum,
27 nec Lēthaea valet Thēseus abrumpere cārō
28   vincula Pīrithoō.

Discussion

1. How is this ode structured?
    a. Can the poem be divided into sections, and, if so, where are the divisions?
    b. What particular role does the central stanza (13–16), the fourth of seven, play in the structure of the poem?
    c. In the final lines we are far from the opening vision of springtime. How does the final stanza bring the poem to an appropriate conclusion? What oppositions can you find between the closing stanzas and the opening ones?
2. The poem revolves around a fundamental contrast between the life of nature and the life of human beings.
    a. What are the distinguishing qualities of the two types of life?
    b. How then does the poem represent a blending of the two by describing one in terms of the other?
    c. What overall conclusion does the poem draw concerning the world of nature and the life of humans?
3. Compare the ode, and particularly lines 13–24, with Catullus 5, quoted in Passages for Comparison I following these questions.
    a. What specific words, phrases, effects, and ideas does Horace's poem have in common with that of Catullus?
    b. What are the differences between the points of view of the two poems?
4. a. Keeping in mind the depiction of human life and the life of nature in *Odes* 4.7, consider the simile from Homer *Iliad* 6.146–49 quoted in Passages for Comparison II following these questions. How does the sense of Homer's simile relate to Horace's poem?
    b. Consider also a related passage in Vergil *Aeneid* 6.305–12, quoted in Passages for Comparison II following these questions. What are the similarities and differences between this passage, Homer's simile, and Horace's poem?
5. Compare *Odes* 4.7 with A. E. Housman's translation of the poem, quoted in Passages for Comparison III following these questions.

Passages for Comparison

I.

Catullus 5:

1   Vīvāmus, mea Lesbia, atque amēmus,
2   rūmōrēsque senum sevēriōrum
3   omnēs ūnius aestimēmus assis!
4   Sōlēs occidere et redīre possunt:
5   nōbīs cum semel occidit brevis lūx,
6   nox est perpetua ūna dormienda.
7   Dā mī bāsia mīlle, deinde centum,
8   dein mīlle altera, dein secunda centum,

9   deinde ūsque altera mīlle, deinde centum.
10   Dein, cum mīlia multa fēcerīmus,
11   conturbābimus illa, nē sciāmus,
12   aut nē quis malus invidēre possit,
13   cum tantum sciat esse bāsiōrum.

> Let us live, my Lesbia, and let us love, and let us value all the gossip of
> those rather stern old men as worth just one cent. Suns can set and rise
> again; whenever [our] brief light has once set, one uninterrupted night
> must be slept by us. Give me a thousand kisses, then a hundred, then a
> second thousand, then a second hundred, then yet another thousand,
> then a hundred. Then, when we will have reached many thousands, we
> will confound them, so that we may not know [how many they are], or
> some evil person may not be able to cast a spell on us, once he knows
> there to be so great a number of kisses.

II.

Homer *Iliad* 6.146–49; the lines come from a conversation on the battlefield between
two opposing warriors:

> Such as the generations of leaves, so also are the generations of men. For the
> wind scatters the leaves to the ground, but wood grows and blooms, and the
> season of spring returns. So the generations of men: one grows, another dies off.

Vergil *Aeneid* 6.305–12:

305   Hūc omnis turba ad rīpās effūsa ruēbat,
306   mātrēs atque virī, dēfūnctaque corpora vītā
307   magnanimum hērōum, puerī innuptaeque puellae
308   impositīque rogīs iuvenēs ante ōra parentum:
309   quam multa in silvīs autumnī frīgore prīmō
310   lāpsa cadunt folia, aut ad terram gurgite ab altō
311   quam multae glomerantur avēs, ubi frīgidus annus
312   trāns pontum fugat et terrīs immittit aprīcīs.

> And here towards the banks the whole crowd flowed and rushed, moth-
> ers and men and the bodies of great-hearted heroes having fulfilled life,
> boys and unmarried girls, young men placed on their biers in front of
> their parents' faces: as many as the leaves that drop and fall in the forests
> at the first frost of autumn, or as many as the birds that gather to land from
> the deep sea when the cold season chases them over the ocean and sends
> them to sunny lands.

III.

A. E. Housman, the famous classicist and poet of the early twentieth century, pronounced *Odes* 4.7 "the most beautiful poem in ancient literature." He also at-
tempted his own version of the poem, the only Horatian ode he translated:

The snows are fled away, leaves on the shaws
And grasses in the mead renew their birth,
The river to the river-bed withdraws,
And altered is the fashion of the earth.

The Nymphs and the Graces three put off their fear
And unapparelled in the woodland play.
The swift hour and the brief prime of the year
Say to the soul, *Thou wast not born for aye.*

Thaw follows frost, hard on the heel of spring
Treads summer sure to die, for hard on hers
Comes autumn, with his apples scattering;
Then back to wintertide, when nothing stirs.

But oh, whate'er the sky-led seasons mar,
Moon upon moon rebuilds it with her beams;
Come *we* where Tullus and where Ancus are,
And good Aeneas, we are dust and dreams.

Torquatus, if the gods in heaven shall add
The morrow to the day, what tongue has told?
Feast then thy heart, for what thy heart has had
The fingers of no heir will ever hold.

When thou descendest once the shades among,
The stern assize and equal judgment o'er,
Not thy long lineage nor thy golden tongue,
No, nor thy righteousness shall friend thee more.

Night holds Hippolytus the pure of stain,
Diana steads him nothing, he must stay;
And Theseus leaves Pirithous in the chain
The love of comrades cannot take away.

Roman Satire

An Introduction to *Satires* 1.9

With *Satires* 1.9, the last poem in this collection, there is a change of genre, from lyric to satire. The most immediate difference is the meter: the *Satires* are written in dactylic hexameter, the meter of epic and other narrative poetic genres, rather than the lyric meters of the *Odes*. In comparison to the *Odes*, Horace's *Satires* are less highly formalized and more casual, even conversational, in presentation. The title of the work we refer to as the *Satires* was in Latin **Sermōnēs,** meaning *conversations, talks,* or *chit-chat.* The first book of Horace's *Satires*, from which *Satires* 1.9 is drawn, was published probably in 35 B.C. and was Horace's first work of poetry. It contained ten "conversations," ranging in topic from common morality to Horace's life story and his relationship with Maecenas to current events to humorous anecdotes. This was followed by a second collection of eight poems in 30 B.C. Whereas the *Odes* often imitate singing in the private setting of a symposium, the *Satires* evoke settings that are both more public and more casual, such as the chance encounter in the forum that is the subject of *Satires* 1.9. Where the *Odes* hearken back to the archaic Greek poetic traditions of Sappho and Alcaeus and others, the *Satires* look to more recent years and to Roman figures, while also paying homage to a type of conversational, street-corner philosophy from the Hellenistic Greek world known as diatribe. Roman satire, and *Satires* 1.9 in particular, also has much in common with drama, especially Roman comedy, in its representation of direct speech and its use of often casually idiomatic language.

Horace's most important predecessor in writing verse satire was Gaius Lucilius. Writing in roughly the middle of the second century B.C., Lucilius was himself a member of the Roman elite. He was an equestrian but had relatives who were senators, and he mingled directly with the politically powerful of his day. He used the venue of verse satire to address current events, to engage in criticism of other poets and other poetic genres, and to attack and ridicule his personal enemies. In his *Satires*, Horace is very interested in both acknowledging his literary debts to Lucilius (*Satires* 1.9, for instance, both begins and ends with verbal reminiscences of Lucilius's poems) and clarifying how his own brand of satire is different. Horace, for one thing, considers himself a much more refined poetic craftsman than Lucilius had been, which is in keeping with the general trend in Roman poetry since the time of Catullus and the neoterics towards ever greater attention to fine technique. Horace's satires are also different in spirit from Lucilius's. Lucilius was notorious as an outspoken and even excessively harsh critic of his Roman contemporaries. Horace's criticisms of society and of individuals in his *Satires* are restrained and mild by comparison. It is more often than not the case in Horace's *Satires* that the poet himself, or his "persona" who speaks within the poem, is the figure whose moral shortcomings, lack of social grace, or even foolishness are held up for humorous criticism. While "satire" in the modern sense of the word as humorous criticism of society or individuals thus does have a place in Horace's *Satires*, it is not the only, or even the primary, concern. The first and most important subject of Horace's *Satires* is the poet's presentation of himself.

The word "satire" derives from the Latin word **satira**, which may be related to the Latin noun **satura** (feminine of the adjective **satur, satura, saturum**, *full of food, stuffed; rich*). The noun **satura** was used inter alia of a dish containing various igredients such as dried grapes, barley-meal, edible pine-cone seeds, honey, and wine. If the noun **satira** is related to the noun **satura**, it would reflect the grab-bag style of subject matter, tone, and even metrical form in the early Roman satirists.

In addition to Horace and Lucilius, other Roman authors of satire include Ennius (239–169 B.C.), the great national poet who is the first known author of **satirae**, but whose more lasting influence was as a writer of epic and drama, and Varro (116–27 B.C.), whose style of satire (called "Menippean") blends poetry and prose. In the years after Horace, the tradition of verse satire was notably continued by Persius (A.D. 34–64), whose disgusted denunciations of Roman society and literature were written under the emperor Nero, and, most importantly, by Juvenal, who wrote his satires at the end of the first century and beginning of the second century A.D. and filled them with angry denunciations of foreigners, the rich, patrons and clients, men and women, that is, just about everybody in Roman society.

The literary critic Quintilian, writing around A.D. 90, famously said **satira quidem tōta nostra est**, *satire, at least, is entirely ours* (*Institutio oratoria* 10.1.93). For Quintilian, satire was *entirely ours* in the sense that it was not derived, like other literary genres at Rome, from Greek models. This might be overstated, since there are in fact important Greek precedents for many aspects of Roman satire, but still at Rome satire was always identified as a national product, part of a native tradition of free speech and humorous verses going back to the earliest days of the Republic.

Horace's *Satires* 1.9 is a good introduction to the genre. It well demonstrates Horace's humor, his mild-mannered social commentary, and his deft touch with turning a critical eye on himself and his own foibles. Written in a crucial period in Roman history, between the battles of Philippi and Actium, i.e., before the *Odes*, it also shows the way in which Horace observes the workings of high Roman society (in this case Maecenas and his circle of literary associates) as an insider, but also manages to cultivate a sense of personal distance from the controversies and difficulties of the day.

Meter: Dactylic hexameter

1   **Ībam forte viā Sacrā**: these words echo phrases in two poems of Lucilius,
     Horace's Roman predecessor in writing verse satire, fragments 258 and
     559, **Ībat forte domum** and **Ībat forte ariēs** (*ram*). The narrator in *Satires*
     1.9 uses the first person, where Lucilius used the third. By this we are per-
     haps alerted to a fictional element in the narrator's presentation of himself
     here. He is telling a tale in the Lucilian manner, but about himself.
          viā Sacrā: *along the Sacred Way*, ablative of route, a type of ablative of
          means. The Sacred Way was the oldest street in Rome and the main
          route through the **Forum Rōmānum**; its name probably derives from
          the presence on this street of many of the most sacred buildings of the
          Roman state religion such as the temple of Vesta.
     sīcut, adv., *just as, as.*
          sīcut . . . mōs: take with both the preceding and the following clauses.
2   **nescio quis, nescio quid**, *someone; something.*
     meditor, -ārī, -ātus sum, *to ponder; to muse on.*
     nūgae, -ārum, f., *nonsense; trifles* (Catullus uses the word **nūgās** of his verse
          in line 4 of his poem 1).
          nūgārum: partitive genitive dependent on **nescio quid**.
     tōtus: *totally [absorbed].*
4   **"Quid agis . . . ?"**: a casual greeting, *How are you doing?*
     dulcis, -is, -e, *sweet.*
          dulcissime rērum: an exaggeratedly friendly form of address; translate
          [my] dearest fellow in the world or the like.
               rērum: partitive genitive.
          "Quid . . . rērum?": understand a verb meaning *he asks.*
5   **ut nunc est**: *as things are at present*; perhaps ironic, "until I met you."
     inquam, *I say*, defective verb, used to introduce a quotation and always
          placed after one or more words of the quotation.
     cupiō omnia quae vīs: *I desire everything that you wish*, a polite formula not
          intended by the speaker to carry literal force.
6   **adsector** [ad-, *toward* + **sequor, sequī, secūtus sum**, *to follow*, + **-tor**, itera-
          tive suffix], **-ārī, -ātus sum**, *to wait upon, escort; to follow closely.*
          Cum adsectārētur: note the five long/heavy syllables.
     Num quid: = **Num aliquid.**
          "Num quid vīs?": *"You don't want anything, do you?"* This was said when
          taking leave of someone and was not necessarily to be taken literally.
     occupō [ob-, *in front of* + **capiō, capere, cēpī, captus**, *to take*], **-āre, -āvī**,
          -ātus, *to take beforehand; to do something before someone else, to anticipate; to get
          the jump on.*
               occupō: *I get the jump on [him]*; the narrator slips in an expression of
               leave-taking in order, he hopes, to forestall the pest from continuing
               the conversation.

Satires 1.9

The Poet's Encounter with a Pest

Misplaced poetic ambitions and too much eagerness to join the circle of Maecenas represent the wrong way to advance in society.

1 Ībam forte viā Sacrā, sīcut meus est mōs,
2 nescio quid meditāns nūgārum, tōtus in illīs.
3 Accurrit quīdam nōtus mihi nōmine tantum,
4 arreptāque manū, "Quid agis, dulcissime rērum?"
5 "Suāviter, ut nunc est," inquam, "et cupiō omnia quae vīs."
6 Cum adsectārētur, "Num quid vīs?" occupō. At ille

continued

Explorations

1. How does the narrator present himself in the first two lines? What interests him and what does not?
2. In lines 3–4, the narrator meets another person. Who is it? How is this figure's behavior characterized? What specific Latin words contribute to this characterization?

7   **nōscō, nōscere, nōvī, nōtus**, *to get to know.*
       Nōris: syncope, = **Nōveris**, perfect subjunctive in an optative (wish) clause
          introduced by an understood **velim ut** in response to **"Num quid vīs?"**
          (6a); *[Yes, I would like] you to get to know me* [lit., *us*]. The pest takes **"Num**
          quid vīs?" literally and not as a formula of leave-taking.
       inquit: cf. **inquam** (5); third person singular, present, *he says.*
       doctus, -a, -um, *learned* (a favored epithet for poets, especially those who
          identified with the artistic values of Catullus and his neoteric peers; cf.
          Odes 1.1.29 and Catullus 1.6–7); as substantive, *a literary man, a poet.*
          nōs . . . doctī sumus: plural used pompously for the singular.
       "Plūris / . . . eris" (8a): *You will be of greater value to me because of this*, geni-
          tive of value, with **hōc** (8a) as causal ablative.
8   **Miserē**: here and in line 14, colloquial, *desperately.*
9   **īre . . . cōnsistere . . . / dīcere** (10): historical infinitives, conveying a sense
       of lively, speedy narration; translate as past tense with subject "I."
       modo, adv., *only; at one point.*
       ōcius, comparative adv., of which no positive degree form was in use, *more*
          quickly.
       auris, auris, f., *ear.*
10   **nescio quid**: see line 2.
       puerō: the narrator's slave, who accompanies him on his morning errands;
          possessive dative with **aurem** (9) or indirect object with **dīcere.**
       sūdor, sūdōris, m., *sweat.*
       īmus, -a, -um, *the lowest*; when used attributively (as here), *the lowest point of,*
          the bottom of.
11   **tālus, -ī**, m., *ankle, anklebone; heel.*
       ad īmōs (10) **/ . . . tālōs**: *to the bottoms of my feet.*
       Bōlānus, -ī, m., *Bolanus* (a Roman name; not a known person).
       "Ō tē, Bōlāne . . . ": apostrophe.
       cerebrum, -ī, n., *brain*; metaphorically, *anger, hot temper.*
       cerebrī: the genitive of respect defines the sphere in which an adjective, in
          this case **fēlīcem** (12), is in force.
          "tē . . . cerebrī / fēlīcem!" (12): exclamatory accusative, *[how] lucky*
             you [are] in your hot temper! or *blessed with a hot temper!*
12   **āiō**, defective verb, *to say.*
       āiēbam: pronounce as three syllables, = **ājēbam**; imperfect indicative, first
          person singular, *I was saying.*
       tacitus: adverbial, *silently, under my breath.* Note that the pest does not actu-
          ally hear the narrator's exclamation in praise of Bolanus and his hot tem-
          per.
       cum: *while* or *since*, with the imperfect subjunctives in the next line.
       quīlibet, quaelibet, quodlibet or **quidlibet**, *whoever, whatever; whoever you*
          like, whatever you like; someone or other, something or other.

7   "Nōris nōs," inquit; "doctī sumus." Hīc ego, "Plūris
8   hōc," inquam, "mihi eris." Miserē discēdere quaerēns,
9   īre modo ōcius, interdum cōnsistere, in aurem
10   dīcere nescio quid puerō, cum sūdor ad īmōs
11   mānāret tālōs. "Ō tē, Bōlāne, cerebrī
12   fēlīcem!" āiēbam tacitus, cum quidlibet ille

continued

Explorations

3. How is the characterization of the narrator and the pest further developed in lines 5-8a?
4. In lines 8b-11a, how does the narrator react to the pest's words and behavior?
5. In light of the situation, why does the narrator praise Bolanus as *blessed with a hot temper* (11b–12a)?

13 **garriō, -īre**, *to chatter.*
vīcus, -ī, m., *street with houses, neighborhood.*
garrīret, vīcōs, urbem laudāret: note the two examples of asyndeton.
15 **iamdūdum**, adv., *for a long time now.*
videō: Latin requires a present tense verb with adverbs such as **iamdūdum**, where English uses a perfect tense; translate *I have seen.* In translation, supply *it* as object of **videō**.
nīl agis: *it's no use*, literally, *you're accomplishing nothing.*
ūsque, adv., *all the way.*
tenēbō: *I will hold [to my course], persevere.*
16 **persequar**: supply **tē**.
hinc, adv., *hence, from here.*
Nīl opus est: *There is no need for*, here followed by an accusative + infinitive construction.
17 **circumagō [circum-**, *around* + **agō, agere, ēgī, āctus**, *to lead*], **circumagere, circumēgī, circumāctus**, *to lead around.*
volo: the final syllable is short by "iambic shortening," i.e., when the second syllable of an iambic word (˘ -) is shortened. This metrical phenomenon is common in Roman comedy.
vīsō, vīsere, vīsī, vīsus, *to go to see; to visit* (often of calling on a sick person).
18 **cubō, cubāre, cubuī, cubitūrus**, *to lie down; to sleep; to recline* (for instance at the dinner table); *to lie sick in bed.*
Caesar, Caesaris, m., *Caesar* (C. Julius Caesar, 100–44 B.C., the general, politician, and victor in the Roman civil wars who was named "dictator for life" and subsequently assassinated in a senatorial conspiracy).
Caesaris hortōs: the *gardens of Caesar* were an estate located on the Janiculum, across the Tiber and at least an hour's walk from the Sacred Way. They were left to the Roman people by a provision in Caesar's will.
19 **quod agam**: relative clause of characteristic.
piger, pigra, pigrum, *reluctant; slow, lazy.*
20 **auricula [dim. of auris, auris**, f., *ear*], **-ae**, f., *ear.*
dēmittō auriculās: perhaps a play on the meaning of Horace's cognomen, **Flaccus**, which means *having drooping, floppy, or pendulous ears.*
inīquus, -a, -um, *uneven, unequal; adverse; resentful.*
asellus [dim. of asīnus, -ī, m., *ass*], **-ī**, m., *donkey.*
21 **dorsum, -ī**, n., *back.*
dorsō: dative with **gravius**, *too heavy for. . .* or ablative with **subiīt**, *on . . .*
subeō [sub-, *under* + **eō, īre, iī** or **īvī, itūrus**, *to go*], **subīre, subiī, subitūrus**, *to go under*; transitive + acc., *to take on.*
subiīt: the final syllable is lengthened due to the meter. A short final syllable can be lengthened when it falls on the initial long of a foot in dactylic hexameter. This is an example of diastole.

13   garrīret, vīcōs, urbem laudāret. Ut illī
14   nīl respondēbam, "Miserē cupis," inquit, "abīre;
15   iamdūdum videō: sed nīl agis; ūsque tenēbō;
16   persequar hinc quō nunc iter est tibi." "Nīl opus est tē
17   circumagī: quendam volo vīsere nōn tibi nōtum:
18   trāns Tiberim longē cubat is, prope Caesaris hortōs."
19   "Nīl habeō quod agam et nōn sum piger: ūsque sequar tē."
20   Dēmittō auriculās, ut inīquae mentis asellus,
21   cum gravius dorsō subiīt onus. Incipit ille:

continued

Explorations

6. While the narrator was praising Bolanus under his breath (11b–12a), what was the pest doing (12b–13a)?
7. What does the repetition of the word **miserē** in line 14 from line 8b reveal about the pest?
8. How is the characterization of the pest advanced in lines 14b–16a?
9. It appears that the excuse the narrator offers in lines 16b–18 is invented on the spot as a way to get rid of the pest. What specific words and details give the indication that the narrator is describing his appointment in ways designed to discourage the pest from accompanying him?
10. Why does the narrator's attempt to get rid of the pest fail?
11. How does the simile in lines 20b–21a effectively convey the narrator's displeasure at his inability to get rid of the pest?

22 **"Sī bene mē nōvī"**: loosely, "Unless I'm badly underestimating myself."

Vīscus, -ī, m.,*Viscus* (a member of Horace's circle of literary friends; not much is known about him beyond brief mention in the *Satires*. At *Satires* 1.10.83, two brothers named Viscus are mentioned among the group of friends whose approval Horace says he seeks with his verse. See Passages for Comparison I following the discussion questions).

plūris: *of greater value*, genitive of value.

23 **Varius, -ī**, m., *Varius* (L. Varius Rufus, an eminent epic and tragic poet of the Augustan period. Varius was, along with Vergil, a close poetic associate of Horace throughout his career. He is mentioned a number of times in the *Satires*, including in the same list of friends that includes Viscus; cf. on line 22. In *Satires* 1.6.55 Horace says that Varius, along with Vergil, recommended him to Maecenas (see Passages for Comparison II following the discussion questions). *Odes* 1.6 names Varius as a suitable poet to write the epic for Agrippa that Horace claims he is himself incapable of).

> **nōn Vīscum (22) . . . / nōn Varium**: anaphora and asyndeton; Viscus and Varius are Horace's fellow guests at a dinner party described in *Satires* 2.8, which is also attended by Maecenas.

faciēs: *you will consider*.

24 **citō**, adv., *quickly*.

citius: comparative of **citō**.

possit: potential subjunctive.

> **scrībere plūrīs (23) / aut citius possit versūs**: a dubious talent for someone wishing to ingratiate himself with the narrator. In a poem earlier in the first book of *Satires*, Horace criticizes his predecessor Lucilius specifically for writing abundantly, quickly, and sloppily (*Satires* 1.4.7b–13a; see the passage for comparison quoted with lines 31–34).

membrum, -ī, n., *member, limb*.

25 **mollis, -is, -e**, *soft; tender; flexible; delicate*.

> **membra mōvere (24b) / mollius**: i.e., in dancing, another dubious talent from the perspective of someone in the narrator's elite circles. The alliteration reinforces the silliness of the speaker's pride in this talent. From the perspective of traditional notions of Roman masculinity, **mollitia**, *softness*, meant a gracefulness, elegance, or refinement that bordered disreputably on effeminacy.

Hermogenēs, Hermogenis, m., *Hermogenes* (Tigellius Hermogenes is mentioned several times in Book 1 of the *Satires*, always in a critical and negative light. Incessant, unwelcome, and bad singing is singled out for mention among Hermogenes' faults in *Satires* 1.3.1–8).

> **Invideat quod et Hermogenēs ego cantō**: the word order is somewhat strained; in prose it would be **ego cantō quod et** (*even*) **Hermogenēs invideat**.

22 "Sī bene mē nōvī, nōn Vīscum plūris amīcum,
23 nōn Varium faciēs: nam quis mē scrībere plūrīs
24 aut citius possit versūs? Quis membra movēre
25 mollius? Invideat quod et Hermogenēs ego cantō."

continued

Explorations

12. How does the pest's description of himself and his talents in lines 22–25 seem
     designed to earn the narrator's respect? How does it fail?

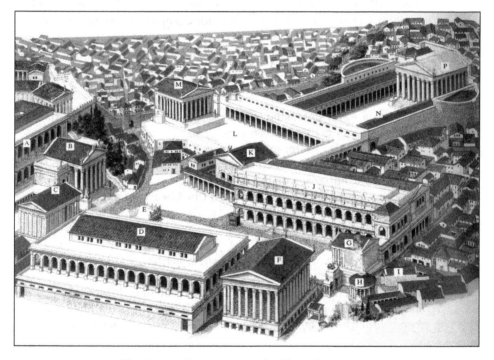

*The **Forum Rōmānum** at the Time of Augustus*

A Tabularium   I Regia
B Temple of Concord   J Basilica Aemilia
C Temple of Saturn   K Curia Julia
D Basilica Julia   L Forum of Julius Caesar
E *rostra*   M Temple of Venus Genetrix
F Temple of Castor and Pollux   N Forum of Augustus
G Temple of the Deified Julius Caesar   P Temple of Mars Ultor
H Temple of Vesta

26   **Interpellandī**: note the five long/heavy syllables.
      tibi: dative of possession.
27   **cōgnātus, -a, -um**, *relative*.
      quīs: = **quibus**, dative plural.
      est opus: *there is need for*, here governing a dative (**quīs**) of the persons in
         need and an ablative **(tē salvō)** of the thing needed; cf. lines 16b–17a.
      quisquam, quisquam, quicquam, *anyone, anything*.
28   **compōnō [con-**, *together* + **pōnō, pōnere, posuī, positus**, *to put, place*], **com-
         pōnere, composuī, compositus**, *to put together; to bury* (i.e., to put the
         bones of the cremated dead together in a funerary urn).
      "Fēlīcēs!": this and the remainder of the narrator's words to the end of line
         34 are best understood not as spoken aloud but as something whispered by
         the narrator under his breath (cf. lines 11b–12a) or as a representation of his
         thoughts.
         "Fēlīcēs!": mock epic exclamation; see Homer *Iliad* 5.306–7, and Vergil
            Aeneid 1.94–96a, quoted in Passages for Comparison on the opposite
            page.
      restō [re-, *back* + **stō, stāre, stetī, stātūrus**, *to stand*], **restāre, restitī**, *to with-
         stand, resist; to remain, be left*.
29   **Cōnfice**: supply **mē**.
      namque, conj., *for*.
      īnstō [in-, *upon* + **stō, stāre, stetī, stātūrus**, *to stand*], **īnstāre, īnstitī** + dat., *to
         approach; to pursue; to threaten, loom over*.
         īnstat fātum mihi trīste: an ironic echo of statements by epic heroes at
            critical moments on the battlefield; see *Iliad* 22.300–305, quoted in Pas-
            sages for Comparison on the opposite page.
      Sabellus, -a, -um, *of/belonging to the Sabelli* (the Oscan speaking Italic peo-
         ples, Sabine in origin), *Sabellian*.
         Sabella: take with **anus** (30).
30   **puerō**: supply **mihi**.
      dīvīnus, -a, -um, *divine; inspired by the gods, prophetic*.
      urna, -ae, f., *urn*.
         dīvīnā mōtā . . . urnā: in this method of fortune telling, lots or tokens were
            shaken in a vessel before being spilled or drawn out so that they could
            then be interpreted by the fortune teller; cf. *Odes* 2.3.26 and 3.1.16.

26 Interpellandī locus hīc erat: "Est tibi māter,

27 cōgnātī, quīs tē salvō est opus?" "Haud mihi quisquam:

28 omnīs composuī." "Fēlīcēs! Nunc ego restō.

29 Cōnfice; namque īnstat fātum mihi trīste, Sabella

30 quod puerō cecinit dīvīnā mōtā anus urnā:

continued

Explorations

13. Why does the narrator ask if the pest has any relatives concerned about his well-being (26b–27a)? How does the pest respond (27b–28a)?

Passages for Comparison

I.

Homer *Odyssey* 5.306–7; Odysseus, storm-tossed at sea, speaks in desperation:

"Three times and four times blessed are the Greeks who died back then in the wide land of Troy, bringing pleasure to the sons of Atreus."

II.

Vergil *Aeneid* 1.94–96a; Aeneas, storm-tossed at sea, speaks in desperation:

94 Talia vōce refert: "Ō terque quaterque beātī,
95 quīs ante ōra patrum Trōiae sub moenibus altīs
96a contigit oppetere!

He says the following aloud: "O three times and four times blessed, for whom it fell to meet death before the faces of their fathers beneath the high walls of Troy!"

III.

Homer *Iliad* 22.300–305; Hector speaks after hurling his spear at Achilles in vain during their duel to the death; Hector realizes that his fate has caught up with him.

"Now indeed evil death is close to me and no longer far away, nor do I have a way out. Thus long ago it must have pleased Zeus and the far-shooting son of Zeus, who previously gladly protected me, but now my fate overtakes me. May I not die without a struggle and without glory, but after I have done something for men still to come to learn of."

31   'Hunc . . . aetās' (31–34): the narrator quotes the prophecy given to him as a
      boy by the old Sabellian fortune teller. The language of the prophecy is
      humorously exaggerated and mock-epic in tone (see notes below). Note
      the anaphora: **neque . . . nec . . . / nec . . . nec** (31–32).
      dīrus, -a, -um, *dire, terrible; evil.*
          dīra: a high-register word.
      venēnum, -ī, n., *potion; poison.*
      hosticus, -a, -um, *hostile, of an enemy.*
          hosticus: an epic-style archaism.
      ēnsis, ēnsis, m., *sword.*
          ēnsis: here used as a grand word for **gladius**.
          nec hosticus auferet ēnsis: we might think of Horace's escape from the
              battle of Philippi, as related in *Odes* 2.7.
32   **latus, lateris**, n., *side* (of the body), *flank.*
      dolor, dolōris, m., *grief; pain.*
          laterum dolor: *a pain in the flanks,* a reference to pleurisy, a painful disease
              characterized by inflammation of the lining around the lungs.
      tussis, tussis, f., *cough.*
      podagra, -ae, f., *gout* (a disease causing painful inflammation in the joints,
          especially in the feet).
          tarda podagra: a transferred epithet; *gout* is not itself *slow,* but it does
              cause a person who suffers from it to be slowed or hobbled. The adjec-
              tive **tarda** attached to **podagra** personifies the disease.
33   **garrulus, -a, -um**, *garrulous, talkative, chattering.*
          garrulus: cf. **garrīret** (13a) and *Satires* 1.4.12, quoted in Passage for Compar-
              ison on the opposite page.
      quandō . . . cumque: tmesis, = **quandōcumque**, adv., *at some time or other.*
      cōnsūmō [**cōn-**, *thoroughly, completely* + **sūmō, sūmere, sūmpsī, sūmptus**,
          to take; to use], **cōnsūmere, cōnsūmpsī, cōnsūmptus**, *to use up; to devour,*
          waste; to destroy.
      loquāx, loquācis, *talkative*; as substantive, *chatterbox.*
34   **sapiō, sapere, sapīvī**, *to have taste; to be intelligent, be sensible, be wise.*
          simul atque: = **simul ac**, *as soon as.*
      adolēscō, adolēscere, adolēvī, adultus, *to grow up, mature.*
      aetās, aetātis, *age; time; time of life.*

31   'Hunc neque dīra venēna nec hosticus auferet ēnsis,

32   nec laterum dolor aut tussis, nec tarda podagra;

33   garrulus hunc quandō cōnsūmet cumque: loquācēs,

34   sī sapiat, vītet, simul atque adolēverit aetās.'"

continued

Explorations

14. What is the tone of the old fortune teller's prophecy? How does it invoke the
     language and ideas of epic poetry? What is its effect in this context?
15. How is the prophecy being fulfilled in the present circumstances?
16. How does the criticism Horace offers of his predecessor Lucilius in *Satires* 1.4,
     quoted below, compare with both the cause of death foretold in the prophecy
     and the characterization of the pest in this poem?

Passage for Comparison

Satires 1.4.7b–13a:

7b   .   .   .   Facētus,
8   ēmūnctae nāris, dūrus compōnere versūs:
9   nam fuit hōc vitiōsus: in hōrā saepe ducentōs,
10   ut magnum, versūs dictābat stāns pede in ūnō:
11   cum flueret lutulentus, erat quod tollere vellēs:
12   garrulus atque piger scrībendī ferre labōrem,
13a scrībendī rēctē: nam ut multum, nīl moror. . . .

> [Lucilius was] witty, with a discerning nose, [but] tough at writing
> verses; for he was at fault in this respect: often in an hour, as if it were a
> great thing, he would dictate two hundred verses while standing on one
> foot: when he flowed along muddily, there was stuff you'd want to take
> out; [he was] verbose and lazy at putting up with the effort of writing, of
> writing correctly[, that is]; that he could really churn it out, I do not object.

35   **Ventum erat**: the impersonal passive of the intransitive verb places empha-
     sis on the action of the verb, as opposed to the person performing the ac-
     tion.

     Vesta, -ae, f., *Vesta* (Roman goddess of the hearth).

     ad Vestae: understand **aedem** [**aedēs, -is**, f., *shrine, temple*] as object of the
     preposition **ad**. The round *temple of Vesta* was located in the southern
     part of the Roman Forum, near the Regia on the Sacred Way. Unlike
     most temples it did not contain an image of the goddess, but rather
     housed the eternal flame that was tended by the Vestal Virgins. The
     Basilica Julia, where court cases were heard, was located further along on
     the Sacred Way.

     quartā iam parte diēī / praeteritā (36a): the time indicated is approximately
     9 o'clock in the morning. The Romans divided the available daylight into
     twelve hours of varying length depending on the time of year. In this case
     three hours have passed since dawn.

36   **respondēre**: + dat., *to answer* (to a plaintiff by appearing in court); without
     dative, *to appear in court* (to answer a charge).

     vador, -ārī, -ātus sum, *to accept bond* (**vadimōnium**, from someone to guar-
     antee that the person would appear or reappear in court on a particular
     date and at a particular time); *to institute proceedings against*.

     vadātō: perfect participle, active in meaning, as is usual with deponent
     verbs, used as a substantive and serving as the dative object of **re-
     spondēre**, i.e., *to answer to [a person] who had instituted proceedings
     against [him]*, i.e., *to answer to a plaintiff*. Some take the perfect participle
     of the deponent verb in a passive sense as a one-word ablative abso-
     lute, i.e., *since bond had been accepted*; **respondēre vadātō** would then
     mean *to appear in court since he had given bond*, with **respondēre** used in
     a technical sense, *to appear in court*.

37   **nī**: = **nisi**, *unless, if not*.

     perdō [**per-**, *through* + **dō, dare, dedī, datus**, *to give*], **perdere, perdidī,
     perditus**, *to destroy; to lose*.

     līs, lītis, f., *dispute; lawsuit, case*.

     quod nī fēcisset, perdere lītem: virtual indirect statement, quoting the
     language of the original bond or contract guaranteeing the pest's ap-
     pearance in court, which would have read **nisi reponderit, lītem
     perdet**, *if he does not answer/fails to appear in court, he will lose his case*. The
     future perfect indicative of the direct statement is represented by a plu-
     perfect subjunctive in the virtual indirect statement. The infinitive
     perdere is dependent on **dēbēbat** in the preceding clause.

35 Ventum erat ad Vestae, quartā iam parte diēī
36 praeteritā, et cāsū tunc respondēre vadātō
37 dēbēbat; quod nī fēcisset, perdere lītem.

continued

Temple of Vesta
Forum Rōmānum
Rome, Italy

38   **Sī me amās**: a polite formula; translate *if you please* or simply *please*.
      me: because **mē** does not elide with **amās** (hiatus) its vowel is shortened.
      adsum [**ad-**, *to, toward* + **sum, esse, fuī, futūrus**, *to be*], **adesse, adfuī**, *to be present; to lend aid, support, assist*; in a technical sense, *to appear in support of someone in court, lend legal aid*.
      ades: present imperative.
      intereō [**inter-**, *among* + **eō, īre, iī** or **īvī, itūrus**, *to go*], **interīre, interiī, interitūrus**, *to go among, be lost; to die*.
      Interéam: optative subjunctive in a mild oath, *May I die if. . . .*
39   **valeō stāre**: i.e., have the strength to stand up in court for a long time.
      nōvī: the perfect of **nōscō** (cf. on line 7) should be translated as a present: *I have learned = I know*.
      cīvīlis, -is, -e, *of citizens, civil*.
      iūs, iūris, n., *law*.
40   **properō, -āre, -āvī, -ātūrus**, *to hurry*.
      dubius, -a, -um, *doubtful, in doubt, uncertain*.
      quid faciam: *what I should do*; the subjunctive verb in the indirect question here represents a deliberative subjunctive.
41   **Tēne:** = **Tē** + **-ne**.
      relinquam: deliberative subjunctive.
      relinquam . . . rem: cf. **perdere lītem** (37b).
         rem: *the matter*, either *the case* or *the bond* [**vadimōnium**] that the pest had given to guarantee his appearance in court at the appointed time; the meaning here will depend on how the words **respondēre vadātō** are translated in line 36b.
      sōdēs: = **sī audēs**, *if you will, if you please, please*. **Audeō** here and in earlier Latin means *to have a mind* (to do something), *to intend*, not *to dare*.
      "Nōn faciam," ille: supply **inquit**.
42   **contendere** [**con-**, *thoroughly* + **tendō, tendere, tetendī, tentus**, *to stretch; to exert oneself*], **contendere, contendī, contentus**, *to aim; to strive for; to dispute, fight, contend*.
      dūrus, -a, -um, *hard, difficult*.
43   **Maecēnās, Maecēnātis**, m., *Maecenas* (C. Cilnius Maecenas, Roman knight, advisor to Augustus, and patron of Horace. Maecenas was the most important patron of literature in the Augustan era. In addition to being Horace's patron, he was the patron of Vergil and Propertius as well).
      quōmodo: i.e., on what terms?
      Maecēnās quōmodo tēcum: ellipsis; supply **est** or **agit**.

38   "Sī me amās," inquit, "paulum hīc ades." "Interream sī
39   aut valeō stāre aut nōvī cīvīlia iūra;
40   et properō quō scīs." "Dubius sum quid faciam," inquit,
41   "Tēne relinquam an rem?" "Mē, sōdēs." "Nōn faciam," ille,
42   et praecēdere coepit. Ego, ut contendere dūrum est
43   cum victōre, sequor. "Maecēnās quōmodo tēcum?"

continued

Explorations

17. What are the narrator's three excuses for not accompanying the pest into court (38b–40a)? How do they make him appear?
18. What are the two options facing the pest in lines 40b–41a? What does his choice say about him?
19. What effect is achieved by the absence of speech tags (**inquit** and the like) and connecting words in line 41?
20. How does the prefix **prae-** in the phrase **praecēdere coepit** (42a) help you to visualize the scene? Compare lines 41–42a with lines 6a, 15b–16a and 19. How have the relative positions of the narrator and the pest changed?
21. How does the narrator now characterize his interaction with the pest (42b–43a)? What explains his attitude?
22. What does the pest's question (**"Maecēnās quōmodo tēcum?"**, 43b) reveal about him and about his motivation for accosting the narrator? What lines earlier in the poem prepare for this moment?

44   **hinc**, adv., *from here.*
     repetō [**re-**, *back, again* + **petō, petere, petīvī, petītus**, *to look for, seek; to attack*],
        repetere, repetīvī, repetītus, *to attack again; to begin again.*
        repetit: i.e., he resumes his attack from where he left off in line 25.
     Paucōrum hominum: *of few men;* i.e., of selective company.
     bene: here used as an intensifier, *very, thoroughly.*
     sānus, -a, -um, *healthy, sound.*
        Paucōrum hominum et mentis bene sānae: genitives of description, de-
           pendent on an implied phrase such as **est vir**; Maecenas is being de-
           scribed. Note that as punctuated here these words are spoken by the
           pest. Some editors prefer to assign the words to the narrator, as his reply
           to the question **"Maecēnās quōmodo tēcum?"** (43b).
45   **dexter, dext(e)ra, dext(e)rum**, *right; skillful.*
        nēmō . . . ūsus: as punctuated here, these words continue the pest's
           thought from the previous line, and the implied comparison must be
           "than Maecenas." Others prefer to read the lines so that the implied
           comparison is "than you," i.e., the narrator.
     Habērēs: apodosis of the condition introduced by **vellēs sī trādere** (47a).
46   **adiūtor, adiūtōris**, m., *assistant, helper* (sometimes used of a subordinate ac-
        tor).
     posset quī: relative clause of characteristic with delayed conjunction.
     secundus, -a, -um, *second; following; supporting.*
        ferre secundās: supply **partēs**, *role*; translate *to play a supporting role.*
47   **hunc hominem**: *this fellow here, yours truly*; the pest is referring to himself.
     sī: delayed conjunction.
     trādere: here, *to introduce.*
     dispereō [**dis-**, *badly* + **per-**, *thoroughly, completely* + **eō, īre, iī** or **īvī, itūrus**, *to
        go*], **disperīre, disperiī**, *to go to ruin, to perish.*
        dispeream, nī: cf. **Interam sī** (38b).
48   **summoveō** [**sub-**, *under* + **moveō, movēre, mōvī, mōtus**, *to move*], **sum-**
        movēre, summōvī, summōtus, *to remove; to shove aside.*
        nī summōssēs: syncope, = **summōvissēs**, literally, *if you hadn't shoved*
           X *aside*, pluperfect subjunctive in a mixed condition; the pluperfect is
           used instead of the imperfect for vividness, representing instanta-
           neously completed action, *if you wouldn't [immediately] have shoved*
           X *aside.*
     omnīs: all the other people whom the pest imagines the narrator is compet-
        ing with for Maecenas's attention.
     iste, ista, istud, *that* (often pejorative).
        istō . . . / . . . modō (49a): *in that way*, ablative of manner.
     illīc, adv., *there, in that place.*

44   hinc repetit: "Paucōrum hominum et mentis bene sānae;
45   nēmō dexterius fortūnā est ūsus. Habērēs
46   magnum adiūtōrem, posset quī ferre secundās,
47   hunc hominem vellēs sī trādere: dispeream, nī
48   summōssēs omnīs." "Nōn istō vīvimus illīc,

continued

Explorations

23.   As punctuated here, lines 44–45a are the pest's assessment of Maecenas.
      What is his view of Maecenas? What role does the pest assign to luck or good
      fortune (**fortūnā**, 45a) in Maecenas's life? Assuming that the pest's remarks
      are designed to ingratiate himself with the narrator, is he likely to succeed?
      Why or why not?
24.   In lines 45b–48a what benefits does the pest suggest he could give the narra-
      tor, if the narrator were willing to introduce him to Maecenas? What do his
      remarks say about what he believes the narrator's relationship with Maece-
      nas to be like?

49   **reor, rērī, ratus sum**, *to reckon, suppose, think.*
      rēre: = **rēris**, second person singular, present indicative.
      hāc: ablative of comparison, feminine in agreement with **domō** understood.
50   **aliēnus, -a, -um**, *of/belonging to others;* + dat., *remote from, free from.*
      nīl: adverbial, *not at all.*
      officiō [**ob-**, *in front of* + **faciō, facere, fēcī, factus**, *to make; to do*], **officere,**
        offēcī, offectus + dat., *to get in the way of; to hinder; to injure, cause X harm.*
      inquam: here perhaps an emphatic parenthesis, *I'm telling you.* If taken this
        way, **inquam** would go within the quotation marks as part of the speech
        that begins in line 48b.
51   **dītis, -is, -e**, *wealthy.*
      hic: adjective, *this [man];* the word scans long or heavy because the original
        spelling, **hicc(e)**, was still felt.
      doctus, -a, -um, *learned.*
        doctior: cf. "**doctī sumus**" (7a).
          dītior hic aut est quia doctior: this clause is the subject of the imper-
            sonal verb **officit** (50) with the conjunction, **quia**, *because; the fact that,*
            that, significantly delayed; the prose word order would be **nīl mī of-**
            ficit quia hic [homō] dītior est aut doctior.
      locus . . . / . . . suus (52a): *his own place.*
      ūnī: dative of possession.
52   **quisque, quaeque, quidque**, *each.*
      Magnum: substantive, *a great thing.*
      crēdibilis, -is, -e, *believable, trustworthy, to be believed.*
      atquī, conj., *but anyway, and yet.*
53   **sīc habet**: colloquial shortened form of the expression **sīc sē rēs habet**, *that's*
        how it is.
      Accendis: understand **mē** as object, *You're enflaming/encouraging [me].*
      quārē: = **ut eā rē**, *so that therefore,* introducing a result clause.
      illī: i.e., Maecenas.
54   **tantummodo**, adv., *merely, only.*
      Velīs tantummodo: *only wish [it],* jussive subjunctive.
      virtūs, virtūtis, f., *manly spirit, valor; moral excellence.*
      quae tua virtūs: *[that] which is your valor/moral excellence,* = causal, *since your*
        valor/moral excellence is such.
55   **expugnō** [**ex-**, *thoroughly, completely* + **pugnō, -āre, -āvī, -ātūrus**, *to fight*],
        -āre, -āvī, -ātus, *to storm; to overcome; to take* (a fortified position) *by storm.*
          expugnābis: ellipsis, supply **eum.**
      et est: the subject is Maecenas.
      quī vincī possit: relative clause of characteristic.
      eō, adv., *therefore.*

49   quō tū rēre modō; domus hāc nec pūrior ūlla est
50   nec magis hīs aliēna malīs; nīl mī officit," inquam,
51   "dītior hic aut est quia doctior; est locus ūnī
52   cuique suus." "Magnum nārrās, vix crēdibile." "Atquī
53   sīc habet." "Accendis, quārē cupiam magis illī
54   proximus esse." "Velīs tantummodo: quae tua virtūs,
55   expugnābis; et est quī vincī possit, eōque

continued

Explorations

25.   How does the narrator in lines 48b–52a respond to the pest's comments in
      lines 44b–48a? What are the *evils* that he says Maecenas's circle is free from
      (**hīs aliēna malīs**, 50a)? What has changed in the way the narrator interacts
      with the pest?
26.   What is the pest's reaction (52b) to the narrator's praise of Maecenas's circle?
      What does it tell us about him, his character, and his qualifications for joining
      Maecenas's circle?
27.   What is the pest's further reaction in lines 53b–54a? Do you think it is the
      one the narrator intended? How so?

56   **aditus, -ūs**, m., *way of approach, access; approach.*

    aditūs: the basic meaning here is *approaches*, but the word **aditus** also has
        military meanings, = *a hostile approach, attack; a chance of attacking, an open-*
        ing for attack.

    habet: i.e., *he makes;* **difficilīs** is predicate, *he makes X difficult.*

    dēsum [dē-, *away* + **sum, esse, fuī, futūrus**, *to be*], **dēesse, dēfuī, dēfutūrus**
    + dat., *to be neglectful in one's duty* (to), *to fail.*

        dēerō: scanned as two syllables by synezesis.

57   **corrumpō [con-**, *thoroughly* + **rumpō, rumpere, rūpī, ruptus**, *to break*], **cor-**
    rumpere, corrūpī, corruptus, *to destroy; to corrupt, seduce; to bribe.*

58   **exclūdō [ex-**, *out* + **claudō, claudere, clausī, clausus**, *to shut*], **exclūdere,**
    exclūdī, exclūsus, *to shut out, exclude, deny entry.*

        exclūsus fuerō: = **exclūsus erō**.

    dēsistō [dē-, *down* + **sistō, sistere, stitī, status**, *to place, set up*] **dēsistere,**
    dēstitī, dēstitus, *to desist, stop; to give up.*

    tempora: *appropriate times, auspicious moments.*

59   **occurram**: supply **eī**, i.e., Maecenas.

    trivium, -ī, n., *place where three roads meet;* pl., *street corners.*

    dēdūcō [dē-, *down, away* + **dūcō, dūcere, dūxī, ductus**, *to lead*], **dēdūcere,**
    dēdūxī, dēductus, *to lead away; to accompany, escort.*

        dēdūcam: supply **eum**; the pest would be thinking of escorting Maece-
        nas from his house to the Forum as a mark of respect, but given the
        general tone of the pest's remarks, the sense *lead in a triumph* may pos-
        sibly be felt as well; cf. *Odes* 1.37.30–32 and lines 42b–43a above.

    "Nīl . . . / . . . mortālibus" (60a): compare the Greek maxims quoted in Pas-
    sages for Comparison on the opposite page.

61   **Fuscus Aristius, Fuscī Aristī**, m., *Aristius Fuscus* (another friend of Horace
    and a fellow poet, the addressee of *Odes* 1.22 and *Epistles* 1.10. Like Viscus,
    22, and Varius, 23, he appears in *Satires* 1.10.82–83 in the list of literary
    associates whose approval Horace desires; see Passages for Comparison I
    following the discussion questions).

    Fuscus Aristius: note that the usual order of nomen and cognomen is
        reversed.

    occurrit: supply **nōbīs**.

    illum: i.e., the pest.

62   **pulchrē**: here, = **bene**, a colloquialism found in Roman comedy.

    nōsset: syncope, = **nōvisset**; for the tense, cf. above on **nōvī** (39); translate as
    present.

        illum (61) **/ quī pulchrē nōsset**: **illum**, the direct object of **nōsset**, is
        placed ahead of the pronoun **quī**, which introduces the relative clause
        of charactreristic, *the sort who would. . . .*

    cōnsistō [cōn-, *together* + **sistō, sistere, stitī, status**, *to place, set up*], **cōnsis-**
    tere, cōnstitī, cōnstitus, *to stand still; to halt, stop.*

        cōnsistimus: i.e., Aristius Fuscus and I; the narrator does not mean to in-
        clude the pest.

56   difficilīs aditūs prīmōs habet." "Haud mihi dēerō:
57   mūneribus servōs corrumpam; nōn, hodiē sī
58   exclūsus fuerō, dēsistam; tempora quaeram;
59   occurram in triviīs; dēdūcam. Nīl sine magnō
60   vīta labōre dedit mortālibus." Haec dum agit, ecce
61   Fuscus Aristius occurrit, mihi cārus et illum
62   quī pulchrē nōsset. Cōnsistimus. "Unde venīs?" et,

continued

Explorations

28. Lines 54b–56a represent a further change in the narrator's interaction with the pest. What is different?
29. What is the dominant imagery in lines 54b–56a? Identify all the words and ideas that contribute to that imagery. How does it apply to the pest on the one hand and to Maecenas on the other? How does the picture of Maecenas here compare to the picture of the relationship of Maecenas and Horace in *Odes* 1.1.1–2?
30. How does the pest characterize his own intentions in lines 56b–59a? How do the pest's intentions here link up with his behavior as represented previously in the poem?
31. What is the tone of the maxim cited by the pest in lines 59b–60a? What is the application of the maxim that the pest intends? How is it incongruous in its context here?
32. Two characteristics of Aristius Fuscus are singled out for mention when he suddenly appears (60b–62a). What are they? Why is the narrator glad to see him?

Passages for Comparison

I.

Phocylides (a 6th century B.C. writer of maxims in hexameters) 162:

Men have no good thing without hard work.

II.

Sophocles *Electra* 945:

Without effort nothing succeeds.

63   **tendō, tendere, tetendī, tentus**, *to stretch; to direct oneself, go.*
      rōgat et respondet: with **respondet**, supply **mihi rogantī**; Fuscus both asks
         the questions and answers them when the narrator asks them of him in
         turn.
      vellō, -ere, *to pluck; to pull, tug at.*
         vellere: understand **togam** as direct object.
64   **prēnsō** [iterative form related to **prehendō, prehendere, prehendī, pre-
         hēnsus**, *to lay hold of*], **-āre, -āvī, -ātus**, *to lay hold of, grab, grip.*
      lentus, -a, -um, *slow; slow to feel emotion, unresponsive.*
      bracchium, -ī, n., *arm.*
         lentissima bracchia: Fuscus makes no sign of acknowledging the narra-
            tor's repeated tugs and grips; his *arms* are *totally unresponsive.*
      nūtō, -āre, -āvī, -ātūrus, *to nod.*
65   **distorqueō** [**dis-**, *apart* + **torqueō, torquēre, torsī, tortus**, *to turn*], **dis-
         torquēre, distorsī, distortus**, *to turn aside, twist.*
         ut mē ēriperet: indirect command dependent on the implied plea for
            help contained in the words **nūtāns, / distorquēns oculōs** (64b–65a).
      salsus, -a, -um, *salted, salty; witty.*
         Male salsus: *with a mischievous sense of humor.*
66   **dissimulō** [**dis-**, *apart* + **simulō, -āre, -āvī, -ātus**, *to make like, imitate*], **-āre,
         -āvī, -ātus**, *to make unlike; to disguise, dissimulate, to pretend one does not
         understand.*
         dissimulāre: historical infinitive (see on line 9); translate as past tense;
            the subject is Fuscus.
      iecur, iecoris, n., *liver.*
      ūrō, ūrere, ūssī, ūstus, *to destroy by fire; to cause to burn with intense emotion;
         to enrage, inflame.*
         ūrere: historical infinitive; the subject is **bīlis**.
      bīlis, bīlis, f., *bile.*
         iecur ūrere bīlis: a sign of anger; cf. *Odes* 1.13.3b–4.
67   **"Certē . . . / . . . mēcum"** (68a): the narrator is speaking.
      nescio quid: see line 10.
68   **āiēbās**: trisyllabic, from **āiō**, see line 12.
      "Meminī . . . / . . . / . . . oppēdere?" (70a): Fuscus is speaking.
69   **trīcēsimus, -a, -um**, *thirtieth.*
      sabbata, -ōrum, n., *Sabbath (the Jewish holy day).*
         trīcēsima sabbata: *the thirtieth Sabbath* is not attested as a particular Jewish
            festival; Fuscus is making up a ridiculous excuse not to stay and rescue
            the poet.
      vīn: = **vīsne**, i.e., **vīs** + **-ne**.
70   **curtus, -a, -um**, *shortened; clipped; circumcised.*
      Iūdaeus, -a, -um, *Jewish*; substantive, *a Jew.*
         curtīs Iūdaeīs: the Jewish practice of circumcision particularly puzzled the
            Romans.
      oppēdō [**ob-**, *in front of* + **pēdō, pēdere, pepēdī, pēditūrus**, *to fart*], **op-
         pēdere** + dat., *to fart in the face of; to mock, insult.*
71   **rēligiō, rēligiōnis**, f., *religious awe; religious scruple.*

63   "Quō tendis?" rōgat et respondet. Vellere coepī,
64   et prēnsāre manū lentissima bracchia, nūtāns,
65   distorquēns oculōs, ut mē ēriperet. Male salsus
66   rīdēns dissimulāre: meum iecur ūrere bīlis.
67   "Certē nescio quid sēcrētō velle loquī tē
68   āiēbās mēcum." "Meminī bene, sed meliōre
69   tempore dīcam: hodiē trīcēsima sabbata: vīn tū
70   curtīs Iūdaeīs oppēdere?" "Nūlla mihi," inquam,
71   "rēligiō est." "At mī: sum paulō īnfirmior, ūnus

continued

Explorations

33.   What words and phrases in lines 60b–63a suggest the suddenness and speed
      of Fuscus's appearance and of his initial exchanges with the narrator?
34.   How does the style of lines 63b–66 continue the effect of rapidity? How
      might the style reflect the narrator's state of mind at this point?
35.   Describe in your own words the actions of the narrator in lines 63b–65a.
      What does the choice of the word **ēriperet** (65a) suggest about the narrator's
      attitude? What does Aristius Fuscus do (65b–66a)? How does the narrator
      react (66b)?
36.   What is the purpose behind the narrator's statement to Fuscus in lines 67–
      68a?
37.   How does Fuscus characterize himself through the excuse he offers in lines
      68b–70a? How does his excuse and the language he uses to express it accord
      with the narrator's description of him as **male salsus** (65b)?
38.   What does the narrator's claim that he has *no religious scruple(s)* (70b–71a)
      say about him?

72   ignōscō [in-, negative prefix + (g)nōscō, (g)nōscere, (g)nōvī, (g)nōtus, *to get to know, learn*], ignōscere, ignōvī, ignōtus + dat., *to pardon, forgive*.
        ignōscēs: supply mihi.
     loquar: supply tēcum.
     Huncine: when the enclitic particle -ne is added to certain forms of the demonstrative pronoun, an *i* is inserted between the pronoun and the particle.
73   surrēxe: syncope, = surrēxisse.
        Huncine (72b) . . . / surrēxe mihī: the enclitic particle -ne here introduces an indignant exclamation using an accusative and infinitive construction rather than a question; translate *To think that this sun/day.* . . .
     mihī: note that the second *i* is scanned as long here.
     improbus, -a, -um, *wicked;* as substantive, *a/the scoundrel/jerk*.
        improbus: referring to Aristius Fuscus.
74   culter, cultrī, m., *knife*.
        sub cultrō: *under the knife,* an idiom meaning *in extreme peril;* the image suggests an animal waiting to be sacrificed.
     Cāsū: the same word was used in line 36.
     obvius, -a, -um, *in the way;* + dat., *situated so as to meet*.
        venit obvius illī: *runs into him*.
75   adversārius, -a, -um, *opposite; hostile;* as substantive, *plaintiff, opponent* (in a legal proceeding).
        "Quō tū": understand a verb such as īs, *you are going;* the adversārius addresses the pest.
     turpis, -is, -e, *ugly, repulsive; disgraceful, vile*.
76   inclāmō [in-, *against* + clāmō, -āre, -āvī, -ātūrus, *to shout*], -āre, -āvī, -ātus + dat., *to shout at* X.
     et, "Licet antestārī?": the adversārius now addresses the narrator.
        Licet: supply mihi, *Is it allowed to me? May I?*
     antestor [either ambi-, *around,* or ante-, *in front of, beforehand* + testor, -ārī, -ātus sum, *to testify*], -ārī, -ātus sum, *to call* X *as a witness*.
        antestārī: the object tē is understood. In Roman legal practice, the adversārius has the authority physically to compel his opponent to appear in court. Before doing so in this case, the adversārius calls on the narrator to witness his arrest of the pest, who has failed to appear in court at the appointed time (cf. lines 40b–42a). Compare the fragment from the Twelve Tables, the oldest Roman law code, dating from the fifth century B.C., quoted in Passage for Comparison on the opposite page.
77   oppōnō [ob-, *in front of* + pōnō, pōnere, posuī, positus, *to put, place*], oppōnere, opposuī, oppositus, *to place before, offer up*.
        oppōnō auriculam: offering the ear to be touched was the traditional way of acknowledging a request to appear as a witness.
     rapit: the subject is the adversārius; supply eum, i.e., the pest, as object.
     iūs: see line 39; here *court*.

72   multōrum: ignōscēs: aliās loquar." Huncine sōlem
73   tam nigrum surrēxe mihī! Fugit improbus ac mē
74   sub cultrō linquit. Cāsū venit obvius illī
75   adversārius et, "Quō tū turpissime?" magnā
76   inclāmat vōce, et, "Licet antestārī?" Ego vērō
77   oppōnō auriculam. Rapit in iūs: clāmor utrimque:

continued

Explorations

39.   What is the narrator's state of mind when Aristius Fuscus departs? What
      specific words and ideas in lines 72b–74a contribute to this impression?
40.   How is the arrival of the **adversārius** characterized?

Passage for Comparison

The Twelve Tables 1.1:

Sī in iūs vocat, <ītō>. Nī it, antestāminō. Igitur em capitō.

If [a plaintiff] calls [a defendant] into court, let him go. If he does not go, let [the
plaintiff] call a witness. Then, let him arrest him.

78   **concursus, -ūs**, m., *a running about.*

        clāmor utrimque: (77b) / **undique concursus:** note the ellipses, chiasmus, and enjambment.

        Sīc mē servāvit Apollō: cf. Homer *Iliad* 20.441b–44 and Lucilius 267–68a, quoted in Passages for Comparison I and II on the opposite page.

           Apollō: Apollo is, among other things, the god of poetry and patron of poets.

78   undique concursus. Sīc mē servāvit Apollō.

Explorations

41.   What is the result of the appearance of the **adversārius**?
42.   What does the narrator mean when he comments **Sīc mē servāvit Apollō**
       (78b)? Why does he designate Apollo as the god who rescued him?
43.   With line 78b, compare the passages from Homer and Lucilius quoted below.
       What is the same and what is different? Why would the narrator choose to
       allude to these passages at the conclusion of the satire?
44.   Apollo's salvation comes, and the poem ends, very suddenly (cf. **Cāsū**, 74).
       There are a number of other chance and sudden occurrences in the poem (see
       lines 1a, 3, 36b–37a, and 60b–61a). How is the emphatic representation of for-
       tuitous events appropriate for the genre of satire?

Passages for Comparison

I.

Homer *Iliad* 20.441b–44; Achilles attacks Hector in battle:

> But Achilles rushed forward eagerly intending to kill him, shouting terribly,
> but Apollo snatched him [i.e., Hector] away from danger (τὸν δ' ἐξήρπαξεν
> Ἀπόλλων), very easily, as a god, and hid him in a thick mist.

II.

Lucilius 267–68a

267   nīl ut discrepet ac τὸν δ' ἐξήρπαξεν Ἀπόλλων
268a   fīat.

> so that it be no different and become an example of "and Apollo snatched
> him away from danger."

Satires 1.9

1	Ībam forte viā Sacrā, sīcut meus est mōs,
2	nescio quid meditāns nūgārum, tōtus in illīs.
3	Accurrit quīdam nōtus mihi nōmine tantum,
4	arreptāque manū, "Quid agis, dulcissime rērum?"
5	"Suāviter, ut nunc est," inquam, "et cupiō omnia quae vīs."
6	Cum adsectārētur, "Num quid vīs?" occupō. At ille
7	"Nōris nōs," inquit; "doctī sumus." Hīc ego, "Plūris
8	hōc," inquam, "mihi eris." Miserē discēdere quaerēns,
9	īre modo ōcius, interdum cōnsistere, in aurem
10	dīcere nescio quid puerō, cum sūdor ad īmōs
11	mānāret tālōs. "Ō tē, Bōlāne, cerebrī
12	fēlīcem!" āiēbam tacitus, cum quidlibet ille
13	garrīret, vīcōs, urbem laudāret. Ut illī
14	nīl respondēbam, "Miserē cupis," inquit, "abīre;
15	iamdūdum videō: sed nīl agis; ūsque tenēbō;
16	persequar hinc quō nunc iter est tibi." "Nīl opus est tē
17	circumagī: quendam volo vīsere nōn tibi nōtum:
18	trāns Tiberim longē cubat is, prope Caesaris hortōs."
19	"Nīl habeō quod agam et nōn sum piger: ūsque sequar tē."
20	Dēmittō auriculās, ut inīquae mentis asellus,
21	cum gravius dorsō subiīt onus. Incipit ille:
22	"Sī bene mē nōvī, nōn Vīscum plūris amīcum,
23	nōn Varium faciēs: nam quis mē scrībere plūrīs
24	aut citius possit versūs? Quis membra movēre
25	mollius? Invideat quod et Hermogenēs ego cantō."
26	Interpellandī locus hīc erat: "Est tibi māter,
27	cōgnātī, quīs tē salvō est opus?" "Haud mihi quisquam:
28	omnīs composuī." "Fēlīcēs! Nunc ego restō.
29	Cōnfice; namque īnstat fātum mihi trīste, Sabella
30	quod puerō cecinit dīvīnā mōtā anus urnā:
31	'Hunc neque dīra venēna nec hosticus auferet ēnsis,
32	nec laterum dolor aut tussis, nec tarda podagra;
33	garrulus hunc quandō cōnsūmet cumque: loquācēs,

34   sī sapiat, vītet, simul atque adolēverit aetās.'"
35   Ventum erat ad Vestae, quartā iam parte diēī
36   praeteritā, et cāsū tunc respondēre vadātō
37   dēbēbat; quod nī fēcisset, perdere lītem.
38   "Sī me amās," inquit, "paulum hīc ades." "Inteream sī
39   aut valeō stāre aut nōvī cīvīlia iūra;
40   et properō quō scīs." "Dubius sum quid faciam," inquit,
41   "Tēne relinquam an rem?" "Mē, sōdēs." "Nōn faciam," ille,
42   et praecēdere coepit. Ego, ut contendere dūrum est
43   cum victōre, sequor. "Maecēnās quōmodo tēcum?"
44   hinc repetit: "Paucōrum hominum et mentis bene sānae;
45   nēmō dexterius fortūnā est ūsus. Habērēs
46   magnum adiūtōrem, posset quī ferre secundās,
47   hunc hominem vellēs sī trādere: dispeream nī
48   summōssēs omnīs." "Nōn istō vīvimus illīc,
49   quō tū rēre modō; domus hāc nec pūrior ūlla est
50   nec magis hīs aliēna malīs; nīl mī officit," inquam,
51   "dītior hic aut est quia doctior; est locus ūnī
52   cuique suus." "Magnum nārrās, vix crēdibile." "Atquī
53   sīc habet." "Accendis, quārē cupiam magis illī
54   proximus esse." "Velīs tantummodo: quae tua virtūs,
55   expugnābis; et est quī vincī possit, eōque
56   difficilīs aditūs prīmōs habet." "Haud mihi dēerō:
57   mūneribus servōs corrumpam; nōn, hodiē sī
58   exclūsus fuerō, dēsistam; tempora quaeram;
59   occurram in triviīs; dēdūcam. Nīl sine magnō
60   vīta labōre dedit mortālibus." Haec dum agit, ecce
61   Fuscus Aristius occurrit, mihi cārus et illum
62   quī pulchrē nōsset. Cōnsistimus. "Unde venīs?" et,
63   "Quō tendis?" rōgat et respondet. Vellere coepī,
64   et prēnsāre manū lentissima bracchia, nūtāns,
65   distorquēns oculōs, ut mē ēriperet. Male salsus
66   rīdēns dissimulāre: meum iecur ūrere bīlis.
67   "Certē nescio quid sēcrētō velle loquī tē
68   āiēbās mēcum." "Meminī bene, sed meliōre

69   tempore dīcam: hodiē trīcēsima sabbata: vīn tū
70   curtīs Iūdaeīs oppēdere?" "Nūlla mihi," inquam,
71   "rēligiō est." "At mī: sum paulō īnfirmior, ūnus
72   multōrum: ignōscēs: aliās loquar." Huncine sōlem
73   tam nigrum surrēxe mihī! Fugit improbus ac mē
74   sub cultrō linquit. Cāsū venit obvius illī
75   adversārius et, "Quō tū turpissime?" magnā
76   inclāmat vōce, et, "Licet antestārī?" Ego vērō
77   oppōnō auriculam. Rapit in iūs: clāmor utrimque:
78   undique concursus. Sīc mē servāvit Apollō.

Discussion

1. Consider the following questions about the pest:
   a. What makes the pest a pest? That is to say, what particular characteristics, attitudes, and behaviors that he exhibits in the poem are held up for criticism?
   b. How is the pest a lot like the historical Horace? He has, in fact, been called Horace's "distorted double" (Oliensis, p. 36). How is that true?
   c. What do both the differences and the similarities between the pest and the historical Horace say about the purpose of *Satires* 1.9?
2. What is the picture of Maecenas, of his group of associates, and of Horace's place in that group that emerges from the poem?
3. Consider the following questions about the author/narrator of *Satires* 1.9:
   a. How might the author figure we meet in *Satires* 1.9 be taken not as a historically accurate representation of Horace, but as a "persona" crafted with specific appropriateness for the *Satires*?
   b. What picture of Horace himself emerges from *Satires* 1.9?
   c. What unflattering characteristics are ascribed to the narrator?
   d. How are the presentations of the narrator and the pest generically appropriate to satire?
4. Compare the picture of Horace that you have built up during your reading of the *Odes*. How is the satiric Horace different from the lyric Horace?
5. Compare *Satires* 1.9 with *Odes* 1.22. How are they similar and different in their depiction of Horace in his guise as poet?

Passages for Comparison

I.

Satires 1.10.81–90a:

81 Plōtius et Varius, Maecēnās Vergiliusque,
82 Valgius, et probet haec Octāvius, optimus atque
83 Fuscus, et haec utinam Vīscōrum laudet uterque!
84 Ambitiōne relēgātā tē dīcere possum,
85 Pollio, tē, Messalla, tuō cum frātre, simulque
86 vōs, Bibule et Servī, simul hīs tē, candide Furnī,
87 complūrīs aliōs, doctōs ego quōs et amīcōs
88 prūdēns praetereō; quibus haec, sint quāliacumque,
89 arrīdēre velim, ditūrus sī placeant spē
90a dēterius nostrā.

> May Plotius and Varius, Maecenas and Vergil, Valgius, and Octavius, and the eminent Fuscus approve these things [i.e., my poems], and I hope both of the Viscus brothers may praise them! Ambition banished, I can also name you, Pollio, you, Messalla, along with your brother, and at the same time you too, Bibulus and Servius, and together with them, you, brilliant Furnius, many others, learned men who are also my

friends, I modestly pass over; to whom these things, such as they are, I
would hope are charming, and I will be saddened, if they are pleasing
less than is my hope.

II.

Horace *Satires* 1.6.52b–64:

52b   .   .   .   Fēlīcem dīcere nōn hōc
53   mē possim, cāsū quod tē sortītus amīcum;
54   nūlla etenim mihi tē fors obtulit: optimus ōlim
55   Vergilius, post hunc Varius, dīxēre quid essem.
56   Ut vēnī cōram, singultim pauca locūtus,
57   īnfāns namque pudor prohibēbat plūra profārī,
58   nōn ego mē clārō nātum patre, nōn ego circum
59   mē Saturēiānō vectārī rūra caballō,
60   sed quod eram nārrō. Respondēs, ut tuus est mōs,
61   pauca: abeō; et revocās nōnō post mēnse iubēsque
62   esse in amīcōrum numerō. Magnum hoc ego dūcō
63   quod placuī tibi, quī turpī sēcernis honestum,
64   nōn patre praeclārō sed vītā et pectore pūrō.

I would not be able to say that I am lucky for this reason, that by chance I
was allotted you [i.e., Maecenas] as a friend; for no chance brought you to
me; once the eminent Vergil, and after him Varius, told you what I was.
When I came before you, having spoken a few choked words, for speech-
less shame prohibited me from saying more, I did not say that I was born
from a famous father, nor that I was conveyed around my country estate
on a Satureian [i.e., Apulian] nag, but I told you what I was. You answer,
as is your custom, briefly; I go away, and you call me back nine months
later and tell me to join your circle of friends. I consider it a great thing
that I found favor with you, who distinguish the upstanding from the
base, [I who am a man] not born from a distinguished father, but of a pure
life and heart.

In this passage from *Satires* 1.6 Horace describes his own introduction to Maecenas, and the contrast between his attitudes and behaviors and those of the pest in *Satires* 1.9 is very strongly marked. The
comparison serves to put further emphasis on just how thoroughly
wrong the pest's approach to gaining an introduction to Maecenas is.
In *Satires* 1.6, Horace, in the first place, disavows luck or chance as a
factor in his introduction to Maecenas (52b–54a), whereas the pest
hopes that what is no more than a chance encounter with Horace on
the street will lead to an introduction to Maecenas (cf. Explorations
44). The pest further misconstrues the situation by attributing
Maecenas's own success to his clever exploitation of his good luck
(*Satires* 1.9.45a). In contrast to the pest, Horace, as he tells us himself,
did not seek out an introduction to Maecenas at all, but rather relied
on knowledgeable friends to take the initiative (*Satires* 1.6.54b–55),

based not on any pressure coming from Horace, but on a true assessment of his worth (**quid essem**, *Satires* 1.6.55b). Once in Maecenas's presence, Horace distinguished himself by his shyness and taciturnity (**singultim pauca locūtus**, *Satires* 1.6.56b; **īnfāns ... pudor**, 57), which is in very strong contrast with the pest's aggressive talkativeness and self-promotion. In further contrast, Horace offered an honest self-presentation (*Satires* 1.6.58-60a), whereas the pest is a boaster with an inflated self-estimation (*Satires* 1.9.7a, 22–25, 45b–48a). Horace shows his respect for Maecenas by going away (**abeō**, *Satires* 1.6.61b) and patiently awaiting further word from Maecenas (**revocās nōnō post mēnse**, 61b); the pest, by contrast, refuses to leave Horace alone (*Satires* 1.9.14b–16a, 19, 40b–42a) and plans worse for Maecenas himself (56b–60a). Horace credits both his own purity of life and heart (*Satires* 1.6.63–64; cf. *Satires* 1.9.48b–52a, where a comparable purity is acribed to Maecenas's house) and Maecenas's ability to distinguish the good from the base (*Satires* 1.6.63b) for his acceptance. On these criteria, the pest will have no hope of gaining Maecenas's approval.

VOCABULARY

A

ā or **ab**, prep. + abl., *from; by*

abeō, abīre, abiī, abitūrus, *to go away; to get away*

absum, abesse, āfuī, āfutūrus, *to be away, be absent, be distant*

ac, conj., *and*

accendō, accendere, accendī, accēnsus, *to set on fire*

accurrō, accurrere, accurrī, accursūrus, *to run toward/up to*

ad, prep. + acc., *to, toward; at, near*

adimō, adimere, adēmī, adēmptus + dat., *to take away* (from)

aequor, aequoris, n., *sea*

aestās, aestātis, f., *summer*

ager, agrī, m., *field*

agō, agere, ēgī, āctus, *to do; to drive*

albus, -a, -um, *white*

aliās, adv., *at another time*

aliquis, aliquid, *someone, something*

alius, alia, aliud, *another, other*

alō, alere, aluī, altus, *to feed, nourish, rear*

alter, altera, alterum, *a/the second, one (of two), the other (of two), another*

altus, -a, -um, *tall; high; deep*
    altum, -ī, n., *the deep, the sea*

amīcus, -ī, m., *friend*

amō, -āre, -āvī, -ātus, *to love*

amor, amōris, m., *love*

an, conj., *or*

annus, -ī, m., *year*

anus, -ūs, f., *old woman*

Apollō, Apollinis, m., *Apollo* (son of Jupiter and Latona; god of prophecy, music, archery, and medicine).

appāreō, -ēre, -uī, -itūrus, *to appear*

aqua, -ae, f., *water*

arbiter, arbitrī, m., *master*
    arbiter bibendī, *master of the drinking*

arbor, arboris, f., *tree*

ārdeō, ārdēre, ārsī, ārsūrus, *to burn, blaze;* + abl., *to burn with love/passion* (for)

ārea, -ae, f., *open space; threshing floor*

arripiō, arripere, arripuī, arreptus, *to grab hold of*

at, conj. *but*

atque, conj., *and, also*

ātrium, -ī, n., *atrium, main room*

audeō, audēre, ausus sum + infin., *to dare* (to)

audiō, -īre, -īvī, -ītus, *to hear, listen to*

auferō, auferre, abstulī, ablātus, *to carry off*

aureus, -a, -um, *golden*

auricula, -ae, f., *ear*

aut, conj., *or*

avis, avis, m./f., *bird*

B

bellum, -ī, n., *war*

bene, adv., *well*

bibō, bibere, bibī, *to drink*

bis, adv., *twice*

bonus, -a, -um, *good*

brevis, -is, -e, *short*

C

cadō, cadere, cecidī, cāsūrus, *to fall; to set*

caelum, -ī, n., *sky, heaven*

Caesar, Caesaris, m., *Caesar; emperor*

campus, -ī, m., *plain, field*
    Campus Mārtius, -ī, m., *the Plain of Mars* (on the outskirts of Rome)

candidus, -a, -um, *white; fair-skinned; beautiful*

canō, canere, cecinī, cantus, *to sing*

cantō, -āre, -āvī, -ātus, *to sing*

capillī, -ōrum, m. pl., *hair*

caput, capitis, n., *head*

careō, carēre, caruī, caritūrus + abl., *to need; to lack*

cārus, -a, -um, *dear; beloved*

castra, -ōrum, n. pl., *camp*

cāsū, *by chance, accidentally*

celer, celeris, celere, *swift*

cēna, -ae, f., *dinner*

centum, indecl., *a hundred*

certus, -a, -um, *certain*

cēterī, -ae, -a, *the rest, the others*

cithara, -ae, f., *lyre*

clāmor, clāmōris, m., *shout, shouting*

clārus, -a, -um, *bright; famous; glorious*

cliēns, clientis, m., *client, dependent*

coepī, *I began*

cōgō, cōgere, coēgī, coāctus, *to compel, force*

colō, colere, coluī, cultus, *to cultivate*

cōnficiō, cōnficere, cōnfēcī, cōnfec- tus, *to accomplish, finish; to finish off*

coniūnx, coniugis, m./f., *husband; wife*

cōnsistō, cōnsistere, cōnstitī, *to halt, stop*

cor, cordis, n., *heart*

corōna, -ae, f., *garland, wreath; crown*

corōnō, -āre, -āvī, -ātus, *to crown*

corpus, corporis, n., *body*

crās, adv., *tomorrow*

crēdō, crēdere, crēdidī, crēditus + *dat.*, *to trust; to believe; to entrust*

cum, prep. + abl., *with*

cum, conj., *when; since; whenever*

cūnctī, -ae, -a, *all*

cupiō, cupere, cupīvī, cupītus, *to desire, want*

cūr, adv., *why*

cūra, -ae, f., *care*

cūrō, -āre, -āvī, -ātus, *to look after, take care of*

D

dē, prep. + abl., *down from; from; concern- ing, about*

dēbeō, -ēre, -uī, -itus, *to owe*; + infin., *ought; to have to*

dēdicō, -āre, -āvī, -ātus, *to dedicate*

dēmittō, dēmittere, dēmīsī, dēmissus, *to let down, lower, drop*

dēpōnō, dēpōnere, dēposuī, dēposi- tus, *to lay down, put aside, set down*

dēscendō, dēscendere, dēscendī, dēscēnsūrus, *to come/go down*

dēsīderō, -āre, -āvī, -ātus, *to long for, de- sire*

dēsinō, dēsinere, dēsiī, dēsitus, *to stop*

deus, -ī, nom. pl., **dī**, dat., abl. pl., **dīs**, m., *god*

dextra, -ae, f., *right hand*

diēs, diēī, m., sometimes f., *day*

difficilis, -is, -e, *difficult*

digitus, -ī, m., *finger*

dīligō, dīligere, dīlēxī, dīlēctus, *to love, have special regard for*

discēdō, discēdere, discessī, discessūrus, *to go away; to get away*

dīves, dīvitis, *rich*

dīvitiae, -ārum, f. pl., *wealth, riches*

dō, dare, dedī, datus, *to give*

doleō, -ēre, -uī, -itūrus, *to be in pain, hurt*

dominus, -ī, m., *master, owner*

domus, -ūs, f., *house*

dormiō, -īre, -īvī, -ītūrus, *to sleep*

dūcō, dūcere, dūxī, ductus, *to lead*

dum, conj., *while, as long as*

dux, ducis, m., *leader*

E

ē or ex, prep. + abl., *from; out of*

ēbrius, -a, -um, *drunk*

ecce, interj., *look*

effundō, effundere, effūdī, effūsus, *to pour out*

ego, *I*

ēheu, interj., *alas*

enim, conj., *for*

eō, īre, iī or īvī, itūrus, *to go*

equus, -ī, m., *horse*

ēripiō, ēripere, ēripuī, ēreptus, *to snatch from, rescue*

errō, -āre, -āvī, -ātūrus, *to wander*

et, conj., *and, also*

et . . . et, conj., *both . . . and*

exeō, exīre, exiī or exīvī, exitūrus, *to go out*

F

facilis, -is, -e, *easy*

faciō, facere, fēcī, factus, *to make; to do*

iter facere, *to travel*

fāma, -ae, f., *fame*

fātum, -ī, n., *fate*
fax, facis, f., *torch*
fēlīx, fēlīcis, *lucky; happy; fortunate*
fenestra, -ae, f., *window*
feriō, -īre, -īvī, -ītus, *to hit, strike*
ferō, ferre, tulī, lātus, *to bring; to carry, bear*
ferōx, ferōcis, *fierce*
fēstus, -a, -um, *festive; festival/feast* (day)
fidēlis, -is, -e, *faithful*
fidēs, fideī, f., *good faith; reliability; trust*
fīlius, -ī, m., *son*
fīlum, -ī, n., *thread*
fīnis, fīnis, m., *end*
fīō, fierī, factus sum, *to become; to be made, be done; to happen*
fleō, flēre, flēvī, flētus, *to weep, cry*
flōs, flōris, m., *flower*
forte, adv., *by chance*
fortis, -is, -e, *brave*
fortūna, -ae, f., *fortune; luck*
frangō, frangere, frēgī, frāctus, *to break*
frīgidus, -a, -um, *cool, cold*
frōns, frontis, f., *forehead*
frūstrā, adv., *in vain*
fugiō, fugere, fūgī, fugitus, *to flee; to flee from*
fundus, -ī, m., *farm*
fūnus, fūneris, n., *funeral*
furor, furōris, m., *frenzy; rage; madness*
fūrtim, adv., *stealthily*

G
gaudeō, gaudēre, gavīsus sum, *to be glad, rejoice*
geminus, -a, -um, *twin*
gēns, gentis, f., *family, clan*
gracilis, -is, -e, *slender*
grātus, -a, -um + dat., *loved* (by); *pleasing* (to); *dear* (to)
gravis, -is, -e, *heavy*

H
habeō, -ēre, -uī, -itus, *to have; to hold*
haud, adv., *not*
hedera, -ae, f., *ivy*
hērēs, hērēdis, m., *heir*

heu, interj., *alas*
hīc, adv., *here*
hic, haec, hoc, *this*
hiems, hiemis, f., *winter*
hodiē, adv., *today*
homō, hominis, m., *man*
hōra, -ae, f., *hour*
hortus, -ī, m., *garden*
hostis, hostis, m., *enemy*
  hostēs, hostium, m. pl., *the enemy*
hūc, adv., *here, to here*
humilis, -is, -e, *humble*

I
iaceō, -ēre, -uī, -itūrus, *to lie, be lying down*
iaciō, iacere, iēcī, iactus, *to throw*
iam, adv., *now; already*
  nōn iam, adv., *no longer*
iānua, -ae, f., *door*
īdem, eadem, idem, *the same*
ignis, ignis, m., *fire*
ille, illa, illud, *that; he, she, it*
imāgō, imāginis, f., *likeness; mask*
imber, imbris, m., *rain*
immemor, immemoris + gen., *forgetful*
immortālis, -is, -e, *immortal*
imperium, -ī, n., *power; empire*
impetus, -ūs, m., *attack*
impōnō, impōnere, imposuī, impositus, *to place on; to put*
in, prep. + abl., *in*
in, prep. + acc., *into*
incipiō, incipere, incēpī, inceptus, *to begin*
īnfirmus, -a, -um, *weak*
ingēns, ingentis, *huge*
inquam, *I say*
  inquit, *(he/she) says*
interdum, adv., *from time to time*
interpellō, -āre, -āvī, -ātus, *to interrupt, break in*
inveniō, invenīre, invēnī, inventus, *to come upon, find*
invideō, invidēre, invīdī, invīsus + dat., *to envy, be jealous* (of)
ipse, ipsa, ipsum, *himself, herself, itself,*

themselves

īrācundus, -a, -um, *prone to anger, irritable; in a bad temper*

ita, adv., *thus, so, in this way, in such a way*

Ītalia, -ae, f., *Italy*

Ītalus, -a, -um, *Italian*

iter, itineris, n., *journey*
  iter facere, *to travel*

iubeō, iubēre, iussī, iussus, *to order, bid*

iungō, iungere, iūnxī, iūnctus, *to join*

Iuppiter, Iovis, m., *Jupiter, Jove*

iuvenis, iuvenis, m., *young man*

L

lābor, lābī, lāpsus sum, *to slip*

labor, labōris, m., *work, toil*

laedō, laedere, laesī, laesus, *to harm*

laetus, -a, -um, *happy, glad*

lapis, lapidis, m., *stone*

lateō, -ēre, -uī, *to lie in hiding, hide*

laudō, -āre, -āvī, -ātus, *to praise*

lentus, -a, -um, *slow*

leō, leōnis, m., *lion*

lepus, leporis, m., *hare*

levis, -is, -e, *light*

lēvis, -is, -e, *smooth*

līberō, -āre, -āvī, -ātus, *to set free*

licet, licēre, licuit + dat., *it is allowed*

līmen, līminis, n., *threshold, doorway*

lingua, -ae, f., *tongue*

linquō, linquere, līquī, *to leave*

lītus, lītoris, n., *shore*

locus, -ī, m.; n. in pl., *place*

longus, -a, -um, *long*
  longē, adv., *far*

loquor, loquī, locūtus sum, *to speak, talk; to speak of*

lūctor, -ārī, -ātus sum, *to wrestle*

lūna, -ae, f., *moon*

lupus, -ī, m., *wolf*

M

magis, adv., *more*

magnus, -a, -um, *big, great, large*

maior, maior, maius, gen., **maiōris**, *bigger*

malus, -a, -um, *bad, evil*

male, adv., *badly*

maneō, manēre, mānsī, mānsūrus, *to remain, stay*

mānō, -āre, -āvī, *to flow*

manus, -ūs, f., *hand*

mare, maris, n., *sea*

māter, mātris, f., *mother*

melior, melior, melius, gen., **meliōris**, *better*

meminī, meminisse, *to remember*

mēns, mentis, f., *mind; disposition*

mercātor, mercātōris, m., *merchant*

Mercurius, -ī, m., *Mercury* (messenger god)

merum, -ī, n., *undiluted wine*

mēta, -ae, f., *goal; turning-post*

metus, -ūs, m., *fear*

meus, -a, -um, *my, mine*

mī = **mihi**

mināx, minācis, *menacing*

minimus, -a, -um, *very small, smallest*

minus, adv., *less*

minuō, minuere, minuī, minūtus, *to lessen, reduce, decrease*

misceō, miscēre, miscuī, mixtus, *to mix*

miser, misera, miserum, *unhappy, miserable, wretched*
  miserē, adv., *wretchedly; desperately*

mittō, mittere, mīsī, missus, *to send, let go*

modus, -ī, m., *way; manner; limit*

mōlēs, mōlis, f., *mass, huge bulk*

mollis, -is, -e, *soft; mild; gentle; delicate*

moneō, -ēre, -uī, -itus, *to advise, warn*

mōns, montis, m., *mountain*

monumentum, -ī, n., *monument, tomb*

morbus, -ī, m., *illness; disease*

morior, morī, mortuus sum, *to die*

moror, -ārī, -ātus sum, *to delay; to remain, stay, linger*

mors, mortis, f., *death*

mortālēs, mortālium, m. pl., *mortals*

mōs, mōris, m., *custom*, pl., *character*

moveō, movēre, mōvī, mōtus, *to move; to shake*

mox, adv., *soon, presently*

mulier, mulieris, f., *woman*

multus, -a, -um, *much; great*
    multī, -ae, -a, *many*
    multum, adv., *greatly, much*

mūnus, mūneris, n., *gift*

Mūsa, -ae, f., *Muse* (goddess of song and poetry)

mūtuus, -a, -um, *mutual*

myrtus, -ī, f., *myrtle*

N

nam, conj., *for*

nārrō, -āre, -āvī, -ātus, *to tell* (a story)

nāscor, nāscī, nātus sum, *to be born*

nāvis, nāvis, f., *ship*

nec, conj., *and . . . not; nor*
    nec . . . nec/neque . . . , conj., *neither . . . nor*

nēmō, nēminis, m./f., *no one*

neque, conj., *and . . . not*
    neque . . . neque/nec, conj., *neither . . . nor*

nesciō, -īre, -īvī, -ītus, *to be ignorant, not to know*

niger, nigra, nigrum, *black*

nihil, *nothing*
    nīl, *nothing*

nisi, conj., *unless, if . . . not*

nōbilis, -is, -e, *noble*

noceō, -ēre, -uī, -itūrus + dat., *to do harm* (to); *to harm*

nōmen, nōminis, n., *name*

nōn, adv., *not*

nōs, *we, us*

nōscō, nōscere, nōvī, nōtus, *to get to know*

nōtus, -a, -um, *known*

novus, -a, -um, *new*

nox, noctis, f., *night*

nūllus, -a, -um, *no, none*

num, adv., *surely not* (introduces a question that expects the answer "no")

numerus, -ī, m., *number*

numquam, adv., *never*

nunc, adv., *now*

nympha, -ae, f., *nymph, nature spirit*

O

ō, interj., *O* (used with vocative and in exclamations)

occurrō, occurrere, occurrī, occursūrus + dat., *to meet*

oculus, -ī, m., *eye*

ōlim, adv., *once (upon a time); at some future time, one day*

omnis, -is, -e, *all; the whole; every*

onus, oneris, n., *load, burden*

oppidum, -ī, n., *town*

ōra, -ae, f., *shore*

orior, orīrī, ortus sum, *to rise*

ōrnō, -āre, -āvī, -ātus, *to decorate*

Orpheus, -ī, m., *Orpheus* (legendary singer and husband of Eurydice)

P

parcō, parcere, pepercī + dat., *to spare*

pariēs, parietis, m., *wall* (of a house or room)

parō, -āre, -āvī, -ātus, *to prepare*

pars, partis, f., *part*
    partēs, partium, f. pl., *role*

pater, patris, m., *father*

patior, patī, passus sum, *to suffer, endure*

paucī, -ae, -a, *few*

paulō, adv., *a little*

paulum, adv., *little*

pauper, pauperis, *poor*

pavīmentum, -ī, n., *floor* (tiled, marble, or mosaic)

pendeō, pendēre, pependī, *to be suspended, hang*

per, prep. + acc., *through*

pereō, perīre, periī, peritūrus, *to die, perish*

perpetuus, -a, -um, *lasting, permanent*

persequor, persequī, persecūtus sum, *to pursue*

pēs, pedis, m., *foot*

pius, -a, -um, *dutiful, devoted; worshipful; pious*

placeō, -ēre, -uī + dat., *to please*

plūrēs, plūrēs, plūra, gen., **plūrium**, *more*

plūs, plūris, n., *more*

pōculum, -ī, n., *cup*

pōnō, pōnere, posuī, positus, *to put, place*

populus, -ī, m., *people*

poscō, poscere, poposcī, *to demand, ask for*

possum, posse, potuī, irreg., *to be able; I can*

post, prep. + acc., *after, behind*

posteā, adv., *afterward*

posterus, -a, -um, *next, following; future, later*

postis, postis, m., *door-post*

potior, -īrī, -ītus sum + abl., *to obtain; to seize; to acquire; to take possession of*

praebeō, -ēre, -uī, *to display, show, provide*

praecēdō, praecēdere, praecessī, praecessūrus, *to go in front; to lead the way*

praeter, prep. + acc., *except*

praetereō, praeterīre praeteriī or praeterīvī, praeteritus, *to go past*

prīmus, -a, -um, *first*

prius, adv., *earlier, previously*

prīscus, -a, -um, *of olden times, ancient; original, first*

prō, prep. + abl., *for, on behalf of*

prope, prep. + acc., *near*

proximus, -a, -um, *nearby, near*

puella, -ae, f., *girl*

puer, puerī, m., *boy; slave*

pulcher, pulchra, pulchrum, *beautiful, handsome*

    pulchrē, adv., *finely; excellently; well*

pulvis, pulveris, m., *dust*

pūrus, -a, -um, *spotless, clean; pure*

Q

quaerō, quaerere, quaesīvī or quaesiī, quaesītus, *to seek, look for, ask (about)*

quam, adv., *than*

    quam, adv. + superlative adj. or adv., *as . . . as possible*

quamquam, conj., *although*

quandō, adv., *when*

quārtus, -a, -um, *fourth*

-que, enclitic conj., *and*

quī, quae, quod, relative pronoun, *who, which, that*; interrogative adjective, *what, which*

quīdam, quaedam, quoddam, *a certain*

quīntus, -a, -um, *fifth*

quis, quid, interrogative pronoun or adjective, *who, what*

quō, adv., *there, to that place, to which place, to there*

quō, interrogative adv., *where, to where*

quod, conj., *because; that*

quōmodo, interrogative adv., *in what way*

quoque, adv., *also*

R

rāmus, -ī, m., *branch*

rapiō, rapere, rapuī, raptus, *to snatch, seize*

rēctus, -a, -um, *right, proper*

reddō, reddere, reddidī, redditus, *to give back, return*

redeō, redīre, rediī, reditūrus, *to return*

redigō, redigere, redēgī, redāctus, *to bring, bring back*

redūcō, redūcere, redūxī, reductus, *to lead/bring back*

reficiō, reficere, refēcī, refectus, *to re-make, rebuild, repair*

refugiō, refugere, refūgī, *to shrink back, recoil*

rēgīna, -ae, f., *queen*

rēgnō, -āre, -āvī, -ātūrus, *to rule*

regō, regere, rēxī, rēctus, *to rule*

relinquō, relinquere, relīquī, relictus, *to leave behind, abandon*

rēs, reī, f., *thing, matter, situation, affair*

respondeō, respondēre, respondī, respōnsūrus, *to reply, make a response, answer*

rēx, rēgis, m., *king*

rīdeō, rīdēre, rīsī, rīsus, *to laugh (at), smile*

rīpa, -ae, f., *river bank*

rīsus, -ūs, m., *laugh, laughter*

rīvus, -ī, m., *stream*
rixa, -ae, f., *quarrel*
rogō, -āre, -āvī, -ātus, *to ask*
Rōmānus, -a, -um, *Roman*
rosa, -ae, f., *rose*
rota, -ae, f., *wheel*
ruīna, -ae, f., *collapse, ruin*
rumpō, rumpere, rūpī, ruptus, *to burst*
rūrsus, adv., *again*
rūs, rūris, n., *country, country estate*

S

sacer, sacra, sacrum, *sacred*
saepe, adv., *often*
 saepius, adv., *more often*
saevus, -a, -um, *fierce, savage*
salvus, -a, -um, *safe*
sanguis, sanguinis, m., *blood*
satis, adv., *enough*
scelus, sceleris, n., *crime*
sciō, -īre, -īvī, -ītus, *to know*
scrībō, scrībere, scrīpsī, scrīptus, *to
 write*
sēcrētō, adv., *secretly; in private*
sed, conj., *but*
sedeō, sedēre, sēdī, sessūrus, *to sit*
sēdēs, sēdis, f., *seat; place*
semper, adv., *always*
sentiō, sentīre, sēnsī, sēnsus, *to feel; to
 notice*
sequor, sequī, secūtus sum, *to follow*
serēnus, -a, -um, *clear, bright; serene,
 calm*
sērius, adv., *later*
servō, -āre, -āvī, -ātus, *to save; to keep*
servus, -ī, m., *slave*
sī, conj., *if*
sīc, adv., *thus, so*
silva, -ae, f., *woods, forest*
similis, -is, -e + dat., *similar (to), like*
simul, adv., *together, at the same time*
simulac or simul ac, conj., *as soon as*
sine, prep. + abl., *without*
sōl, sōlis, m., *sun*
soleō, solēre, solitus sum + infin., *to be
 accustomed (to), be in the habit (of)*
sōlus, -a, -um, *alone; lonely*

solvō, solvere, solvī, solūtus, *to loosen,
 untie, release, set free*
somnus, -ī, m., *sleep*
sonitus, -ūs, m., *sound*
soror, sorōris, f., *sister*
spērō, -āre, -āvī, -ātus, *to hope*
stō, stāre, stetī, statūrus, *to stand*
suāvis, -is, -e, *sweet, delightful*
sub, prep. + abl., *under, beneath*
sum, esse, fuī, futūrus, *to be*
summus, -a, -um, *greatest, very great;
 highest; the top of*
super, prep. + acc. or abl., *over, above*
superbus, -a, -um, *proud, arrogant,
 haughty*
surgō, surgere, surrēxī, surrēctūrus, *to
 get up; to rise*
suspendō, suspendere, suspendī,
 suspēnsus, *to suspend, hang*
suus, -a, -um, *his, her, one's, its, their
 (own)*

T

tabula, -ae, f., *tablet*
taceō, -ēre, -uī, -itus, *to be quiet*
tam, adv., *so, such*
tamen, adv., *however, nevertheless*
tandem, adv., *at last, at length*
tangō, tangere, tetigī, tāctus, *to touch*
tantum, adv., *only; so much*
tardus, -a, -um, *slow*
temptō, -āre, -āvī, -ātus, *to try*
tempus, temporis, n., *time*
teneō, tenēre, tenuī, tentus, *to hold*
ter, adv., *three times*
terra, -ae, f., *earth; land*
Tiberis, Tiberis, m., *the Tiber River*
tigris, tigris, m./f., *tiger*
timeō, -ēre, -uī, *to fear*
 timendus, -a, -um, *to be feared*
timor, timōris, m., *fear*
tollō, tollere, sustulī, sublātus, *to lift,
 raise*
tōtus, -a, -um, *all, the whole; total(ly)*
trādō, trādere, trādidī, trāditus, *to hand
 over; to introduce*
trāns, prep. + acc., *across*

tremō, tremere, tremuī, *to tremble*

trēs, trēs, tria, *three*

trīstis, -is, -e, *sad*

tū, *you* (sing.)

tum, adv., *then*

turba, -ae, f., *crowd, mob*

tuus, -a, -um, *your* (sing.)

U

ubi, adv., conj., *where, when*

ūllus, -a, -um, *any*

umbra, -ae, f., *shadow, shade* (of the dead)

unda, -ae, f., *wave*

unde, interrogative adv., *from where*

undique, adv., *on all sides, from all directions*

unguentum, -ī, n., *ointment; perfume; oil*

ūnus, -a, -um, *one*

urbs, urbis, f., *city*

urgeō, urgēre, ursī, *to press, weigh heavily upon*

ūsque, adv., *all the way*

ut, conj. + indicative, *as, when*

ut, conj. + subjunctive, *so that*

ūtor, ūtī, ūsus sum + abl., *to use*

utrimque, adv., *on both sides*

uxor, uxōris, f., *wife*

V

valeō, -ēre, -uī, -ītūrus, *to be strong*

-ve, enclitic conj., *or*

vel, conj., *or*

velut, adv., *just as*

veniō, venīre, vēnī, ventūrus, *to come*

ventus, -ī, m., *wind*

Venus, Veneris, f., *Venus* (the goddess of love); *the highest throw of the knuckle-bones*

verberō, -āre, -āvī, -ātus, *to beat*

versus, -ūs, m., *verse, line* (of poetry)

vērus, -a, -um, *true*

vērō, adv., *truly, really, indeed*

vēscor, vēscī + abl., *to feed* (on)

vestīmentum, -ī, n., *clothing;* pl., *clothes*

vetus, veteris, *old*

via, -ae, f., *road, street*

victima, -ae, f., *sacrificial victim*

victor, victōris, m., *conqueror, victor*

videō, vidēre, vīdī, vīsus, *to see*

videor, vidērī, vīsus sum, *to seem; to be seen*

vīlla, -ae, f., *country house*

vincō, vincere, vīcī, victus, *to conquer*

vīnea, -ae, f., *vineyard*

vīnum, -ī, n., *wine*

vir, virī, m., *man*

virga, -ae, f., *stick; rod; switch*

virgō, virginis, f., *maiden; virgin*

vīta, -ae, f., *life*

vītō, -āre, -āvī, -ātus, *to avoid*

vīvō, vīvere, vīxī, vīctūrus, *to live*

vix, adv., *scarcely*

volō, velle, voluī, *to wish, want*

vōs, *you* (pl.)

vōx, vōcis, f., *voice*

vultus, -ūs, m., *face; expression*

THE GREEK ALPHABET

Letter		Name	Transliteration	Pronunciation
Α	α	ἄλφα	alpha	= the sound in *top*
Β	β	βῆτα	bēta	= *b*
Γ	γ	γάμμα	gamma	= *g* (but before γ, κ, ξ, or χ = the sound in *sing*)
Δ	δ	δέλτα	delta	= *d*
Ε	ε	ἒ ψῑλόν	epsīlon	= the sound in *get*
Ζ	ζ	ζῆτα	zēta	= σ + δ = *sd* as in *wisdom*
Η	η	ἦτα	ēta	= the sound in *bed*, but held longer
Θ	θ	θῆτα	thēta	= aspirated *t* as in *top*
Ι	ι	ἰῶτα	iōta	= the sound in *it* or when long the sound in *keen*
Κ	κ	κάππα	kappa	= the sound of *k* (without aspiration), as in *sack*
Λ	λ	λάμβδα	lambda	= *l*
Μ	μ	μῦ	mū	= *m*
Ν	ν	νῦ	nū	= *n*
Ξ	ξ	ξῖ	xī	= κ + σ = the sound of *x* in *axe*
Ο	ο	ὂ μῑκρόν	omīcron	= the sound in *boat* or *goat*
Π	π	πῖ	pī	= *p* (without aspiration), as in *sap*
Ρ	ρ	ῥῶ	rhō	= a trilled *r*
Σ	σ, ς	σίγμα	sigma	= *s* as in *sing*, but = *z* before β, γ, δ, and μ (written ς when last letter of a word)
Τ	τ	ταῦ	tau	= *t* (without aspiration), as in *sat*
Υ	υ	ὒ ψῑλόν	upsīlon	= the sound in French *tu*
Φ	φ	φῖ	phī	= aspirated *p* as in *pot*
Χ	χ	χῖ	chī	= aspirated *k* as in *kit*
Ψ	ψ	ψῖ	psī	= π + σ = *ps* as in *lips*
Ω	ω	ὦ μέγα	ōmega	= the sound in *caught*, but held longer

Reprinted with modifications from Maurice Balme and Gilbert Lawall, *Athenaze: An Introduction to Ancient Greek: Book I*, Second Edition, Oxford University Press, 2003, p. xii.

ACKNOWLEDGMENTS

ILLUSTRATIONS:

- **43:** Ted Smykal
- **63:** Ted Smykal
- **87:** XNR Productions, Inc.
- **100:** Ted Smykal
- **106:** Ted Smykal
- **259:** Ted Smykal
- **299:** Peter Connolly (from Peter Connolly and Hazel Dodge, *The Ancient City: Life in Classical Athens & Rome*, Oxford University Press, 1998, p. 110)

PHOTOGRAPHS:

- **17:** Corcoran Gallery, Washington, D.C. William A. Clark Collection #26.3
- **19:** Alinari / Art Resource, N.Y.
- **21:** Erich Lessing / Art Resource, N.Y.
- **33:** Erich Lessing / Art Resurce, N.Y.
- **51:** Courtesy Andrew Aronson
- **75:** Erich Lessing / Art Resource, N.Y.
- **115:** Erich Lessing / Art Resource, N.Y.
- **112:** Courtesy John Higgins
- **123:** Bildarchiv Preussischer Kulturbesitz / Art Resource, N.Y.
- **136:** Scala / Art Resource, N.Y.
- **145:** Vatican Museums and Gallewries, Vatican City, Italy / Bridgman Art Library
- **153:** Museum of Fine Arts, Boston
- **163:** Mimmo Jodice / CORBIS
- **167:** Erich Lessing / Art Resource, N.Y.
- **179:** Rockefeller Center, Manhattan, New York City, U.S.A. / Bridgeman Art Library
- **192:** Alinari / Art Resource, N.Y.
- **203:** The Art Archive / Heraklion Museum / Dagli Orti
- **217:** Courtesy Rebecca Chodes
- **239:** Ashmolean Museum, Univeristy of Oxford, U.K. / Bridgman Art Library
- **246:** Courtesy Edmund DeHoratius
- **258:** G. E. Kidder Smith / CORBIS
- **275:** Scala / Art Resource, N.Y.
- **305:** Scala / Art Resource, N.Y.

TEXT:

- **334:** Extract from *Athenaze: An Introduction to Ancient Greek: Book I*, by Maurice Balme and Gilbert Lawall. Second Edition, copyright © 2003 by Oxford University Press. Used with Permission.

The Latin texts of poems of Catullus included in this book are taken from *C. Valerii Catulli Carmina*, edited by R. A. B. Mynors, Scriptorum Classicorum Bibliotheca Oxoniensis (Oxford Classical Texts), Oxford University Press, 1958, and are reproduced here by permission of Oxford University Press.

The Latin texts of poems of Horace included in this book are taken from *Q. Horati Flacci Opera*, edited by Eduardus C. Wickham, 2nd edition edited by H. W. Garrod, Scriptorum Classicorum Bibliotheca Oxoniensis (Oxford Classical Texts), Oxford University Press, 1901, 1912, and are reproduced here by permission of Oxford University Press.

The Greek and Latin texts of all other authors included in this book are taken from Loeb Classical Library editions published by Harvard University Press, Cambridge,